Employment relations in the Asia-Pacific

Changing approaches

Edited by Greg J. Bamber, Funkoo Park,
Changwon Lee, Peter K. Ross and
Kaye Broadbent

Business Press

Thomson Learning™

Australia • Canada • Denmark • Japan • Mexico • New Zealand •
Philippines • Puerto Rico • Singapore • South Africa • Spain •
United Kingdom • United States

FOREWORD
Thomas A. Kochan

A major challenge for scholars, practitioners and students in our field is to try to diagnose the key employment relations (ER) issues and problems in our own countries and in other countries. This book helps to meet such a challenge by providing up to date analyses of ER, including human resource initiatives in the workplace and larger-scale industrial relations reform, in seven important Asia-Pacific countries: Australia; Indonesia; Japan; New Zealand; the Peoples' Republic of China (PRC); Republic of (South) Korea; and Taiwan (Republic of China, ROC).

The book is very useful for people in those countries and for others who aim to learn more about those countries. Students and practitioners can evaluate their local trends and practices against the experiences of other countries in the Asia-Pacific region. The first chapter offers a valuable comparative analysis in terms of three contrasting groups of countries in this region. This discusses the links between ER, industrialisation and democratisation. The analysis in the last chapter implies that the Asia-Pacific Economic Co-operation (APEC) forum is a microcosm of the World Trade Organisation (WTO). Hence this helps our understanding of the controversies about the WTO that were illustrated in 1999 in Seattle.

In recent years, ER policies and practices have been transformed in older industrialised market economies and in newly industrialising economies. It is particularly interesting to compare the various recovery strategies of different countries following the Asia-Pacific region's economic and financial turmoil of the late 1990s. Japanese companies appear to continue with many of the institutional aspects of their pattern of long-term employment, though internationally competitive market forces are putting increasing pressures on such traditional Japanese ER practices. In Australia and New Zealand there have been attempts to discontinue the award-wage system to foster increased labour market flexibility and international competitiveness. But preliminary data from New Zealand suggest that such increases in productivity may not be so easily achieved.

There has also been much change in the Peoples' Republic of China (PRC), with State owned enterprises (SOEs) being induced to break the 'iron rice bowl' and reduce staff in an effort to remain competitive in a 'socialist market' economy. In addition Taiwan has been reviewing its ER practices as its industries move into increasingly high-tech areas—traditional Taiwanese small family businesses and associated paternalistic management styles may no longer be suitable for the emerging industries of the 'new economy'. Indonesian ER are also in a state of flux: after years of state suppression, the emergence of the country from its present political and economic problems may present opportunities for worker groups to have more say in labour-related issues. In South Korea, companies have demanded more flexibility to make it easier to dismiss workers—in some cases precipitating considerable labour unrest.

In the space available here, I will comment on the issues in just one of these countries: Korea, which is the subject of three chapters of this book, and currently at a crossroads in terms of ER. But some of my tentative comments on Korea, in an international perspective, may have a more general applicability to other countries. I hope that they might encourage readers to reflect on the situation in Korea and other countries too.

The essence of problems in Korea is not the ER climate, but the structure and design of the ER system. Korea must decide what type of system is best for its future economy and society. The choice it makes now will determine whether ER will merely be a problem to be contained or an asset for competing in the global economy.

Currently, Korea is caught in a hybrid phase between two models—an American model and an Asian one that is a variant of the Japanese system. Recent developments, and the effect of the International Monetary Fund (IMF) loan provisions pertaining to corporate governance and layoffs (see below ch. 5), suggest the country is drifting toward the American model and will be likely to move further in this direction in the absence of a government strategy to do otherwise. This is not in the best interests of the Korean economy or society. It will reinforce Korea's past patterns of adversarial ER (characterised by periods of apparent industrial peace—low strike rates and low time lost to strikes, low levels of union activity/growth—that are interrupted periodically by industrial conflict, worker unrest and crisis). The difference from past patterns will be that the base level of industrial conflict will be higher and the periodic bursts of conflict and crisis will be more frequent and more costly. This is not a system that is in the long-term interests of most of the people. Therefore the most critical ER problem facing

Korea is to take active steps to break out of this anticipated adversarial cycle and system, and to build the institutional capacity and labour-management relationships capable of sustaining an alternative model.

A *caveat* is in order before discussing the options open to Korea. ER problems cannot be separated from the other choices made in economic and industrial organisational policy. Indeed, the effort to introduce more American-style corporate finance, governance, and employment flexibility will have profound long-term effects on ER, as it moves the ER system in the direction of an American model. This is one of the perhaps unintended, but I would suggest, unfortunate and perverse effects of the requirements imposed by the IMF loan agreements with Korea in the late 1990s. It is a problem that the world's financial institutions need to attend to in future policy interventions, not just in Korea, but in other countries as well.

To illustrate the choices facing Korea, let me briefly outline the broad features of two contrasting models of ER. (These are only general caricatures, not detailed analyses.)

An *American* approach starts with a corporate model that gives strong influence to shareholders and financial agents. Human resource policies are subordinate to financial considerations, management culture carries a strong anti-union ethos, and there is limited labour-management consultation and information sharing. Unionisation levels are low, but union influence in politics and in the economy is greater than would be expected by membership numbers. Wages are rather rigid except in periods of crisis or fundamental shifts in power. Work organisation tends to reflect Frederic Taylor's ideas, with rigid work rules and limited employee involvement. In the past twenty years, in response to pressures from growing international and domestic competition, the model has moved toward more flexible work arrangements, greater employee involvement and some labour-management partnerships (though these partnerships are fragile and more the exception than the rule). The American management culture remains strongly anti-union and unions distrust efforts to introduce new forms of employee participation for fear that it will further undermine their role in the workplace. As a result, labour policy has been in a stalemate for twenty years.

An *Asian/Japanese* model is designed to support an economic strategy that emphasises human resources as a competitive asset—a strategy that requires a highly-skilled and committed workforce and a cooperative labour-management culture and system. It rests on an organisational governance model that stresses enterprise growth and employment continuity, builds a strong role for human resources into the governance and senior management structures, and engages union representatives in consultation and information sharing processes at the enterprise and national levels. At the workplace, this system rests on a foundation of flexible work structures and employee participation in problem solving to improve quality and productivity. Unions are mostly enterprise-based and accepted as legitimate institutions by management. Union and management relations at the national level revolve around annual negotiations that, informed by considerable macro-economic information, set a framework for wage movements. In the past decade, in response to its own economic problems, the Japanese system has moved to allow more employment flexibility and openness to US-oriented financial institutions and investment, but its basic employment system features remain intact.

Korean ER are currently an uneasy blend of the two models. Historically, Korean industrial organisation and corporate governance shared some of the Japanese corporate features and employment stability was given high priority. But Korea also had a history of repressive labour policies prior to 1987. Since the democratisation of labour market policies was announced in 1987, unions have grown in influence as membership grew, though membership has declined again in recent years. The Korean management culture, however, is still rather authoritarian and reluctant to accept unions, share information, or engage in consultation or labour-management partnerships. Unions, in turn, are more militant and sceptical of cooperation with management. Labour laws enacted in 1997 were designed to allow more flexibility for layoffs and acknowledged multiple unions and federations. The new labour laws also created national administrative structures to provide mediation and settle labour-management disputes in a fashion similar to the American model. The corporate finance reforms introduced as part of the IMF loan package move in the direction of an American model of corporate governance emphasising shareholder rights and finance as the most powerful force within executive decision making, with little regard for the role of human resources. In the short run, this has produced wage concessions and real wage declines, increased income inequality, higher unemployment, and a movement toward more dispatched (temporary) employment.

At the same time Korea is attempting to use tripartite structures at the national level to discuss labour and economic policies; these, however have proved to be unstable, as first unions then employers walk out of the talks as pressures from their political constituents intensify. Meanwhile union membership falls, labour conflicts decline in the short run but, as in the past, labour unrest may be simmering under the surface.

Given these circumstances, if no changes are made to Korean

ER policy, we might expect a future scenario characterised by periodic resurgence of militancy as the economy improves but worker welfare lags, persistent inequality in income, and further deepening of adversarial relations as management resistance of unions and union resistance of cooperative efforts intensify and reinforce each other. Union membership may remain relatively low but the impact of unions and union-management relations on the economy will be high. Efforts at national tripartite dialogue on economic, social, or labour policies are not likely to be fruitful or sustainable in the absence of a major economic or social crisis. Pressures on government leaders and employers to repress unions during crisis periods will intensify. Government policy will end up either in a stalemate similar to the US or will reflect a see-saw pattern (favouring unions or management depending on the particular leanings of the elected leaders).

Under this scenario, ER will be a problem to be contained, not an asset for competing in the global economy. This is not likely to be a viable strategy for Korea, given its high wage position relative to its neighbours in Asia.

An alternative approach that would support a high productivity and innovation-oriented economic strategy would focus on seeking to build a more inclusive, participatory, and cooperative ER system. This will not be easy; it will require support from the key international financial institutions, strong national leadership, a sustained effort to break out of the adversarial pattern and culture that is now gaining strength, and the building of institutional capacity to support this alternative model.

I hope that these remarks will stimulate people to read the rest of this interesting book and to form their own conclusions about Korea and the other countries that are considered.

Thomas A. Kochan
George M. Bunker Professor of Management,
MIT Institute for Work & Employment Research,
Sloan School of Management, Massachusetts Institute of Technology,
USA
and President of the Industrial Relations Research Association (US)
1999–2000

Contents

xi

Figures and tables

Figures

Tables

Abbreviations

ABAC	APEC Business Advisory Council
ABS	Australian Bureau of Statistics
ACCI	Australian Chamber of Commerce and Industry
ACFTU	All-China Federation of Trade Unions (PRC)
ACOSS	Australian Council of Social Services
ACSPA	Australian Council of Salaried and Professional Associations
ACTETSME	APEC Centre for Technology Exchange and Training for SMEs
ACTU	Australian Council of Trade Unions
AECS	All Employees Contract System
AFL-CIO	American Federation of Labor–Congress of Industrial Organizations
AIRC	Australian Industrial Relations Commission
ALP	Australian Labor Party
APEC	Asia–Pacific Economic Co-operation
APESMA	Association of Professional Engineers, Scientists and Managers, Australia
APINDO	Asosiasi Pengusaha Indonesia—Indonesian Employers' Association
APLN	Asia Pacific Labour Network
APRO	Asia Pacific Regional Organisation
ASEAN	Association of South East Asian Nations
AWA	Australian Workplace Agreements
AWIRS	Australian Workplace Industrial Relations Surveys
BCA	Business Council of Australia
BMN	Business Management Network of APEC's HRDWG
CA	Certified Agreement (Australia)
CAGEO	Council of Australian Government Employee Organisations

CAI	Confederation of Australian Industry
CAW	Canadian Auto Workers
CCP	Chinese Communist Party
CEC	Collective employment contract (New Zealand)
CEDA	Chinese Enterprise Directors' Association (PRC)
CFL	Chinese Federation of Labour (Taiwan)
CLRC	Central Labour Relations Commission
CMA	Chinese Management Association (Taiwan)
CNCA	Collective negotiation and collective agreement
COE	Collectively owned enterprise
CTU	Council of Trade Unions
DGB	Deutscher Gewerkschaftsbund—German Confederation of Unions
DPP	Democratic Progressive Party (Taiwan)
EPA	Economic Planning Agency (Japan)
ER	employment relations
EU	European Union
FBSI	Federasi Buruh Seluruh Indonesia—All Indonesia Labour Federation
FDI	foreign direct investment
FFE	foreign funded enterprise (PRC)
FKTU	Federation of Korean Trade Unions (Hankuk Nochong)
FLSL	Fair Labour Standards Law (Taiwan)
FSPSI	Federasi Serikat Pekerja Seluruh Indonesia—All Indonesia Workers' Union Federation
GATT	General Agreement on Tariffs and Trade
GDP	gross domestic product
HRD	human resource development
HRDWG	HRD Working Group of APEC
HRM	human resources management
HURDIT	Human Resources Development in Industry Technology Network of APEC's HRDWG
IC	integrated circuit
ICFTU	International Confederation of Free Trade Unions
IEC	Individual employment contract (New Zealand)
ILO	International Labour Organisation
IME	industrialised market economy
IMF	international monetary fund
IR	industrial relations
IRCC	Industrial Relations Reform Committee
ITF	International Transport Federation
ITO	Industry Training Organisation (New Zealand)
JV	joint venture
KCIA	Korean Central Intelligence Agency

KCTU	Korea Confederation of Trade Unions (Minjunochong)
KLI	Korea Labor Institute
KORPRI	Indonesian Civil Servants' Corps
LPC	Low Pay Commission (UK)
M&A	Merger and acquisition
MF	Manufacturers' Federation, New Zealand
MUA	Maritime Union of Australia
NAFTA	North American Free Trade Agreement
NEDM	Economic Development Management Network of APEC's HRDWG
NFF	National Farmers Federation (Australia)
NGO	Non-governmental organisation
NIE	newly industrialised economy
Nikkeiren	Japan Federation of Employers' Associations
NZBRT	New Zealand Business Round Table
NZCTU	New Zealand Council of Trade Unions
NZEF	New Zealand Employers' Federation
NZMF	New Zealand Manufacturers' Federation
OECD	Organisation for Economic Co-operation and Development
OJT	on the job training
OOS	occupational overuse syndrome (New Zealand)
PBEC	Pacific Basin Economic Council
PECC	Pacific Economic Co-operation Council
PIR	Pancasila industrial relations (Indonesia)
PKI	Partai Kommunis Indonesia—Indonesian Communist Party
PMD	Performance Management and Development
PRC	People's Republic of China
PSA	Public Service Association (New Zealand)
PUK	Perwakilan Unit Kerja (Indonesia)—SPSI enterprise level units
Rengo	Japan Trade Union Confederation
ROC	Republic of China on Taiwan
SBLP	Serikat Buruh Lapangan Pekerjaan—industrial sector unions (Indonesia)
SBM	Serikat Buruh Merdeka—independent union committed to human rights (Indonesia)
SBSI	Serikat Buruh Sejahtera Indonesia—The Indonesian Prosperous Workers' Union
SDA	Shop Distributive and Allied Employees Association (Australia)
SEZ	Special Economic Zone (PRC)
SMEs	Small and medium-sized enterprises

SOBSI	Sentral Organisasi Buruh Seluruh Indonesia—All Indonesian Organisation of Trade Unions
SOE	State owned enterprise (PRC)
SPSI	Serikat Pekerja Seluruh Indonesia—All Indonesia Central Workers' Union
SPTP	Serikat Pekerja Tingkat Perusahaan—enterprise based union (Indonesia)
TSMC	Taiwan Semiconductor Manufacturing Company
UMAP	University Mobility in the Asia Pacific
UMR	minimum regional wage (Indonesia)
WTO	World Trade Organisation
YLBHI	Yayasan Lembaga Bantuan Hukum Indonesia—Indonesian Legal Aid Institute

Contributors

Greg J. Bamber is Professor and Director of the Graduate School of Management, Griffith University, Queensland. He was formerly Director of the Australian (Key) Centre in Strategic Management, Queensland University of Technology, and previously was at the University of Queensland and at Durham University Business School (UK); he also was an independent mediator/arbitrator for the British Advisory, Conciliation and Arbitration Service. His (joint) books include: *Managing Managers*, Blackwell; *Organisational Change Strategies: Case Studies of Human Resource and Industrial Relations Issues*, Longman; and *International and Comparative Employment Relations* and *New Technology: International Perspectives on Human Resources and Industrial Relations*, both Allen & Unwin/Routledge. His publications have been translated into several languages including French, German, Spanish, Italian, Russian, Chinese, Korean and Japanese. He researches and consults with international organisations, governments, employers and unions. His current research includes studies of changing employment relations and organisational strategies and structures in several sectors including car manufacturing, retailing, fast food and telecommunications. He is a past President of the Australian & New Zealand Academy of Management. He is currently President of the International Federation of Scholarly Associations of Management.

Kaye Broadbent received her PhD from Griffith University for a thesis focusing on the gendered construction of part-time employment in Japan. She is currently an Associate Lecturer in the School of Industrial Relations, Griffith University where she teaches Australian and comparative industrial relations. She has been a visiting research fellow at the Institute of Social Science, Tokyo University; her research interests include gender and work and gender and unions.

Edward M. Davis is Professor of Management, Director of the Labour-Management Studies Foundation and a Deputy Director at the Macquarie Graduate School of Management. He is joint editor of the *Economic and Labour Relations Review* and author and co-editor of several books. His most recent books are *Making the Link: Affirmative Action and Industrial Relations* No.10, Jackson and *Managing Together: Consultation and Participation at Work* (Melbourne, Longman, 1996). The first was co-edited with Valerie Pratt and the second with Russell Lansbury. Professor Davis has acted as a consultant on industrial relations to employers, unions and government and he has also undertaken assignments for the International Labour Organisation. He is currently National President of the Industrial Relations Society of Australia.

Jan Elliott was awarded a PhD from the University of New South Wales in 1998 for a thesis on the history of workers and unions in Indonesia from 1945–65. Currently, she is a Research Fellow for CAPSTRANS (Centre for Asia Pacific Social Transformation Studies) at the University of Wollongong, Australia. She has published on labour legislation and gender and women workers in Indonesia. Her publications include: (1994) 'Labour legislation and gender in Indonesia', *Asian Studies Review*, 17, 3:33–42 and in (1997) 'Separate but equal? Women and wage labour in Indonesia', in Jean Gelman Taylor (ed.) *Women Creating Indonesia: The First Fifty Years*, Clayton: Monash Asia Institute, Centre of Southeast Asian Studies, Monash University.

Meiyu Fang is an Assistant Professor in the Institute of Human Resource Management at the National Central University in Taiwan. She studied Psychology in the National Chengchi University in Taiwan, and received the degree of Bachelor of Science in 1990. After graduation, she started her graduate education in the School of Industrial and Labor Relations at Cornell University, US. She gained a Master of Science degree in 1993 and her PhD degree in 1997. Her research activities include work attitudes, employee motivation, the compensation system, staffing and general human resources management. Her current research interest is in human resources management of Taiwan's high-tech industry.

Nigel Haworth is Professor of International Business at the University of Auckland. After taking an undergraduate degree in Economics, he completed a doctorate in Latin America Studies based on research in Peru. He has published widely, particularly in the areas of Latin American labour studies (in relation to Peru and Chile), the role of foreign direct investment in regional policy and employment relations, the relationship between internationalisation and sovereignty and, more recently, the issue of international labour standards, regional integration in the Asia-Pacific region (with particular reference to HRD issues), and Maori strategies for sustainable commercial development. A member of the New Zealand APEC Study Centre Committee, he is also a New Zealand delegate to the APEC HRD Working Group and National Co-ordinator of the BMN network in New Zealand. He is head of the Department of International Business in the University of Auckland which has a strong teaching and research interest in the Asia-Pacific region.

Stephen Hughes is at the University of Newcastle upon Tyne. In 1984 he graduated with a BA (Hons) in Human Studies from Bradford and in 1985 he gained an MA in Industrial Relations from Warwick. He has also worked at Oxford Brookes University and the University of Auckland. His research activities include trade and labour standards, regionalism, supra-national and intergovernmental organisations, and employment relations systems. His teaching and research are from an international perspective. He has published articles in *Work, Employment and Society* and *Industrial Relations Journal*.

Young-Kee Kim is the Vice President, Human Resources, LG Electronics (LGE), part of the LG Group (formerly Lucky Gold Star). He is in charge of human resources and labour–management relations. Mr Kim has devoted much of his career to labour relations. He began as a labour relations expert at LG Chemical in 1979, moved on to become a manager in 1983, and was promoted to General Manager of Labour Relations at the Chairman's Office in 1987. He spent two years as an adjunct professional at the Marriott School of Management, Brigham Young University. Mr Kim was promoted to his current position in 2000. Mr Kim holds an MA in Industrial and Labor Relations from Marriott School at Brigham Young University and a BA in Economics from the Sogang University in Seoul, South Korea.

Thomas A. Kochan is the George M. Bunker Professor of Management, Sloan School of Management, Massachusetts Institute of Technology, USA. He was President of the International Industrial Relations Association from 1992 to 1995 and President of the Industrial Relations Research Association (US) in 1999. He is the author, co-author or co-editor of many articles and books including: *Introduction to Collective Bargaining and Industrial Relations, The Transformation of American Industrial Relations, The Mutual Gains Enterprise, Employment Relations in a Changing World Economy, Employment Relations in the Growing Asian*

Economies; The Changing Nature of Work: Implications for Occupational Analysis, and *The New Relationship: Human Capital and the American Corporation.*

Felicity Lamm is at the Department of Management Studies and Employment Relations at the University of Auckland. With a background in environmental science and employment relations, she is a specialist in occupational health and safety and employment in small businesses. She has completed research projects for New Zealand and overseas public and private sector organisations in areas such as employment programs, regulatory compliance behaviour, small business employment and occupational health and safety in small businesses. She is currently the Chairperson of the New Zealand branch of the Australian and New Zealand Small Business Association, Chairperson of the Australian and New Zealand Occupational Health and Safety Educators Association and on the editorial board of the *British Journal of Safety Science.*

Changwon Lee graduated from Yonsei University in Seoul. He has since studied at the University of Chicago, US, where he completed a Masters degree in 1992 and a PhD in 1994 in the field of Sociology. From 1994 to 1995, he worked for the First Economic Research Institute in Seoul as a Chief Research Fellow. He joined the Korea Labor Institute (KLI) in 1996. As a Research Fellow at the KLI, he studied white-collar union movements and their career development. Currently he is Director for Labor Policy in the Office of the President, Republic of Korea. His interests include the changing nature of industrial relations and the transformation of corporate structures.

Joseph S. Lee is currently Professor of Human Resource Management and Director of the Research Centre for Taiwan Economic Development at the National Central University, Taiwan. He received his BA in Economics from the National Taiwan University, his MA in Labour Relations and his PhD in Labour Economics from the University of Massachusetts-Amherst, Mass. After graduation he taught at Minnesota State University at Mankato for 22 years. He then served as Vice-President for the Chung Hua Institution for Economic Research in Taiwan between 1992 and 1997. In 1997 he was appointed Director of the newly established Research Centre for Taiwan Economic Development. Professor Lee's major research interest is in labour relations and human resources. He has published several books and many articles, including *Labor Standards and Economic Development, Changing of Employment Relations in Asian Countries* and *The Emergence of the South China Growth Triangle, Capital and Labor Mobility in Taiwan.* Professor Lee also serves as a member on the Executive Council of the International Industrial Relations Association and is a member of the Council of Labor Affairs, Republic of China, and a board member of the Chinese Economic Association.

Bill Mansfield is an Assistant Secretary of the ACTU, a position he has held since 1985. He has been a union official since 1963 when he took up a full-time role in the Victorian Branch of the Australian Telecommunications Employees' Association. He was Federal Secretary of that union when he left to join the ACTU in 1985. He is Deputy Chair of the Australian National Training Authority and a member of the Governing Body of the International Labour Organisation (ILO). In addition, he is a Board member of the Australian Quality Council. He left school in 1957 and trained as a telecommunications technician. After taking up his full-time union post, he undertook further studies and completed a law degree at Melbourne University in 1972.

Funkoo Park is President of the Korea Labor Institute (KLI), Seoul, South Korea. He was formerly Secretary to the President for Labour Affairs, Office of the President, and previously was a Senior Fellow at the Korea Development Institute. He has a PhD in Economics from the University of Minnesota. His publications include: *Social Issues in Korea* (co-edited), KDI (1993), *Emerging Labor Issues in Developing Asia* (co-edited), KDI (1992) and *Industrial Relations in Transition,* Paper presented at KDI-UCSD Conference of Korea's Social Policy, 1992.

Young-bum Park is a Professor of Economics and Business at Hansung University in Seoul, South Korea, and teaches labour economics and industrial relations. He holds a PhD in Economics from Cornell University. From 1988 until May 1997 he was a Senior Research Fellow at the KLI and during 1995–96 was a Visiting Research Fellow at the East-West Centre in Hawaii, US. Professor Park has published extensively on industrial relations, economics and related fields in Korea and Asia; his publications include *Public Sector Industrial Relations*, KLI Press; and 'Korea' in *Telecommunications: Restructuring Work and Employment Relations World-wide*, Cornell University Press.

Erling Rasmussen studied at Odense University, Denmark, where he graduated with the Danish degree CandMag in 1980—this degree is equivalent to a BA in History (1974), a BA in Social Sciences (1977) and an MA in Social Sciences (1980). Erling was awarded the European Doctorate at the European University Institute, Florence, in 1986. During 1980–85, Erling was involved in academic research, first as a Visiting Research Fellow at the Institute of

Applied Economics and Social Research, University of Melbourne, then as a Researcher at the European University Institute, Florence. Following the completion of his doctoral thesis, Erling was employed as Assistant Editor for Incomes Data Services Ltd, London, from 1986 to 1989. He was then employed by the Industrial Relations Service, Department of Labour, in Wellington for three years. In February 1993 Erling joined the Department of Management Studies and Labour Relations at Auckland University.

Peter Ross is a PhD candidate and Associate Lecturer at the School of International Business, Griffith University, where he graduated in 1994. Prior to this he worked as an industrial officer with the Queensland state government. He has specialised in comparative human resources (HR) and industrial relations (IR) practices. He is currently examining the effects of deregulation and privatisation on employment relations in the telecommunications sectors of Australia and New Zealand. His publications include 'Employment, economics and industrial relations: Comparative statistics' (jointly with G.J. Bamber & G. Whitehouse) in Bamber & Lansbury's *International and Comparative Employment Relations: A Study of Industrialised Market Economies* 3rd edn, Allen & Unwin, 1998.

Sutanto Suwarno obtained a bachelor degree (BA/Drs) in 1990 from the University of Islam Syekh Yusef, Jakarta, specialising in public administration, and obtained a Masters degree in Sociology from the University of Wales (Cardiff) in 1993. He completed his PhD on IR through the University of Glamorgan, Wales. He is presently employed by the Ministry of Manpower, Indonesia.

Charles T. Tackney is an Associate Professor in the Japanese Study Programme, Department of Intercultural Communication and Management at the Copenhagen Business School. He received his PhD in the field of International-Comparative Industrial Relations from the Industrial Relations Research Institute of the University of Wisconsin-Madison. Among his publications and translations is a jointly authored study of the postwar adaptive appropriation in Japan of German labour and employment jurisprudence: David Kettler & Charles T. Tackney (Fall 1997), 'Light from a dead sun: The Japanese lifetime employment system and Weimar labor law', *Comparative Labor Law & Policy Journal*, 19. He is currently drafting a manuscript on the legal ecology of the postwar Japanese firm to aid in understanding and evaluating the institutionalised practice of the lifetime employment system and the global transfer of Japanese management practices.

Malcolm Warner is Professor and Fellow, Wolfson College, Cambridge, and the Judge Institute of Management Studies, University of

Cambridge. He took his bachelor and doctoral degrees at the University of Cambridge. After this he held several teaching and research posts on both sides of the Atlantic. He is the author and editor of over 30 books and more than 150 articles on social science and management related topics. He is the Editor-in-Chief of the *International Encyclopedia of Business and Management*, published in 1996 in six volumes, London: International Thomson Business Press and has published several books on China, including (with S.H. Ng) (1998) *China's Trade Unions and Management*, London: Macmillan.

Ying Zhu is Senior Lecturer in the Department of Asian and International Studies, Victoria University of Technology, Melbourne. He was educated at Beijing University where he took his bachelor degree, then held the post of Economist and Research Fellow in the Research Office of Shenzhen Special Economic Zone Development Company. He later completed a PhD at the University of Melbourne on 'The role of export processing zones in East Asian development'. He was a Visiting Scholar at the Institute of Labour Studies of the International Labour Organisation in Geneva, Switzerland. His main publications are on Chinese industrial relations in journals such as *Asian Economies*, *International Labour Review*, and *Labour and Industry*.

Preface

This book examines changing approaches to employment relations (ER) in the Asia-Pacific region. There was rapid economic development in this region in the post-1945 period. Economic turmoil in the late 1990s checked that growth in several countries. But they have tended to make rapid recoveries, for instance, the Republic of (South) Korea (often called Korea). State institutions and government responses to organised labour developed over a comparatively long period in the older institutionalised market economies (IMEs). In view of the high levels of growth in the Asia-Pacific region, decision-makers in many of the newly industrialising economies (NIEs) have had to develop such policies relatively quickly. By including views from government organisations, unions, practitioners and academics, this book covers a range of perspectives to present views on ER at the macro and micro levels.

The book is divided into five parts, with the introductory and concluding chapters focusing on general developments in the Asia-Pacific region. The book begins with a discussion of the experiences of the seven countries that are discussed in the following chapters. The Introduction also considers the impact of industrialisation and democratisation on the development of ER. The concluding chapter explores the treatment of ER in an international institution, the Asia-Pacific Economic Co-operation (APEC) forum, and why ER issues are becoming more important on its agenda.

The central three parts of the book are divided into: analyses of particular countries, perspectives on unions and company case studies. ER in Australia, New Zealand, Japan, South Korea, Taiwan, the PRC and Indonesia are examined in the national studies. A theme explored in each chapter is the impact of economic transformation on the structure and functioning of labour markets. This theme is developed further in part three where challenges facing unions in South Korea and Australia are examined, and in part four which details policies in companies in the microelectronics industries of South Korea and Taiwan.

The countries selected provide an understanding of ER institutions, practices and legislation that have developed from diverse cultural contexts. The structure of the book emphasises this. Having countries with similar institutions and/or cultural and historical links juxtaposed facilitates comparisons while also allowing for reflection on the diversity of 'Asian' values.

The seven national perspectives include discussions of recent developments in ER policies and legislation, and of future directions. As mature economies Australia, New Zealand and Japan demonstrate the impact of restructuring the labour market in an attempt to promote greater flexibility. The chapters on Australia and New Zealand allow comparison of the major institutions—government, employers' associations and unions—against the backdrop of the continuing deregulation of the labour market. Legislation introduced in both countries in the 1990s significantly weakened the role of unions and industrial commissions and altered power relations. Revisions to Japan's Labour Standards Law, while consistent with moves towards deregulation, include the requirement that employers show 'just cause' for dismissing employees. This may represent a move towards the re-regulation of employment law.

Japan also provides a comparison with South Korea and Taiwan. In the pre-1945 period their status as Japanese colonies meant the impact was direct, while in the post-1945 period the relationship has reflected Japan's economic power. The impact of recent political, economic and social transformation on ER in South Korea and Taiwan is explored. While South Korea experienced a reduction in state intervention in the union movement, resulting in increased union membership, 'democratisation' in Taiwan has induced the government to take a more active and regulatory stance on labour policy than previously.

The discussion of the People's Republic of China (PRC) and Indonesia shows that in both of these important developing countries there are differing degrees of economic development in different regions. Also, both of these large countries face demands for greater workers' rights. The PRC's change from a highly regulated to a 'socialist market' economy has had a significant effect on employees as they shift from state run to privately operated companies. For Indonesia, ER has been closely tied to the state doctrine of Pancasila (five state principles governing life and behaviour formulated by Sukarno in 1945). While the end of the Suharto government offers opportunities for greater government recognition of workers' interests, political instability has constrained government action.

Part four explores the impact on unions of deregulating employment policies. Rapid economic growth combined with authoritarian governments has in many instances made it difficult for unions to establish themselves as legitimate partners of government in much of the Asia-Pacific. In South Korea they have become a force which is more difficult for the government to ignore. In contrast, in Australia, traditionally a country of comparatively dense unionisation, the deregulation of the labour market and a move away from manufacturing towards service industries induced a significant decrease in union density. Despite different stages of maturation, union movements in both countries are looking for strategies to promote their continuing relevance.

As both are rapidly growing economies, Taiwan and South Korea provide micro-level studies of the impact of changing ER. South Korea's LG group developed a new model of employment relations in an attempt to achieve the twin goals of higher productivity and enhanced quality of working life for employees. TSMC of Taiwan established a multimillion dollar business as a foundry manufacturing service by establishing facilities in which other companies can manufacture their own semiconductor products. To maintain productivity and profitability, it is moving towards a pay system based on workers' individual performances.

This book, then, offers a broad range of views on ER practices and possible future ER developments in the Asia-Pacific. Exploring how the key players in particular countries are responding to the challenges of globalisation, and the so called 'new economy' of the 21st century should be an exciting and inviting challenge for students and practitioners.

Acknowledgments

In compiling this book we thank especially all of the contributors. We gratefully acknowledge the helpful assistance of the Australia–Korea Foundation, Griffith University and the Korea Labor Institute.

Many people have commented on parts of the draft manuscript, and/or helped in other ways. We thank: Cameron Allan, Bradley Bowden, Peter Brosnan, Warren Chiu, Man-Kee Choe, Bob Elson, Margaret Gardner, Ray Harbridge, Judith Hollows, Seongsu Kim, Leong Liew, Gerry van Klinken, Seung-Ho Kwon, Yul Kwon, Russell Lanbury, Chris Leggett, Ken Lovell, Mary Moloney, Neal Ollett, David Peetz, David Schak, Peter Sheldon, Mindy Thorpe, Nick Wailes and Pat Walsh.

We would always be interested in any further comments on this book.

Greg Bamber, on behalf of all of the editors
Graduate School of Management, Griffith University, Queensland,
4111 Australia
Tel: 07 3875 6497; Fax: +61 7 3875 3900
Email: g.bamber@mailbox.gu.edu.au

PART I

Introduction

1 Industrialisation, democratisation and employment relations in the Asia-Pacific[1]

Greg J. Bamber and Peter K. Ross

The following chapters examine employment relations (ER) at the macro level in seven countries in the Asia-Pacific region. These are supplemented by more specific discussions on the union movements of Australia and South Korea, and case studies at the micro (firm) level in South Korea and Taiwan. This chapter tries to synthesise aspects of these contributions and asks to what extent common factors accompanied the development of ER in these countries. As a starting point we examine the links, if any, between industrialisation, democratisation and ER in these countries.

ER encompasses the varied methods and processes of people management, including human resources management (HRM) and industrial relations. Therefore in this book we generally prefer to use 'ER' as a shorthand term for the broad field of managing people. The ER field, then, includes rules, attitudes, customs, practices, policies and behaviour in and around the employment relationship. The main 'actors' in the field are employees and their organisations, employers and their associations, and the state and its institutions involved in employment issues.[2]

It is also worth considering the terms *transformation* and *democratisation*, because some commentators have used one or both. Transformation can mean a change in appearance or a complete change in character, i.e. a fundamental change (OED 1973). The latter description, involving a radical transformation of ER, can be seen in some countries. However, it is necessary to keep in mind the continuities in ER arrangements and exaggerations of the extent of change which may be made for political or commercial motives: in some cases so-called transformations are more a change in appearance than in substance.

Democratisation means moving towards 'government by the people' which may involve 'direct' or more usually 'indirect' representation (Elliott 1969:120) or 'government where control and power rests [sic] in the majority of the people [but implying] that the rights of the minority will be respected' (Roberts 1986:143). While democratisation of work can occur at both the micro and the macro levels, many ER analysts tend to concentrate on the micro level. This may include the introduction of economic and industrial democracy and employee participation in union and management decisions, perhaps through works councils and/or collective bargaining (Clegg 1960). In the present context it is important to pay attention to the macro (political economy) as well as the micro levels.

When attempts were made by the occupying powers to reinstate democracy in Japan after 1945, considerable attention was paid to the ER institutions, particularly unions, which pluralist reformers saw as offering an important countervailing force to the recently experienced macro-level totalitarianism. In other Asia-Pacific economies, before the Cold War intensified, there was a US-led move to democratise, but a subsequent roll back of militant trade unionism and political parties in much of the Asia-Pacific region helped to transform ER in many countries. In Japan, where industrial conflict had been rife in the early postwar period, militant Japanese trade unionism was eclipsed following the failure of the Miike coalminers' strike in 1960. In 1951, the Australian government had tried (but failed) to ban the Communist Party. In Korea, the union organisation Chun Pyung was banned in 1947 by the American Military government, to be replaced by Daehan Dogrib Chockseong Nodong, the precursor of South Korea's Daehan Nochong or Federation of Korean Trade Unions (FKTU) which, until 1999, remained the only legally recognised peak body.

Since the ending of the Cold War we can discern the growing autonomy of unions in various countries in the region as they have countered their government's attempts to control trade unionism. Since the mid-1990s Minjunochong, the Korean Confederation of Trade Unions (KCTU), has challenged the legitimacy of the government approved FKTU. Since the early 1990s, Serikat Buruh Sejahtera Indonesia, the Indonesian Prosperous Workers' Union (SBSI), has begun to rival the pro-government Serikat Pekerja Seluruh Indonesia, the All Indonesia Workers' Union (SPSI).

The re-emergence of independent labour movements in parts of the Asia-Pacific was confronted by the 'Asian crisis' of the late 1990s. During periods of recession and rising unemployment, unions generally face a difficult task gaining concessions from employers and governments. Nonetheless, attempts by the large Korean family-run conglomerates (*chaebols*), to retrench workers in the late 1990s were still met by vigorous protests from the union movement.

In parallel with the promotion of democratisation in the Asia-

Pacific region, there have been external pressures to improve human rights and union rights. While the International Labour Organisation (ILO) and individual countries including Australia and New Zealand have attempted to induce change, the most powerful pressures have come from North America and the European Union (EU), which have sought to link trading arrangements to human rights issues. Such pressures tend to be viewed with suspicion by governments in the region and seen as meddling in internal affairs. Some countries' leaders alleged that the US government used the regional economic problems of the late 1990s as a lever to force countries in the region to open up previously protected areas of their economies (Gilley 1998).

Industrialisation, democratisation and convergence

A long debated—and contested—argument states that 'there is a global tendency for technological and market forces associated with industrialisation to push national ER systems towards uniformity or convergence'.[3] We use this argument to help us compare Asia-Pacific countries. Our first hypothesis is that as economies move towards becoming industrialised market economies (IMEs), their ER institutions and behaviour tend to converge on those that are more typical in longer established IMEs. Such behaviour includes the increasing autonomy of ER institutions—including unions—and moves towards independent collective bargaining.

The rules, attitudes and behaviour of the ER actors are also shaped by their political context. Against the background of assumptions about the consequences of democratisation, our second hypothesis is that major political changes, such as moves towards democratisation, will induce radical transformations in an economy's ER arrangements.

Industrialisation

To what extent do the experiences of the Asia-Pacific region support these hypotheses, and if they appear to support them, which are the key explanatory factors? There has been a proliferation of commentaries, reports and academic writing which identifies the rapid industrialisation of the Asia-Pacific region and its emergence as a major geo-political entity (Borthwick 1992). The post-1945 period had been one of rapid economic growth for many countries in the region, but the regional economic crisis of the late 1990s highlighted the problems associated with entrenched relationship economies,[4] which in some cases began to overshadow earlier economic successes.

While regional and supra-national trading alliances, including the Association of Southeast Asian Nations (ASEAN) and the Asia-Pacific Economic Cooperation (APEC) forum have emerged, the member countries are more heterogeneous and more loosely grouped than are the countries of the European Union (EU). During the 1990s the ASEAN countries attempted to introduce policies aimed at greater economic co-operation; however, economic problems and political differences have tended to hamper such moves.

Explanations for the rapid industrialisation of many of the Asia-Pacific countries have variously drawn on socioeconomic approaches, political 'strong state' explanations, neo-Confucian ethics and cultural 'collectivist' models (Verma et al. 1995:336). Rather than pursue cultural typologies, we follow an approach advocated by Dore (1979) and discuss the contexts for ER which may reflect the different stages of economic development that the countries discussed in this book are passing through. Classifications may be somewhat arbitrary and there are many differences between the countries in each of the following categories, but a pattern is discernible and may facilitate discussion.

The first group includes the IMEs—Japan, New Zealand and Australia—whose current reforms or structural adjustment programs are in part a response to the spread of industrialisation to other countries of the Asia-Pacific region.

The second group, known as the 'Asian Tigers', includes the newly industrialised economies (NIEs) of South Korea and Taiwan. The 'Tigers' are clearly distinctive as post-Japan industrialisers and some of them moved towards the development of more democratic institutions during the 1990s.

The third group comprises the next generation of industrialisers and includes the People's Republic of China (PRC) and Indonesia. If it sustains the growth rates achieved throughout the 1990s, the PRC will achieve NIE status in the first few decades of the 21st century. However, economic development in the PRC has been uneven, with growth rates in the special economic zones (SEZs) greatly outstripping those of more isolated regions. Indonesia also achieved relatively high growth rates during the early to mid-1990s and had been expected to reach a higher level of industrial development by the early 21st century. However, after being adversely affected by the fallout from the Asian economic crisis, it may face a period of political and economic uncertainty.

Group 1: Restructuring in developed economies: Japan, Australia and New Zealand

Many explanations for the extraordinary growth of several Asia-Pacific economies since the early 1960s, beginning with Japan (Fruin 1992), suggest that ER may make a significant contribution to economic growth. This raises questions of universality and cultural or national uniqueness, either prescriptively, as with *Japan as No. 1: Lessons for America* (Vogel 1980), or analytically, as a justification for the development of a field of comparative human resource management (HRM) (Boxall 1995).

Japan: A post-1945 model

Since the early 1980s, there has been substantial interest in Japanese management (e.g. Suzuki 1995) and in the transferability of Japanese management styles to North America and Europe (e.g. Oliver & Wilkinson 1992). Many studies have tended to oversimplify the Japanese model, focusing on the 'three pillars' typology of enterprise unionism, lifetime employment and seniority pay and promotion. There is little exploration of the legal environment and the impact this has had on shaping Japan's ER practices (see Chapter 4). While ER in Japan is more complex than is demonstrated by the so-called 'three pillars' typology (Kuwahara 1998), a consideration of other institutional sources of jurisprudence suggests that the concept of 'lifetime' employment remains a broadly institutionalised social norm.

Problems in the Japanese economy during the 1990s, and a subsequent rise in its unemployment rate, led to suggestions that the Japanese ER model was under severe strain and required substantial adjustment so that it would converge on a Western 'hire and fire' model.

The Japanese 'model' of ER has been linked to Japan's high economic growth rates in the post-1945 era. While the above evidence suggests that changes during the 1990s tended to be cyclical rather than structural in nature, factors including an ageing population, deregulation and moves towards a service dominated economy suggest the model may have to be adapted to cope more easily with the constraints of lower economic growth—Japan has become a mature IME.

Australia: Towards the decentralisation of bargaining

Many of the moves towards ER reform in Australia since the 1980s reflected a perceived need by employers, unions and governments to improve the competitiveness of Australian enterprises, by stimulating greater labour productivity.

The Australian polity was dominated for thirteen years from 1983 to 1996 by the Australian Labor Party (ALP). Its wage and prices 'Accord' with the Australian Council of Trade Unions (ACTU) was an important cornerstone of the ALP's electoral success at the federal level. The Accord broadly consisted of a trade-off whereby the ACTU agreed to moderate union pay claims and industrial action in exchange for a say in determining political, economic and industry policies, for example, these policies included an increase in the 'social wage' in terms of rights to health and safety at work, consultation, superannuation and the regulation of equal employment opportunities, redundancy and dismissal. The Accord (1983) was intended to enable Australia to pull out of the economic recession of the early 1980s without 'inflationary increases in labour costs'. After periodic revision, it came to form part of a broad framework of economic and social restructuring within which emphasis shifted to microeconomic reform.

Legislation in 1988 simplified and standardised dispute settlement and required the Australian Industrial Relations Commission to take greater cognisance of the interests of the parties and the wider community (Frenkel 1993:259). Legislation in 1993 further challenged the traditional Australian ER system by allowing for the ratification of non-union agreements. At the federal level, the move towards enterprise bargaining favoured by the ALP government and supported by the ACTU was slow, though several states enacted legislation during the 1990s to favour enterprise bargaining rather than follow the tradition of centralised arbitrated awards.[5] Changes in ER legislation were often linked to notions of microeconomic reform.

As shown in Chapter 2, Australia's post-1996 conservative coalition government claimed a mandate to further deregulate and reform ER in Australia and discontinue the previous government's Accord with the unions. The initiators of the *Workplace Relations Act 1996*, then, aimed to further decentralise the Australian ER system. This included limiting the jurisdiction of centralised awards to twenty 'allowable matters' and promoting decentralised enterprise bargaining. Under the Act employees could negotiate collective (enterprise) agreements or individual contracts. The centralised award system was retained as a 'safety net' for employees not covered by any other agreement. However, at the time of writing, the coalition government is proposing another wave of reforms. If it succeeds in implementing most of the proposals, it will move Australia's federal industrial relations system further towards a deregulated model, following a lead from New Zealand.

New Zealand: From welfare state to radical reform

Until the mid-1980s, New Zealand could be regarded as a welfare state with a regulated labour market surrounded by tariff protection. Since then it has experienced radical change, which has included the dismantling of much of the welfare state and the deregulation of its labour market. The economic downturn brought on by the Asian financial crisis in the late 1990s prompted further restructuring and public sector reforms. As in Australia, the change process was initiated by a perceived need in the New Zealand polity to improve the competitiveness of the economy. Begun by a Labour government, ER reform was continued and accelerated by subsequent non-Labour governments that appeared to adopt so-called rational economic policies that were similar to those of Prime Minister Thatcher and President Reagan. However, the implementation of such policies was more thoroughgoing and less constrained in New Zealand than in the UK, the US or Australia due to New Zealand's relatively small population—only 3.6 million—and its unicameral legislative assembly. In this context there are fewer constraints on change than in larger countries (especially those that have two legislative assemblies or houses and those that are federations of states like Australia and the US).

As illustrated in Chapter 3, a particularly significant event in this radical New Zealand program was the deregulation of ER by the *Employment Contracts Act* 1991 which union critics have described as 'an employers' charter' (Anderson 1991). It abolished the Arbitration Court and the award system, de-emphasised collective bargaining and withdrew exclusive jurisdiction rights from unions (Deeks et al. 1994; Walsh & Ryan 1993). The size and role of unions have been severely curtailed so that many employers are no longer confronted by much countervailing power from unions (Harbridge & Honeybone 1995). However, this may change following the election of a Labour government in 1999.

Group 1 countries compared

In the post-1945 era Japan generally achieved higher economic growth rates than either Australia or New Zealand, with some claiming that Japanese ER practices were a contributing factor. Japan was governed for most of this period by a single party, the Liberal Democratic Party, which was much more closely aligned to business than to unions. Although a coalition containing the Japan Socialist Party held office for about 18 months in 1994–95, it resulted in few changes to the employment model. While the model has been resilient, it has been affected by a maturing economy, an ageing population, an expanding service sector and pressures for deregulation. In the 1990s there was ambiguous evidence to confront the assertion that Japan was converging on a Western model.

As domestic demand fell during the 1990s, large Japanese firms reduced the working hours of employees, and were willing to use redundancy only as a last resort (Nitta 1998). Even the 1999 employment reductions announced by Nissan proceeded with a degree of worker participation and efforts to avoid harsh dismissals, despite years of financial decline. Renault, which had bought a stake in Nissan, curiously gained considerable media attention by having a non-Japanese (French) executive (M. Ghosn, Le Cost Killer) announce the personnel reduction scheme. Yet, perhaps, the scheme illustrated that it would still be premature to write the obituary of the institutionalised 'lifetime' employment practice.

In Australia, and even more so in New Zealand, there appears to have been a transformation in terms of ER since the early 1980s. These changes have not been driven by moves towards democratisation at the macro level. Rather, such changes have been induced by explicit political decisions by governments that were not significantly more or less democratic than their predecessors. These decisions were partly a response to globalisation and to the economic growth of other countries in the region, such as Japan, which helped to generate a perception of the need for microeconomic reform. Subsequent changes to labour markets were shaped by policies of economic rationalism and product market considerations that were induced by increasing competition, not least from NIEs.

Group 2: The NIEs—South Korea and Taiwan (ROC)

Industrialisation in NIEs generally begins with the development of labour intensive industries, such as clothing, textile and footwear manufacturing, which allow such countries to exploit their comparative advantage in relatively low wages. The next stage of economic development tends to follow a move to heavy industries, such as steel, ship and motor vehicle manufacturing, often accompanied by government sponsored 'soft' loans. A subsequent move is towards high-tech 'knowledge intensive' industries, requiring a highly educated work force. One of the consequences for ER is the need for increasingly sophisticated HRM practices as countries attempt to move their economies along the value-added path.

Korea: Chaebol led development

South Korea's rapid industrialisation saw its per capita GDP rise from US$87 in 1962 to more than US$10 000 in 1987 (Park &

Leggett 1998:275). During much of this period South Korea was governed by a succession of strong authoritarian governments. There was a great deal of direct state intervention in the economy during this period, with economic development being guided through the *chaebol*. By the early 1990s the five top *chaebol* contributed approximately 60% of South Korea's GDP (BOK 1990). Such a concentration of economic power and government influence was blamed for much of the corruption exposed in the late 1990s, including the collapse of the Hanbo group. This combination of an authoritarian government and big business meant that union jurisdiction was limited; until 1999 the FKTU was the only legally recognised official union confederation. To maintain South Korea's competitive advantage in the export of labour intensive manufactured goods, successive governments tended to limit wage increases.

As discussed in Chapter 9, following student led large-scale protests, the 29 June Democratisation Declaration in 1987 began moves towards more liberalised political institutions. In this environment union membership grew rapidly, along with strikes and increased wage demands. While not officially recognised, there was an associated rapid growth in new independent trade unions. In 1995 a group of these merged to form the KCTU as an alternative to the FKTU. These independent unions co-ordinated some notable large-scale industrial protests that attracted international media interest. These included protests against the 1996 Labor Law amendments— that relaxed laws on retrenching workers—and protests against firms laying off workers during the Asian economic crisis of the late 1990s. Despite such public protests, union membership began to decline during the 1990s. This has been variously attributed to industrial restructuring and the growth of the services sector (Park & Leggett 1998:280). Nevertheless, unions have become a more significant part of the South Korean polity.

The response of firms to increased worker demands has been to seek increased labour market flexibility. To assist such ER reform the government set up the Industrial Relations Reform Commission (IRRC) in 1996. Such reform was also seen as necessary to help move the South Korean economy towards more 'knowledge intensive' industries, with some firms seeking to introduce more participative management styles (see Chapter 9).

Along with the above moves, a major impetus for industrial restructuring and ER reform came from the Asian economic crisis during the late 1990s. Following the regional economic turmoil, the South Korean currency devalued sharply, causing severe problems for firms exposed to offshore loans. Following its call on the International Monetary Fund (IMF) for assistance, the government initiated an austerity drive to implement the IMF conditions. The government also set up a Tripartite Commission in 1998 to deal with the process of structural and ER reform. Interestingly, along with employer and government representatives, it also contained representatives from both the FKTU and the KCTU—the KCTU was still not officially recognised.

While the crisis exposed problems associated with high debt servicing ratios in the *chaebol*, some observers saw the government's willingness to embrace the IMF recommendations as being partially politically motivated, as the downsizing and/or restructuring of these conglomerates could lead to a diminishing of their economic and political power (Liew 1998). President Kim Dae-Jung—elected in 1998—had long campaigned against the concentrated power of the *chaebol*, believing it to be a major cause of corruption.

The lessening of *chaebol* influence could have major implications for South Korean ER. Being Korea's major employers, the *chaebol* developed ER policies and practices that influenced terms and conditions of employment in many other enterprises. Company towns such as Woosan (Hyundai) and, in the public sector, Pohang (POSCO), house and service large numbers of employees. Moves towards the creation of more small to medium-sized enterprises could see a significant change in ER strategies.

Taiwan (ROC): Decentralised industrialisation

During the 1980s and 1990s Taiwan's political and economic landscape changed substantially. The legacy of a strong authoritarian (Kuomintang) government, that had ruled Taiwan since the defeat of the mainland Chinese nationalists in 1949, gave way to a more democratic and liberalised approach. A maturing economy saw the growth of the services sector and moves towards the production of higher value-added, knowledge intensive goods. In contrast to South Korea, where industrialisation was centred on the *chaebol*, Taiwan's private sector has been dominated by small to medium-sized firms. Many such firms had their origins as 'family' run businesses governed by paternal ER practices.

Changes in the economy required a better educated work force and created an awareness of the need for more sophisticated HRM practices. Government regulations, such as the Fair Labour Standards Law 1984, introduced wide-ranging labour standards; however, the government attempted to promote a more voluntarist approach to ER in the 1990s. This in part was a recognition of the need for more flexibility in ER practices in a more open economy. The internationalisation of the economy has been accompanied by large-scale investment in the PRC by Taiwanese firms, with many

Taiwanese managers having to learn new skills to manage mainland Chinese employees (Schak 1997).

As discussed in Chapter 7, democratisation has in part led to the introduction of new social welfare legislation, such as unemployment insurance; however, its effect on the unions has been less clear. The growth of unionism in the services sector, traditionally difficult to organise, has been accompanied by a reduction in union membership in more traditional industries. Unions, however, are more independent than under previous authoritarian governments and more actively promote the welfare of their members. The late 1990s saw the growth of independent, although technically illegal, unions. These grew in response to a perceived increase in worker lay-offs, in part induced by the change of industrial structure; for example, there were moves to re-locate off-shore by many labour-intensive firms and a rapid growth of the electronics industry.

Employer responses to improved social welfare legislation include non-compliance and the conversion of employees into subcontractors. Employers have also put a greater focus on HRM to improve worker productivity, including improved training and incentive programs. The increased use of higher education has resulted in many workers entering the work force at a later age than previously.

Political changes in Taiwan appear to have led to increases in social welfare legislation, that in turn have affected ER practices. Such practices have also been affected by the changing economic environment. While unions have become more independent, the growth of the service sector has been eroding their traditional domination by industrial workers.

Group 2 countries compared

These two NIEs exhibit some similarities. Both underwent rapid industrialisation under strong state authoritarian governments after 1945. In the 1980s and 1990s both countries moved towards more democratic institutions and open economies. There were further changes due to employers reacting to changing product markets (and labour markets). Unions in both countries have become more autonomous; however, moves away from manufacturing towards more service based economies have also been partly responsible for losses of union members.

A major difference between the two IMEs is the industrial concentration of their economies. While South Korea's economy is dominated by the *chaebol*, Taiwan's rapid industrialisation has been largely achieved through the growth of small to medium-sized firms. ER practices in South Korea were developed by the policies and practices of a relatively small number of large conglomerates. Taiwanese firms were often too small to develop sophisticated ER practices, which in part led to the government introducing wide-ranging 'generic' legislation through the Fair Labour Standards Law 1984. Enforcement of the law, however, was often ignored, especially before the moves towards democratisation in the 1990s.

Group 3: The People's Republic of China (PRC) and Indonesia

The ER policies of a third level of Asian industrialisers, including the PRC, have been attracting increasing attention from scholars (O'Leary 1994; Jackson 1994; Kuruvilla & Arudsothy 1995). Echoing the experiences of the NIEs, the third group of countries can get caught in a 'sandwich trap' of cheap labour competition from below and exclusion from higher value-added markets from above (Deyo 1995:23). It is arguable that these market influences have outweighed trends towards democratisation in influencing the claimed transformation of ER in these countries. Political developments in Indonesia since the fall of the Suharto government, however, have been accompanied by more militant worker demonstrations.

The People's Republic of China (PRC): towards 'market socialism'

The economic reforms instituted by Deng Xiaoping in the late 1970s moved the Chinese economy away from its former Maoist doctrines. Foreign owned and domestic private enterprises appeared and in 1992 the goal of a 'socialist market economy' was announced. In China the central planning priorities determined the state level ER policies which shaped enterprise-level ER practices. Subsequent reforms meant that 'the ER policies of Chinese enterprises are driven by product market considerations and by state-level ER policies which are being adjusted to a market-driven economy' (Verma & Yan 1995:317–18). Such changes have had profound effects on ER, as employees shift from state owned to privately operated firms. Disputes arising from the rapid transfer of workers from 'lifetime' to contract employment appeared to provide the trigger for about 50% of all labour disputes in the late 1980s and 1990s; moreover, in spite of restrictions, migration from rural areas to the towns has created heavy urban unemployment (Jackson 1994).

While economic growth throughout the 1990s was relatively high, it was concentrated in the cities and special economic zones

(SEZs) and Hong Kong. Attracted by the promise of jobs, many former rural workers migrated to the SEZs, but were paid substantially lower rates than local workers in similar industries; the practice of hiring workers from other regions was widespread (Hsing 1998). Piecework rates were common and municipal governments tended to turn a blind eye to minimum wage legislation, with local investment being a priority. Thus, the PRC provided some of the cheapest labour in the world to the factories being developed by entrepreneurs in the SEZs (O'Leary 1994:51).

At the national ER level, during the early 1990s a tripartite system was developed consisting of the Labour Ministry, the Chinese Enterprise Directors' Association (CEDA) and the All China Federation of Trade Unions (ACFTU). The State maintains the upper hand in negotiations, with unions traditionally playing a supporting role by implementing state policy (Goodall & Warner 1997), but there are signs that unions are becoming more assertive (Ungar & Chan 1995).

The PRC's transition towards a 'socialist market economy', with its associated ER changes, has been relatively gradual. This has allowed state owned enterprises to recruit and retain workers who would otherwise become unemployed if a rapid transition to free market forces occurred. The PRC's challenge, therefore, is to retrain such workers as its economy becomes increasingly dominated by private firms.

Indonesia: Beyond the New Order?

Following the destruction of the Indonesian Communist Party (PKI) by Suharto's government in the mid-1960s, Indonesian ER were strictly controlled by a strong authoritarian government, supported by the military. A relatively cheap and compliant work force was seen by the government as necessary for economic growth, with the failure of employers to pay minimum wages routinely ignored (Gall 1998). The only union organisation recognised by the State—the SPSI—received much of its funding from the government, with military personnel appointed to many of its positions. The government had linked Indonesian ER to the state sponsored doctrine of *Pancasila*. This includes notions of mutuality of interests, mutual respect and consultation between workers, employers and government (Lambert 1994:87). In practice such concepts rarely appear to have been achieved. While economic growth throughout the 1980s and early 1990s remained relatively high, working conditions, particularly for women, appeared to be harsh (ALU 1991).

Partially in response to the SPSI's perceived lack of effectiveness in representing worker interests, in the 1990s there was a growth of independent unions that were not recognised by the state. The largest of these was the unofficial SBSI (Knowles 1993). While it has attracted international attention and support from agencies such as the ILO, its leaders have been subject to government harassment and imprisonment.

As shown in Chapter 8, the ending of the Suharto government amid the political and economic turmoil of 1998–99 left Indonesian ER at a crossroads. Moves towards the establishment of more democratic processes and institutions could help create greater government recognition for workers' groups and rights—as occurred in Korea after the 1987 democracy declaration. However, continuing political uncertainty, widespread economic problems and a legacy of vested interests makes such a prospect difficult to predict.

Group 3 countries compared

The PRC and Indonesia share some similarities. Both countries have large populations and strong authoritarian governments, although the New Order government in Indonesia was fiercely anticommunist. In both countries the influence of the government on ER has overshadowed that of employer or worker groups and industrialisation has been achieved through the production of labour intensive goods—making use of relatively low-cost labour.

Industrialisation in the PRC has not been accompanied by any significant moves towards democratisation. It remains a one party state with little government tolerance for political dissidents. The greatest effect on ER in the PRC has been the rapid increase in privately owned firms that require a highly committed, more productive work force if they are to compete successfully.

Until the late 1990s industrialisation in Indonesia was not accompanied by any significant moves towards more democratic institutions and processes. The Suharto government maintained tight control over the labour movement, with little tolerance for labour dissidents. While the fall of the Suharto government in 1998 was accompanied by calls for a greater recognition for workers' organisations, political instability has made for an uncertain future. It remains to be seen how the post-1999 Wahid government will change ER arrangements in Indonesia.

Asia-Pacific Economic Co-operation (APEC)

The Asia-Pacific Economic Co-operation (APEC) forum was created in 1989. Its emergence reflects economic and geo-political developments on the international stage. Asia's exceptional industrialisation and export success since World War II was one factor which promoted the formation of such regional linkages. Chapter 13 discusses controversies about human resource development (HRD), HRM and labour-related issues in APEC.

State institutions and government policies on organised labour developed over a comparatively long period of time in the older IMEs of the Group 1 countries. However, rapid recent economic development in the Group 2 and some of the Group 3 countries prompted political and business leaders to develop such policies more quickly. When trying to agree on policies, the participants in the APEC forum had to confront the different stages of development in the diverse countries that they represented. These differences are illustrated in this book.

There has been increasing US-led pressure for the inclusion of labour standards, in particular, and labour-related issues, in general, in trade-related international fora. In July 1999, the US took a firm line in the third APEC HRD ministerial meeting in Washington, promoting a range of initiatives that appeared to be reflecting US union lobbying. However, the pressure exerted by the US in APEC on such issues was less forceful than its support for a trade–labour standards link in the much-publicised December 1999 World Trade Organisation (WTO) meeting in Seattle. It seems that US insistence on a trade–labour standards link contributed significantly to the collapse of that meeting. In light of the Seattle meeting, we can infer that the focus on ER issues within APEC is part of a much larger US agenda on trade and ER issues.

Conclusions

As a point of departure in this chapter, we hypothesised, first, that, as economies move towards becoming IMEs, their institutions and behaviour in ER terms (e.g. the relative autonomy of their ER institutions) would tend to converge on those that are more typical in IMEs. Do the experiences of the Asia-Pacific countries examined in this book support this hypothesis? If so, do technological, market or other forces appear to be key explanatory factors? Second, we hypothesised that major political change, such as moves towards democratisation, will induce radical transformations in an economy's ER arrangements.

Explanations of political and industrial development of economies of the Asia-Pacific region vary, but many in one way or another mention notions of democratisation and the phenomena of ER, including the institutions for settling and regulating collective disputes of conventional ER, and the behavioural-science informed discipline and function for managing employees for the attainment of enterprise goals, known as HRM. Nevertheless, our preliminary observations of the countries examined in this book show differing levels of support for our hypotheses.

Among the first group of countries, Japan's industrialisation has been accompanied by the development of an ER model that is quite distinct from Western IME models. The emergence of a short-lived non-LDP led coalition government in 1994—the first non-LDP government for almost 40 years—did not radically change Japan's ER laws or institutions. In Australia and New Zealand, changes to ER practices were brought about by the perceived need for microeconomic reform in the face of international competition and changing product markets. These changes were hastened by the election of conservative governments in both countries. This led to the introduction of more deregulated ER systems, although the New Zealand approach was more radical.

In the second group of countries, rapid industrialisation was accompanied by political change since the late 1980s. The introduction of more democratic institutions led to changes in the ER practices of both countries. In South Korea this manifested itself with the rise of the independent union movement, while labour regulations in Taiwan were reinforced and expanded. However, there is little evidence that either of these countries' ER institutions and behaviours are converging on a Western-style ER model.

The third group showed little support for either hypothesis. Strong authoritarian governments in the PRC and Indonesia have effectively controlled and guided ER policies in both countries. While industrialisation was not directly linked to moves towards democratisation, the economic turmoil in Indonesia in the late 1990s, brought on by the Asian crisis, helped cause the downfall of the Suharto government. This in turn led to calls for more democratic institutions.

The stimuli for change in ER, therefore, would appear to be more than a product of a country's level of industrialisation. Other factors include the dynamics of local and global product (and labour) markets and actions by governments to address microeconomic reform. Our examination of the above countries suggests that at a certain level of industrialisation, such as in the NIEs of South Korea and Taiwan, political liberalisation may follow economic liberalisation; however, we are cautious about making generalisations on the basis of two countries.

There are strong forces associated with globalisation. Nevertheless, within their own contexts, policy-makers at a national level still have scope for maintaining their national strategic choices and driving further such choices. They are not merely passengers on a train that is converging on a model typified by Western IMEs.

Since product and labour markets and economic and political

changes have not followed an unambiguous path of convergence, it is only to be expected that '. . . human resource management systems in the Pacific Region will differ in many ways' (Moore & Devereaux Jennings 1995:5). We should not expect ER developments in the region to conform to models developed in Western IMEs. The industrialising Asia-Pacific economies are in many ways distinct social formations which deserve systematic analysis based on a growing body of research. The responses of these national policy-makers to the economic, political and social challenges of the late 1990s' Asian crisis helped to shape Asia-Pacific ER institutions in this new century. These responses are exemplified in the chapters that follow.

PART II

National perspectives

2 Changing approaches to employment relations in Australia[1]

Greg J. Bamber and Edward M. Davis

Increasing international competition has encouraged Australian policy-makers to pay more attention to the link between employment relations (ER) and enterprise performance. This chapter examines the Australian ER context, details characteristics of key players and explores ER processes, industrial conflict and pay determination. Included is a summary of debates about: employee participation, equal opportunities, workplace reform, industrial disputes, and changes to industrial law. (Since Federation, there have been more amendments to the Australian legislation on industrial relations than on any other issue except tax.)

The Australian states were separate colonies until 1901, when they federated to become an independent country within the British Empire (subsequently the Commonwealth), but these states still wield considerable power over many issues, including ER. Under the Australian Constitution, the federal government appeared to have only limited ER powers, and was able to make laws only on conciliation and arbitration for the prevention and settlement of industrial disputes extending beyond the limits of any one state (section 51 (xxxv)). Reforms implemented in the 1990s have challenged this traditional interpretation of the powers of the federal government, with the aim of increasing government influence on ER, as discussed later.

Having earlier rejected the notion of compulsory arbitration, unions changed their stance after some disastrous defeats during a wave of strikes in the early 1890s. The *Conciliation and Arbitration Act* 1904 encouraged employers to recognise unions registered under the Act, and empowered these unions to make claims on behalf of all employees within their coverage. Under the 1904 Act, then, unions could ensure that employers were called to the Conciliation and Arbitration Court (later a commission) even if they were unwilling to negotiate. Once the court had made an award (a decision on pay or other terms of employment), its provisions were legally enforceable. Although employers were initially hostile to the federal Conciliation and Arbitration Court established under the Act, they later found that they could use the procedures to their advantage and generally supported them.

There has long been a high degree of state intervention in the Australian labour market, in contrast to Britain, which has often been characterised as having a voluntary approach and relatively little state intervention. (For more such international comparisons, see Bamber & Lansbury 1998, ch. 2.) The advent of arbitration was a significant departure from the British traditions that had been important in Australia before the 1890s, when the foundations of Australia's twentieth century ER system were established.

The political and economic environment

Australian labourism (Hagan 1981:45) differs from that in Britain and other industrialised market economies. There were at least three special characteristics of Australian labourism. First, the 1904 Act and its provision for compulsory arbitration was a key element of Australia's initial 'social contract' (Frenkel 1990). A second element was a law restricting immigration, thereby limiting the supply side of the labour market. The 'white Australia' policy aimed to keep out Asians, in particular, who were seen as threatening union strength and union members' living standards. The third element involved creating a regime of tariffs to protect domestic products from the threat of cheap imports. All political parties maintained such approaches, at least until the post-1945 period.

The tariff policy was originally designed to help create employment for an expanding population. It also enabled commissions to determine wages more on social and equity grounds than in accordance with productivity and market forces. Many protected industries, anticipating the chill winds of international competition, tenaciously lobbied governments to retain high tariff levels. The move of the Whitlam Labor government (1972–75) to reduce tariffs by 25% 'at a single stroke' was strongly criticised by employers and unions as leading to increased levels of unemployment, especially in industries vulnerable to overseas competition.

In the context of protectionist policies, most manufacturing has been oriented to domestic markets. With the reduction of tariff barriers, however, there has been a decline in manufacturing employment. Between 1981 and 1996, manufacturing employment declined from 23% of total employment to below 14%. The proportion of employees in agriculture fell from 7.6% to 5%, but employment in the service sector increased from 63% to 72% (ABS 1997a; OECD 1997).

Australia is a welfare state which provides unemployment benefits, for example, to a greater extent than the US or Japan. Nevertheless, Australia's welfare arrangements are less developed than those in most Western European countries. Since Federation, conservative political parties have generally dominated federal government. However, there were reformist post-war Labor governments in the 1941–49, 1972–75 and 1983–96 periods. Given its links with the unions, the Australian Labor Party (ALP) has been more sympathetic to their interests. In practice, most unions have tended to see wage bargaining or determination via arbitration as a higher priority than improving social welfare benefits. In the Labor government elected in 1983, Prime Minister Bob Hawke was a former president of the Australian Council of Trade Unions (ACTU), and several ministers had also held senior union posts before their entry into parliament. That government, through its Accord with the ACTU, placed more formal emphasis on a range of goals, including job creation, improved social welfare and improved standards of living; wage bargaining, then, was only one of its priorities.

The post-1983 Labor and conservative governments have sought to reduce tariffs to stimulate competition. Such contextual changes may have important implications in terms of employment relations. The lengths to which government should go to protect particular industries and to encourage competition is subject to much debate. These debates are not new but echo some aspects of those of the 1890s.

Relevant laws

The Hawke Labor government, elected in 1983, replaced the *Conciliation and Arbitration Act* 1904 with the *Industrial Relations Act* 1988. In most respects the new Act was similar to its predecessor, which had been extensively amended since 1904. Federal unions generally registered with the Industrial Registrar to gain access to arbitration and to enjoy full legal status. There were also registration requirements for employers and employers' associations, but registration was more significant for unions since it provided them with an important platform. The Act prescribed that a union should not be registered if there was already another in existence to which employees could 'conveniently belong'. While this helped to reduce inter-union disputes, it also inhibited the development of new unions (for example, specific enterprise unions) and helped preserve some whose traditional membership areas had declined.

The arbitration system includes federal and state industrial commissions. The federal Conciliation and Arbitration Court used to
have arbitral and judicial functions. Later, the industrial division of
the Federal Court administered the judicial provisions of the Act,
while the Australian Industrial Relations Commission (AIRC, the
Commission) or its predecessors carried out non-judicial functions.
These changes of function were implemented following the 'Boil-
ermakers' Case' (1956), in which the High Court ruled that, under
the 'separation of powers' doctrine in the Constitution, arbitral and
judicial functions could not be carried out by the same tribunal. This
requirement does not apply to the state industrial commissions,
which administer awards in each state, covering nearly half the work
force. Federal awards cover only about a third of the work force.
The remaining members of the work force are not directly covered
either by the federal or a state jurisdiction.

The main actors

Employers' associations

The early apparent strength of unions in Australia encouraged the
development of employers' associations and led them to place
greater emphasis on employment issues than did their counterparts
in some other countries (Plowman 1989). However, there is great
variation in the size and complexity of employers' associations, from
small, single-industry organisations to large ones which attempt to
cover all employers within a particular state. Most employers' associations offer a range of services to their members, so that industrial
relations advice may be only one of their priorities. Training, trade
and commercial matters are increasingly to the fore. In 1977, the
Confederation of Australian Industry (CAI) was established as
the major national employers' organisation, 50 years after the formation of the ACTU. In 1983, a group of large employers set up
the Business Council of Australia (BCA), partly because the unions
appeared to be a more unified and effective lobby group than
employers. They also formed the BCA as a reflection of their
dissatisfaction with the apparent inability of the CAI to service the
needs of its heterogeneous membership. During the 1980s there were
several important departures from the CAI. These included large
affiliates, such as the Metal Trades Industry Association (1987) and
the Australian Chamber of Manufactures (1989). One repercussion
was the further airing of differences between employers. (These two
former affiliates later merged and became the Australian Industry
Group.)

In an attempt to co-ordinate employers' policies more effectively, the CAI merged with the Australian Chamber of Commerce
to form the Australian Chamber of Commerce and Industry (ACCI)
in 1992. The ACCI comprised some 40 employer organisations,
which represented around 350 000 individual businesses spread
across the economy. Nonetheless, several major employers' associations did not affiliate with the ACCI. The views of Australian
employers, then, are still represented in a fragmented way. The
ACCI argues that there are many policy and other matters over
which employers agree and that their case will be strengthened by
co-ordination and unity. The alternative view is that there are inevitable differences among employers and their associations and that
the diversity of employers' associations reflects this. The disunity
among employers' organisations can be contrasted with the relatively
high level of unity usually demonstrated by unions under the
umbrella of the ACTU.

Unions

The establishment of the legally based federal arbitration system
in the early twentieth century encouraged the rapid growth of
unions. By 1921, approximately 50% of the Australian labour force
was unionised. But union density has fluctuated. During the Depression of the early 1930s it dropped almost to 40%. In the 1940s there
was a steady increase in density, with a peak of 65% (according to
data collected by unions) in 1953. Union density has also been
gauged on the basis of household surveys. This shows a steep
decline since the mid-1970s. In 1976, 51% of all employees were
in unions (56% of males; 43% of females). By 1998 this had fallen
to 28% (30% of males; 26% of females) (ABS 1998). One prediction
is that density will fall to 20% by 2004 (Jost 1994). Contributing
factors have been the relative decline in employment in manufacturing and the public sector (bastions for unions), and the strong
growth in the service sector, which is generally more difficult to
unionise. Significant growth in part-time and casual employment
and in the proportion of women in the work force are additional
factors, as these workers are also difficult to unionise. However, the
unions are trying to improve their recruitment and retention of
members, and some are succeeding (see below, ch. 10).

    The profile of unions has been transformed since 1983. The
Australian Bureau of Statistics (ABS) recorded that in 1983 there
were 319 unions (ABS 1984). Membership was spread unevenly
with, at one end of the scale, 105 unions each with fewer than 500
members and accounting for less than 1% of total membership and,

at the other end, nine unions had 80 000 or more members each, accounting for 34% of membership.

In 1987 the ACTU urged its affiliates to seek mergers and amalgamations to streamline union operations. The ACTU's rationale was that a smaller number of larger unions would be more effective and deliver higher quality services to members. Also, the Labor government introduced legislation that further encouraged and facilitated union mergers. Subsequently, there was rapid change. Union leaders at the 1993 ACTU Congress claimed that 98% of union members were by then covered by only twenty unions or union groups.

The ACTU, formed in 1927, is the main confederation for manual and non-manual unions. Few important unions remain outside it. The high inclusiveness of the ACTU follows the decision of two former white-collar union confederations to join forces with the ACTU: the Australian Council of Salaried and Professional Associations (ACSPA) joined the ACTU in 1979 and the Council of Australian Government Employee Organisations (CAGEO) followed in 1981. The ACTU's considerable influence over its affiliates was reflected at ACTU congresses and conferences throughout the 1980s and 1990s, when nearly all its executive recommendations were endorsed (Davis 1996). Officers of the ACTU also play key roles in the presentation of union cases before the Commission and in the conduct and settlement of important industrial disputes.

As in the US and the UK, then, there is now only one main central union confederation. This is in contrast to many Western European countries, which have several confederations (Bamber & Lansbury 1998: chs. 6–7). Nevertheless, in each of the states, trades and labour councils also play a significant role in ER. Although the state trades and labour councils are formal branches of the ACTU, they generally have a much longer history and display some independence and often considerable power in their localities. (This is unlike trades councils in England and Wales, which have a much smaller role.)

The basic unit of organisation for most unions is the branch, which may cover an entire state or a large district within a state. Workplace organisation tends to be informal, but shop stewards' (or delegates') committees have developed among key groups of manual workers and, especially in the public sector, among non-manual staff too. In another contrast with the British tradition, however, the role of most workplace union delegates is relatively undeveloped. The centralisation of ER decision-making has induced a dependence on union full-time officials at state and federal levels. Nevertheless, greater reliance on enterprise bargaining since the late 1980s has increased the role of workplace delegates.

Government

The federal government has used a range of tools that have influenced the context and substance of ER. For instance, monetary and fiscal policies designed to stimulate or depress the economy have inevitably had an impact on the bargaining power of employers and unions. Governments have enacted or amended legislation on a diverse array of matters connected with ER, conciliation and arbitration. Governments have regularly made submissions to the Commission on pay and conditions, playing a pivotal role at National Wage Cases and in major cases determining conditions on workers' rights in the face of redundancy, and maternity and other leave matters.

The 1983–96 Labor government wielded considerable influence over ER through its Accord with the ACTU. This took the form of an agreement (or social contract) that was a more or less shared vision for economic, industry and social policy. The original Accord of 1983 was renegotiated seven times, often against the background of a forthcoming federal election.

Federal, state and local governments are also major employers in their own right, employing approximately a quarter of the labour force. Their policies as employers are therefore significant. The 1972–75 Whitlam Labor government sought to establish pace-setting conditions for its employees and to encourage the extension of union coverage. The election of the Fraser conservative coalition government in 1975 brought considerable change. The employment conditions of public servants began to fall behind those prevailing in the private sector, and legislation was introduced to strengthen the ability of the government as an employer to lay off or dismiss workers if it chose. It also cancelled the arrangement whereby public service union members' dues were deducted directly from their wages. Such cancellation is a powerful weapon against unions, for it can have serious repercussions in terms of unions retaining their members, and hence their income via members' dues. The post-1983 Labor government repealed those laws regarded as least palatable by the unions and restored the automatic payroll deduction of union dues. Public-sector employees failed, however, to regain their status as pace-setters, so there has been a growing disparity in remuneration for public and private sector employees.

Employee participation

Industrial democracy attracted much attention in the early 1970s, but interest waned with the onset of unemployment under the non-Labor federal government of 1975–83. After 1983 there was renewed interest; the Accord stressed that 'consultation is a key factor in bringing about change in industry [at] industry, company and workplace level' (ALP–ACTU 1983:9).

The Hawke government supported the ACTU at the Commission in its claim for improved job protection standards to be inserted into workers' awards. This led to the Commission's Termination, Change and Redundancy Decision in 1984. Employers were required to consult their employees and unions before introducing major changes to work methods or to organisational structure. Where redundancies were contemplated, the length of notice was increased. Unions welcomed this decision. Many employers were less enthusiastic, however, seeing the decision as increasing costs and impinging on managerial prerogatives.

Some employers had forged agreements that went beyond the employee and union rights determined by the Commission. For example, Telecom (a predecessor to Telstra) and the relevant unions made a Technological Change Agreement. This committed Telecom's managers to provide information to unions and to seek union participation in the process leading up to a decision. Managers and union officials commented that the agreement facilitated the introduction of new technology in this enterprise during the 1980s (Davis & Lansbury 1988). In the mid-1990s, Telstra devised a 'participative approach' in an attempt to facilitate workplace reform and improved productivity. But in anticipation of the change from a Labor to a non-Labor federal government and the subsequent privatisation of Telstra, in the late 1990s Telstra moved away from such management styles towards more directive ones (Ross & Bamber 1998). Telstra reduced its work force by more than a third in the 1990s.

At least at the level of rhetoric, there was a degree of consensus among leaders in government, business and unions on the importance of developing more productive and co-operative workplaces, characterised by higher levels of employee participation. To this end, the parties issued several joint statements. The most obvious formal support for more employee participation was found in the important National Wage Case decisions after 1987, which stressed that co-operation should underpin the approach of unions and employers to the overhaul of work organisation and productivity. For instance, in the 1991 decision the Commission stated that enterprises should 'establish a consultative mechanism and procedures appropriate to their size, structure and needs for consultation and negotiation on matters affecting their efficiency and productivity' (Lansbury & Davis 1992:233).

In spite of such statements, evidence from the two Australian

Workplace Industrial Relations Surveys (AWIRS) suggested that employee participation in decision-making remained limited. In 1995, joint consultative committees were reported in 33% of workplaces with twenty or more employees, compared with only 14% in 1990. Furthermore, in 1995, 16% of workplaces had employee representatives on their boards compared with only 7% in 1990 (Moorehead et al. 1997:188). Some of the increased interest in joint consultative committees may be attributed to the spread of enterprise bargaining in the 1990s. However, while more than 80% of workplaces introduced changes in the two years prior to the 1995 survey, in only 29% of the workplaces surveyed were employees consulted and in only 18% did employees have significant impact on these decisions. Hence, the presence of formal mechanisms for consultation does not necessarily mean that employees will be involved in decision-making by management (Moorehead et al. 1997:244).

The Karpin Report on Leadership and Management Skills in Australia, commissioned by the federal government, criticised the performance of Australian management. Karpin identified weaknesses among Australian managers that included a lack of open-mindedness and a rigidity towards learning; deficiencies in teamwork and empowerment; an inability to cope with differences; and poor 'people skills' (Karpin 1995). These factors may have contributed to the slowness of Australian managers to adopt consultative approaches, despite the advocacy by leading practitioners and academics. While there have been better communications and higher levels of employee participation in some exemplar workplaces, in comparison with best practice in Japan and most Western European countries there remains scope for much greater progress in this area.

Equal opportunities

As female participation in the workforce has increased, there has been more attention paid by the media as well as the industrial parties to women at work. In 1961 women comprised approximately 25% of the work force; by 1981 this had increased to 37% and by 1999 it reached 43.5% (Davis & Harris 1996: ABS 1999).

The federal *Affirmative Action (Equal Employment Opportunity for Women) Act* 1986 covers all private sector employers with 100 or more employees, and obliges employers to take eight specific steps designed to remove discrimination against women and promote equality in employment. Some early evidence suggested indifferent compliance (Davis & Pratt 1990). Also, despite award provisions for equal pay for work of equal value, women's earnings on average have remained below male earnings. In large part, this has been because women have remained concentrated in occupations and industries characterised by relatively low pay and poor conditions.

However, such matters as childcare, maternity and paternity leave, equal employment opportunity, affirmative action and sexual harassment are increasingly seen as being in the ER (and Human Resource Management—HRM) arena, rather than exclusively as women's issues. Further, concern for business performance has induced many employers to improve childcare and related conditions in an attempt to attract and retain women workers.

Many Australian employers have also responded to labour shortages by employing migrant workers. Before 1949, most migrants came to Australia from the British Isles. Since then, Mediterranean countries, Eastern European and South-East Asian countries have also been important sources. In relative terms, the Australian work force is even more multicultural than the American. By 1996 almost a quarter of the Australian work force was born overseas (ABS 1997a) with a much higher proportion in manufacturing born overseas. This mix of languages and cultures poses a challenge for employers, especially when trying to improve two-way communication on health and safety procedures and hazards, or on new technologies and methods of working (Quinlan & Bohle 1991).

Employment relations processes

The Australian ER system has federal and state components. Historically, federal awards have taken precedence, but the state systems have also been important. Problems arising from the overlapping jurisdictions of the state and federal commissions have been a source of concern to reformers. Such concerns are compounded when there is, for instance, a federal Labor government, but non-Labor governments in most states, as there was in the mid-1990s. In effect, there remain seven separate systems of ER regulation; in addition to the federal system, each of the six states has its own legislation and its own distinctive style. In 1997, when there were conservative governments both in Victoria and federally, Victoria ceded most of its ER jurisdiction to the federal government. Following a change to a Labor government in 1999 however, the future directions of industrial relations in Victoria are uncertain.

The federal system has been based on conciliation and arbitration. The federal Commission has encouraged employers and unions to discuss, negotiate and settle matters related to pay and conditions. Conciliation has always been the greater part of the day-to-day work of commissioners. The process of arbitration was compulsory in two senses. First, when activated, it required the parties to submit to a mandatory procedure for presenting their arguments. Second, Commission awards were binding on the parties. Awards specified minimum standards of pay and conditions, which an employer must meet or else face legal penalties.

Pay determination

The arbitration system has usually been associated with the centralisation of pay determination. The Commission has often exercised considerable influence over key wage issues. Its predecessor, the federal Conciliation and Arbitration Court, initially became involved in fixing a minimum wage in 1907 which it described as a 'basic wage'. The basic wage was set at a level sufficient to cover the minimum needs of a male worker and his family unit of five, and became the accepted wage for unskilled work. A custom of pay differentials (margins) for skills was developed in the 1920s, based largely on traditional differentials in the metal and engineering trades.

The Court thus began to regulate wages and differentials through its decisions on the basic wage and margins at the National Wage Case hearings. These have been a much publicised ritual at approximately annual intervals. Employers, unions and governments made submissions to the Commission, which eventually handed down a decision. This then determined a change to pay or conditions for most employees throughout Australia. In 1967, the Commission discontinued the custom of basic wage and margins in favour of a 'total' award. It also introduced a national minimum wage, representing the lowest wage permissible for a standard work week by any employee.

During the early 1970s, the Commission sought to adjust the relative structure of award wages in different industries and to reduce the scope of 'over-award' increases by attempting to bring formal awards more closely into line with actual earnings. But by 1973–74, the contribution of National Wage Cases to total wage increases had declined to approximately 20% as unions bargained directly with employers for large over-award payments. Collective bargaining had therefore become the dominant force in wage increases, its leading settlements soon flowing on to most of the economy.

Faced with the dual problem of rapidly rising inflation and unemployment, the Labor government moved to restore the Commission's authority. In 1974, the federal government and the ACTU sought the introduction of automatic full cost-of-living indexation of wage increases, against the opposition of non-Labor state governments and private sector employers. However, between 1975 and 1981, partial rather than full indexation was the norm, and the Commission abandoned indexation in 1981 (Dabscheck 1989). A round of direct negotiations followed. Some unions won large pay increases and these began to flow on to other sectors. At the same time, there was a sharp fall in demand for goods and services, while unemployment rose.

Labor's 1983–96 Accord

The 1983–96 Labor government returned the Commission to a more powerful role in pay policy. The 1983 Accord agreed between the ALP and the ACTU included a return to centralised wage determination, with guidelines based on wage adjustments for price movements and, at longer intervals, for movements in national productivity. This approach was reflected by the Commission in 1983, which reintroduced wage indexation. However, there was a requirement that each union should pledge to make 'no extra claims' in return for receiving indexation. Most unions accepted this requirement, and there was little movement in wages on top of nationally determined pay rates. Those unions seeking to press for wage increases outside the Accord found themselves isolated and their campaigns were usually unsuccessful (for example, the domestic airline pilots in 1989).

Although opinion has been divided over the effectiveness of the Accord, two researchers have argued that it was responsible for generating an extra 313 000 jobs between 1983 and 1989 (Chapman & Gruen 1990). This represented a 4% rise in employment and a 2% reduction in unemployment. On this reasoning, the Accord produced about one-fifth of the 1.6 million new jobs during this period. A major factor, they estimated, was that real wages fell by 10% between 1983 and 1989.

This estimate sparked debate within the union movement, with some arguing that unions should seek to reverse the fall in real wages. ACTU officials contended, however, that the impact of the fall in real wages was more than offset by increased employment (thereby increasing household incomes), tax reform, improved superannuation and a raft of more generous social welfare provisions. They claimed that such innovations had led to an improvement in living standards. Officials also pointed to the greater influence by union representatives over economic, industry and social policies. The Accord included jointly agreed policies on prices and non-wage incomes, industrial law, social security, occupational health and safety, education, health and Australian government employment.

Between 1983 and 1996 the Accord provided the framework for the development of union and government policies on economic, industrial and social matters.

With regard to pay, the original 1983 Accord (which later became known as Accord Mark I) envisaged federal government support for full wage indexation. However, following the 1985–86 economic crisis, the government abandoned this commitment. It also secured the agreement of the ACTU to support a new-style wages policy, linking pay increases to measures designed to improve productivity and efficiency. Most employers and their organisations welcomed the change; the views of the major parties were put before the Commission in National Wage Case hearings in late 1986.

In the 1987 National Wage Case decision, the Commission introduced a dual system of wage adjustments. A first tier provided $10 for all workers following the decision. A further 4% pay increase depended, in the main, on unions and employers agreeing to improve efficiency in their industry or workplaces. In the following year, wage increases were conditional on discussion of 'structural efficiency' which resulted in a mixture of industry-by-industry and employer-by-employer productivity negotiations. These National Wage Case decisions reflected the central role of the Commission, while also incorporating moves towards devolved industry and enterprise agreements between employers and unions.

Reaffirming these previous National Wage Case decisions, in 1989 the Commission elaborated on the items that unions and employers might consider in their negotiations to improve efficiency. Among their suggestions were issues such as overtime, penalty rates, flexible hours, part-time and casual employment and changes in staffing. Thus the 1989 decision provided the opportunity for unions and employers to begin to address issues that had long bedevilled performance, but had been widely regarded as immutable.

The early 1990s witnessed considerable turbulence in the politics of wage determination. The Business Council had declared in 1989 that enterprise based bargaining was the key to improved competitiveness and the route to the constant adjustment of methods and technologies, the development of a sense of common purpose, better dispute settlement and improved pay systems, linking pay and performance (BCA 1989:8–9). The ACTU stated in 1990 that it wished to see a much greater emphasis on decentralised bargaining rather than on the central determination of wages and conditions. It therefore appeared to endorse the Business Council's call for more enterprise based bargaining. The Labor government joined in the call for greater reliance on bargaining and a diminished role for the Commission. These views were put to the Commission in National Wage Case hearings in late 1990.

In April 1991 the Commission rejected such submissions, arguing that a rapid move to much greater decentralisation might see a surge of wage increases not linked to productivity. This would prove inflationary and would reverse the progress made over the previous few years (AIRC 1991a:18). The Commission was also concerned that although the government, unions and employers all apparently agreed on the need for more bargaining, there were significant differences in interpretation and approach. For instance, should pay increases be linked to enterprise profitability or productivity? How should either or both be measured? What role, if any, should the Commission play? And what would be the nature of bargaining in the large non-unionised sector? (AIRC 1991a:25). The Commission concluded that 'the parties to industrial relations have still to develop the maturity necessary for the further shift of emphasis now proposed' (AIRC 1991a:38). The Commission wished to see a more receptive environment—one more likely to encourage successful bargaining. It therefore deferred the matter until the parties had resolved significant outstanding matters.

Government and union leaders then rejected the Commission's decision and stated that they would pursue more bargaining. Later explaining the reaction of the unions, ACTU Secretary Bill Kelty was very critical of the Commission. He said that centralised wage-fixing removed the main incentive to getting workers active and involved in their workplace. It also reduced the influence of workers at their workplace:

> The result of wages being totally controlled by people who have never visited their workplace, and through a process which workers do not understand or have direct input into, had reduced workers' capacity, willingness and confidence to use their creativity and put forward innovative ideas. The new wage bargaining strategy is a strategy designed to create more interesting and financially rewarding jobs, by stimulating greater worker involvement in all aspects of the way their industry and workplace operates, thereby driving enterprise reform and pushing up productivity levels. (Kelty 1991:1)

In mid-1991 another round of National Wage Case hearings began. This time no submissions for a wage increase were heard; rather the focus was on the appropriate rules for wage fixing. In late 1991 the Commission determined a new enterprise bargaining principle, although it remained concerned about continuing and significant differences between the parties with regard to the implementation of bargaining and that wage outcomes might prove inflationary. Nevertheless, the Commission elaborated the framework for bargaining. Key elements included the provision that pay increases must be based on the implementation of efficiency measures designed to effect real gains in productivity and the demonstration of a broad agenda for negotiation. The Commission therefore sought to retain an important role as overseer of the new system (AIRC 1991b).

In 1992 amendments to the legislation undermined the role of the Commission. A new division in the amended law was designed 'to facilitate the making and certifying of agreements'. This meant that the Commission had to certify agreements, where these agreements involved single enterprises and the appropriate bargaining unit and several tests were met (such as the inclusion of a grievance procedure, specification of the period of operation and employee–union consultation). These amendments therefore diminished the influence of the Commission over bargaining.

In 1993 the Labor government embarked on a further round of legal changes. These were implemented in early 1994 and were designed to facilitate bargaining in the non-unionised sector while at the same time strengthening awards as 'safety nets' and setting minimum rates of pay and conditions. Important features of the newly amended Act included the creation of a sanction-free bargaining period in the negotiation of certified agreements and the establishment of a specialist Industrial Relations Court to replace the former industrial division of the Federal Court.

The Act broke new ground in its reliance on conventions of the International Labor Organisation (an agency of the United Nations). Federal government endorsement of conventions on minimum wages, equal pay for work of equal value, rights to redundancy pay, protection against unfair dismissal and rights to 12 months of unpaid parental leave meant that all employees across Australia were covered. It appeared therefore that the federal government had found a way to spread its influence in ER beyond the federal jurisdiction.

The Coalition's post-1996 reforms

Another significant phase of ER reform began with the election of the Liberal–National coalition government, led by John Howard, in March 1996. Its *Workplace Relations Act* 1996 was one of the first pieces of legislation that it introduced. Because of opposition by Labor and other minority parties, which held the balance of power in Australia's upper house of review, the Senate, the Bill was passed only after a series of amendments by the Democrats was accepted by the government. The Act, which came into force in January 1997, signalled a more radical deregulation of industrial relations although it still provided parties with a choice between remaining in the award system or opting for a workplace agreement. The 1996 Act did not go as far as New Zealand's *Employment Contracts Act* 1991 (see ch. 3), which abolished that country's arbitration system (on which Australia's had been partially modelled). Nevertheless, the Howard government sought to move the system away from a collectivist approach, in which there was a strong role for unions and commissions, to a more fragmented system of individual bargaining between employees and employers. The new system could be characterised as promoting 'fragmented flexibility' rather than the 'co-ordinated flexibility' that had been preferred by the previous Keating Labor government.

Key elements in the *Workplace Relations Act* 1996 included significant changes in the role of the AIRC, which had been able to make determinations about 'industrial matters' pertaining to the relationship between employers and employees. This provided the Commission with wide powers to regulate employment conditions. The new Act restricted the Commission's determinations to a list of 20 'allowable matters', although it could still arbitrate on 'exceptional matters'. Awards were also required to be simplified to cover only 20 issues in order to establish a safety net of minimum standards. New arrangements for enterprise bargaining included a new form of agreement, known as Australian Workplace Agreements (AWAs), to exist alongside Certified Agreements (CAs). Under AWA provisions, employers were able to enter into either a non-union collective agreement or a non-union individual contract with their employees. An AWA had to be lodged with the office of the Employee Advocate to ensure that the AWA met the 'no disadvantage test' (that it did not lead to a reduction in the terms and conditions of employees when compared with their award entitlements). Where there was doubt, the AWA could be referred to the Commission as a final arbiter. The AWA concept was opposed by unions, which saw it as an attempt to undermine the collective basis of ER. For the first time in Australia, registration of individual employment agreements was permitted to prevail over awards and Certified Agreements. While it was generally anticipated that AWAs would play a fairly minor role in regulating wages and conditions, they were part of a broader trend towards greater diversity in labour market arrangements and the growing emphasis on the individualisation of ER.

In 1999, the coalition government proposed a second phase of reforms to the federal legal framework for ER. These included: moves to legislate for secret ballots in union elections, further tighten the provisions for ballots before industrial action, to simplify award conditions and further reduce the power of the Australian

Industrial Relations Commission (*Australian Financial Review*, 3 July 1999). At the time of writing it is not yet clear how much of its new reform program the government will be able to negotiate through the Senate, where the government does not enjoy a majority.

The government also aimed to encourage employers to take more advantage of such reforms. Employers have often appeared reluctant to confront unions. Employers have to maintain a continuing relationship with employees and their unions and this seems to have inhibited many employers from adopting confrontational approaches to the unions covering their employees.

Industrial disputes

One early argument for introducing compulsory arbitration was to render strikes unnecessary. The 'rule of law' provided under arbitration was supposed to displace the 'rude and barbarous process of strike and lockout'. For many years, the *Conciliation and Arbitration Act* rendered strikes illegal and subject to penalties. Although this provision was removed in 1930, Australian workers were not granted the formal right to strike until the implementation of a 1993 federal law. Even this right was limited to situations where there was a dispute between an employer and unions with members employed at a single enterprise and who are covered by an award and negotiating a new enterprise agreement. In 1996 the right to strike was limited to a lawful bargaining period—for example, when the parties were negotiating or renegotiating an agreement. Another 'sanction' sometimes used by the commissions has been to deregister a union that strikes in defiance of a commission order to return to work. In practice, however, union deregistration has been difficult, and those few unions affected have usually been re-registered after making a suitable apology.

One of the main effects of arbitration has been to shorten the duration of strikes. Although international comparisons of strike statistics are notoriously difficult, the experience of Australia is illuminating. It has often been among those countries with a relatively high number of working days 'lost' per 1000 employees. For instance, in an analysis of industrialised market economies, Australia came eighth with an annual average of 176 working days lost per 1000 employees between 1986 and 1995. The seven countries with a higher strike propensity were Spain, Turkey, Finland, Korea, Canada, Italy and New Zealand. The Irish Republic was close behind Australia (see Bamber & Lansbury 1998:Appendix). A relatively adversarial style of industrial relations has prevailed in Australia, in comparison with countries such as Japan, Germany, Switzerland and Austria, which each generally 'lose' significantly fewer working days through disputes.

Industrial disputes have always received a great deal of attention in Australia. The media focus on industrial adversarialism. Conflict is news, while industrial peace is not. Therefore, there remains a popular view that Australian workplaces are rife with industrial conflict and mutual antagonism between management and workers. However, a thorough survey of workplaces with more than four employees showed that nearly three-quarters of all workplaces have never experienced any type of industrial action (Callus et al. 1991). As the then Minister for Industrial Relations, Senator Peter Cook, put it when launching the survey results:

> In the year preceding the survey (1988–89), only 12 per cent of workplaces had been involved in some form of industrial action. In most cases, these were stop-work meetings, including information sessions and the like as well as stoppages per se. Moreover, whether one relies on the account of managers or union representatives, management–employee relations are generally perceived as being reasonably harmonious. About three-quarters of general managers and more than half of all union delegates rated industrial relations as being very good. (Cook 1991:4)

By the late 1990s the average number of working days lost per 1000 employees were less than half of the 1985 level. Since then, annual average numbers of working days lost have ranged between 76 and 269 per 1000 employees, whereas in the previous decade they ranged between 248 and 797 per 1000 employees (ABS 1997b). Beggs and Chapman (1987) argued that while changing macroeconomic conditions have played a part in this absolute and relative decline in the impact of industrial stoppages, so too has the ALP–ACTU Accord. Besides industrial stoppages, however, there are many other expressions of industrial conflict, including accidents, absenteeism, labour turnover, working without enthusiasm and working to rule and bans (Hyman 1989). There is much less comparative data available on such forms of conflict, even though most employers lose many more working days through accidents and absenteeism than through formal stoppages. A 'ban' is 'an individual or a group refusal to undertake certain types of work, to use certain items of equipment or to work alongside some other employees' (Sutcliffe & Callus 1994:19). There is some evidence to suggest that there was an increased implementation of bans in the 1980s. As the decline in the incidence of industrial stoppages tends to correlate with a rise in the number of bans, perhaps the latter are seen as an alternative expression of industrial conflict: 'Bans minimise loss of pay and may make it more difficult for employers to apply legal sanctions against unions' (Frenkel 1990:14). But, even more than with strikes, it is difficult to secure reliable data on bans and other manifestations of industrial conflict.

The 1998 waterfront dispute

After the election of the Howard conservative coalition government, one of the first major disputes was on the docks. As is often the case, there were several related issues and perspectives. This dispute also had significant national and international implications. There had previously been major disputes in the US, UK, New Zealand and elsewhere as attempts were made to reform the docks in those countries. We can illustrate the complexities of, and conflicting interests involved in, such a dispute by summarising some aspects. To simplify, let us broadly categorise the key players as being associated either with the employers' or the employees' interests, but of course there were differences within each of these broad groups.

Employers

In brief, the employers' perspective was that the overpaid dock-workers (wharfies) and their union enjoyed a monopoly of labour supply on the waterfront. Moreover, the union fostered restrictive practices ('rorts') and low productivity on the Australian docks, which were not competitive with the docks in other countries and thereby increased the prices paid by Australian consumers. It was further argued that previous governments and employers had tried to improve the performance of Australian docks by negotiation but that these attempts had failed.

Patrick Stevedores was one of the two main Australian steve-dores, with about 45% of the market (the other was the UK firm P&O, with about 50%). After a series of battles with the union during the previous months, on 7 April 1998 Patrick decided to 'attack' its employees and their union by restructuring (liquidating), appointing an administrator and withdrawing financial support from four subsidiary labour hire companies.

Patrick thereby aimed to avoid its many debts and to make its 1400 dockworkers redundant. The workers generally learnt of the decision by phone or the news media. Those at work were marched off the site by security guards with dogs. Nine new companies were contracted to replace the former dockers with non-union labour ('scabs' in the union lexicon). During the subsequent Easter holiday period a few ships were unloaded in key Australian ports by non-union labour for the first time in 50 years.

The Australian government immediately announced a levy on the movement of containers and vehicles at the docks to support a $250 million scheme to fund the waterfront redundancies. The government had been encouraging Patrick to take a strong line against the dockers (whom it called 'lazy bludgers') and their union (which it branded as being associated with its main political opponent, the Labor Party).

The National Farmers Federation (NFF)—a tough employers' association—had long been one of the leading opponents of what it saw as old-fashioned militant Australian unionism. It had also been encouraging Patrick to take a strong line against the dockworkers and their union. P&C Stevedores was a new company, which the NFF formed with a specially trained workforce ready to replace the former dockers.

Employees

From the employees' perspective, it was argued that the dockworkers were not overpaid in view of their difficult and unsociable working hours and conditions. Productivity had been increased in recent years but was inevitably still lower on the waterfront in Australia than in some overseas ports because in Australia there was a proliferation of relatively small docks, which had outdated equipment. They also held that Patrick was trying to increase its share price and the personal wealth of its chairman, and that big business was trying to smash union power and to generate an issue to help the Howard government win the next federal election—due within the next year. Some argued that the Minister for Workplace Relations was leading this campaign to bolster his own prospects of becoming the next leader of the Liberal Party.

The main union was the Maritime Union of Australia (MUA). To counter a legacy of casual and insecure work on the docks, the MUA and its predecessors had long maintained a closed shop (100% membership) among dockworkers. It was described by one of Australia's national newspapers as 'the toughest union in the country' (*Australian Financial Review*, 11 April 1998). The MUA was affiliated to the ACTU, which also represented most other Australian unions. The ACTU was in a difficult position. On the one hand it was inclined to support its affiliate, the MUA. On the other hand, it was cautious about calling for wider strike action or a national strike which might result in substantial financial damages being awarded against the ACTU and other unions. Hence the support tended to be at the level of demonstrations, legal and financial support, and support by statements to the media.

Under the government's secondary boycott laws, which it had reintroduced into the *Trade Practices Act* (s 45 (d) and (e)) under the *Workplace Relations Act* 1996, any secondary industrial action could render those involved liable to large penalties, which could bankrupt them. (A secondary boycott is traditional union action whereby the workers try to embargo goods or services provided by another party. Around the world such boycotts have long been used to bring pressure on an employer by getting the employees of another enterprise to support them, for example, by refusing to take delivery from, or supply to the employer in question; cf. Sutcliffe & Callus 1994.)

The MUA was also affiliated to the International Transport Federation (ITF). From its head office in London, the ITF was undertaking to mobilise other waterfront, transport and seafarers' unions around the world in an attempt to put pressure on Patrick and the Australian government. From the MUA's perspective, one advantage of invoking such international support was that it would be more difficult for its opponents to take legal action against those participating in secondary boycotts overseas than those in Australia.

The Australian Labor Party also was in a difficult position. The MUA had long been a strong supporter of the ALP; therefore the ALP was inclined to support the MUA in its hour of need. However, the ALP was also concerned about its electoral prospects; opinion polls suggested that, in view of the dockworkers' image as being overpaid and lazy, their cause was not always a popular one.

Third parties

THE JUDICIARY

Australian industrial and business lawyers played a key role in this dispute as each of the parties initiated legal action in various jurisdictions. There was high drama, as one side appeared to be winning a legal battle, then another appeared to be more successful. Along with the parties, legal experts (and academics) were called frequently to give their views to the media.

THE MEDIA

Such disputes attract a great deal of attention in the mass media; there are usually photo opportunities, lots of conflicting and colourful quotes from the various perspectives and, sometimes, violence. Even though the announcement of these dismissals coincided with other big news stories, including the last stage of peace settlement negotiations in Northern Ireland, on 9 April The *Australian* newspaper devoted its entire front page and several other full pages to this dispute. (This is a reminder that conflict is more newsworthy than peace.)

In the print and the electronic media there was much coverage of various details of the dispute, possible repercussions and 'human interest' implications—for instance, how do the families of sacked dockworkers cope? And to a lesser extent what was the experience of the new non-union workers on the Australian docks? To generalise, leader writers and apparently independent commentators tended to argue that, first, it was necessary to reform work practices on the waterfront, but that, second, to achieve this end it was neither necessary nor appropriate for Patrick to dismiss all its employees at night, just before Easter. One extraordinary aspect of the dispute was the conspicuous absence of the Australian Industrial Relations Commission, the traditional conciliator of Australian industrial disputes. The *Workplace Relations Act* 1996 had the impact of removing it from the action. A further question raised by the dispute was to what extent was it an echo of past poor ER, or was it a taste of things to come? Would there be more hard-fought strikes ahead, following an American, rather than an Australian style?

The settlement

By August 1998, after several months of political, industrial and legal drama, the MUA won its case in Federal and High Court proceedings, that its members should be reinstated to their employment on the docks. Members then returned to work, but in subsequent negotiations between the union and Patrick, approximately half opted for voluntary retirement, albeit on relatively generous terms. The talks also secured agreement on higher pay for those remaining and union commitment to changed work practices intended to lift performance. The waterfront dispute illustrated that the unions have the potential to use the federal government's *Workplace Relations Act* in ways that its proponents did not envisage.

Conclusions

Employers, unions and governments have common and divergent concerns about future directions. Employers are concerned with economic performance in the face of increasingly competitive markets. Most of the larger-sized employers continue to give a high priority to ER strategies. The more sophisticated ones are monitoring the outcome of enterprise agreements to see whether promises of increased productivity are realised. Most smaller-sized employers tend to give a much lower priority to such issues.

Unions are also concerned with industry and enterprise performance, since poor performance and low competitiveness constrain economic growth and exacerbate unemployment. Unions are examining their experiences with enterprise bargaining, analysing the repercussions for members' wages, conditions and rights at work. Of particular concern is the position of low-paid workers. In addition, the ACTU and affiliated unions are implementing measures to improve services to members in an attempt to impress upon employees the relevance of unionism. Unions fear that failure to prove their relevance will result in continuing falls in membership and reduced influence.

Federal and state governments of all political persuasions remain preoccupied with the broader economic problems facing Australia and the related calls for microeconomic reform. The federal conservative coalition seems likely to pursue a diminished role for commissions and to curtail union power further. It remains to be seen, however, whether support for the trend towards a decentralised ER system will continue. Whatever the outcome, it seems likely that ER issues will continue to occupy much time and space in the Australian news media.

3 Changing approaches to employment relations in New Zealand

Erling Rasmussen and Felicity Lamm

Employment relations (ER) in New Zealand have undergone radical changes in recent years, commencing with the *Labour Relations Act 1987* and including the *Employment Contracts Act* 1991 and the *Health and Safety in Employment Act* 1992. New Zealanders have witnessed a decline in union membership (facing adverse conditions under the conservative National Party government of 1990–99). There have also been changes in the work force and industry composition, and a shift towards managerial approaches that favour individualism and workplace bargaining.

New Zealand's population of 3.6 million comprises 14% Maori, who are the indigenous people, 72% European descendants, 5% Pacific Island peoples and 9% other ethnicities. Currently New Zealand has a work force of 1.76 million, of which 1.3 million are in full-time employment and 389 200 in part-time employment. Since the introduction of the *Employment Contracts Act*, the 40-hour week has become less prevalent.

While European males are concentrated in the 'primary labour market', Maori, Pacific Island and women workers are found predominantly in the 'secondary labour market' and are overrepresented in the unemployment figures (Statistics NZ 1999a). Changes in the labour force participation rates (that is, the percentage of people aged fifteen years or over who are either employed or unemployed) in the past 40 years have varied markedly according to age, gender, marital status, family and ethnicity. There has been a steady increase in the involvement of women while male labour participation rates have been gradually declining since the mid-1960s. In both these trends, New Zealand has followed a similar pattern to other industrialised market economies (Statistics NZ 1999a).

New Zealand labour patterns have paralleled shifts in business patterns. Since 1992 there has been a 14.5% increase in small businesses (0–49 employees) while there has only been a 9% increase in medium and large businesses (50–100+ employees). It is conservatively estimated that New Zealand's small business sector now employs over 66% of the working population and represents over 95% of business in this country (Industrial Relations Service 1997).

History of New Zealand's employment relations

New Zealand's ER were initially greatly influenced by those of the UK, as British settlers, who started colonising the country in 1770, transplanted the economic arrangements they had known in their homeland. The English law of contract, which used the class conscious terms of 'master' and 'servant', reinforced traditional divisions between capital and labour within the fledgling settlement (Roth 1978; Deeks et al. 1994). However, the effects of the late 1800s depression and a bitter maritime strike saw a newly elected Liberal government determined to manage industrial conflict through mediating institutions. The subsequent statutes enacted by the Liberal government of 1894 provided a framework that was intended to protect workers' wages and conditions by setting minimum standards. The cornerstone of the Liberal government's employment legislation was the *Industrial Conciliation and Arbitration Act* 1894. Its purpose was to strengthen the role of unions as well as provide a legal procedure for settling workplace conflict and enforcing industrial agreements. However, the price for providing statutory methods of dispute resolution was to place strict controls on direct action by unions.

The conciliation and arbitration system lasted, with some modifications, nearly 100 years. The fine-tuning modifications were often constituted in the face of practical enforcement difficulties. Some changes touched on key areas, however, such as the right to strike, and whether arbitration and union membership should be voluntary or compulsory. In addition, an extensive network of supporting legislation covering holidays, minimum wages, shop trading hours and leave entitlements was developed over the years (Rasmussen & Lamm 1999).

The long duration of the arbitration system produced key distinguishing features (Rasmussen et al. 1996b; Deeks et al. 1994; Holt 1986; Walsh & Fougere 1987):

• The legalistic processes fostered and ingrained an adversarial approach.
• The union registration process, where unions obtained sole bargaining rights by 'signing up' to the arbitration system,

perpetuated an organisational structure of many and weak unions.

• Legally binding documents established industry or occupational minima ('blanket coverage').
• Bargaining was restricted to a number of narrowly defined issues ('industrial matters').
• Specialised institutions were created—for example, conciliation councils and an arbitration court.
• Individual employment contracts and conditions were dealt with under common law jurisdiction.

Initially, unions favoured the arbitration system more than did employers as it increased the unions' bargaining and organisational strength. However, the curtailment of collective bargaining rights remained controversial in union circles (Walsh 1993). While employers accepted the legislation as providing predictable wage outcomes and containing industrial conflict, employers were usually less inclined to welcome state intervention. Direct wage bargaining became a tempting option for unions during inflationary times, and employers sought downward adjustments during deflationary periods. Generally, the inability of the arbitration system to implement fast and flexible wage adjustments in both directions was its weakest point during these periods.

From centralised to decentralised bargaining

Boxall (1990) has described the period from the mid-1960s to 1990 as a long, slow drift towards decentralised, direct bargaining. Full employment in the 1950s, 1960s and 1970s increased workplace bargaining. Wage settlements of the arbitration system became less significant as so-called 'second-tier agreements' (that is, above-award pay increases) became more significant, especially for larger employers. The clash between collective bargaining and arbitration came to the fore when employers and unions successfully colluded to overturn the infamous nil pay rise decision by the Arbitration Court in 1968 (Walsh 1994; Deeks et al. 1994). Although the *Industrial Relations Act* 1973 tried to regain control over 'second-tier agreements', it failed in this regard as inflationary pressures and a tight labour market led to endless bargaining which became more and more driven by wage relativity considerations (James 1986). Increased direct state intervention, either in particular disputes or through wage and price restraints, further undermined the support for the arbitration system (Boston 1984).

The ER policy of the fourth Labour government (1984–90) was

based on an uneasy balance between allowing more direct bargaining and keeping the protective mechanisms of the arbitration system (Rasmussen et al. 1996b). Direct bargaining was encouraged by introducing voluntary arbitration, avoiding intervention in industrial disputes and instituting a more permissive legislative framework through the *Labour Relations Act* 1987. This Act supported direct bargaining by making the parties enforce their own agreements, widening the bargaining agenda, allowing a wider choice of collective contracts and stipulating legislative procedures for lawful lockouts and strikes. This was subsequently extended to public sector bargaining through the *State Sector Act* 1988. On the other hand, state regulation became more prevalent by re-instituting compulsory union membership in 1984, strengthening the statutory minimum wage, making 'second-tier agreements' more difficult to achieve, and introducing legislation on parental leave in 1987. Pay equity and the option of final offer arbitration for employee groups with weak bargaining power were introduced in 1990. However, the pay equity and final offer arbitration provisions had little impact as they were abolished after the Labour government lost the general election in November 1990.

The *Employment Contracts Act* 1991

In keeping with its promise of further deregulation, the newly elected 1990 National Party government continued to dismantle the remnants of the arbitration system. The cornerstone of its employment 'package' was the *Employment Contracts Act* 1991 which contained few of the principles associated with the arbitration model. It abolished the award system and union monopoly rights, and promoted an enterprise-bargaining model in the private and public sectors. In short, ER have been shifted away from the collectivist traditions of the past by promoting the rights of individual employees and employers over collective rights (Wailes 1994; Grills 1994). The *Employment Contracts Act* has facilitated a fundamental shift in the locus of ER: from predominantly industry or occupational level towards the individual organisation or workplace. This has prompted a sharp fall in union density and in collective employment coverage, as discussed below.

On the other hand, the *Employment Contracts Act* (ECA) has provided employees in the 'primary labour market' with more leverage and this has influenced ER practices. First, the Act covers *all* employees: whether on collective or individual employment contracts, or whether in the public or private sectors. Previously, employees on individual employment contracts were outside the ER framework and had few employment rights under common law. Second, the Act's institutional set-up reflects the traditional labour institutions: it provides a strong role for the legacy of legal precedence; procedural fairness is crucial in the area of dismissals; the fines and jurisdiction available are substantial; and the personal grievance procedures for all employees (Walsh 1993; Grills 1994). The many cases being taken to the ER institutions since 1991 indicate a more militant pursuit of employee rights among 'primary labour market' employees. There have been well publicised decisions awarding significant compensation to managerial or senior employees. These decisions have influenced managerial attitudes and as a result most managers have become more careful about substantive and procedural fairness in dealing with their staff (see below).

The role of the state and its institutions

New Zealand ER have for many years been treated as a matter of state intervention. Established in 1891, the Department of Labour continues to have responsibility for regulating and promoting compliance with the raft of employment legislation, such as health and safety, hours of work and pay. While the statutory minima contained in employment statutes are regulated through the Labour Inspectorate of the Department of Labour, personal grievances are enforced through the Employment Tribunal.

Early concerns for the working conditions of women and children established a system of statutory minimum conditions. These have become more important following the demise of the award system. The minimum conditions for all employees are: adult and youth minimum wages, parental leave, five days of paid special leave, eleven days of paid statutory holidays, three weeks of paid annual leave, and personal grievance and dispute procedures. Personal grievance procedures (for non-union workers), special leave provisions and the youth minimum wage are extensions of the minimum conditions enshrined in statute before 1991.

The bureaucratic procedures, the possible detrimental employment effects and the associated costs in terms of money and time have deterred some employees from pursuing their rights (Grills 1994). In addition, many vulnerable employees are not aware, or are unsure, of their rights. Nevertheless, many employees have become more interested in knowing about their entitlements. As a result, there has been an increased demand for the services provided by the Labour Inspectorate which in turn has led to a tripling of the Inspectorate staff since the enactment of the *Employment Contracts*

Act contrary to the general trend of public sector employment in the same period. The Labour Department's increase in staff has not met with universal approval. While unions are adamant that the state should continue to provide regulatory protection for workers, many of the employers' associations are not. As a New Zealand Employers' Federation (NZEF) advisor stated previously:

> an army of Government inspectors acting as policemen will not achieve the desired results . . . There should be more emphasis on providing education, information and training . . . [and a] move towards self-regulation where standards, procedures and practices are appropriate to a particular workplace and developed by those responsible for that workplace. (Farlow 1989:190–2)

The employers' associations—such as the NZ Business Round-Table, the Employers' Federation and the Manufacturers' Federation —have criticised the Employment Court. Besides the attempt to fashion all society spheres in line with their philosophical ideas, the employers' attack on the Employment Court is associated with key ER issues. The Court is the icon of separate ER institutions and abolishing the Court and transferring its jurisdiction to the High Court would be a significant step towards abolishing separate ER institutions (Robertson 1996a). The Court's decisions have been attacked and, in particular, the Court's firm intention to uphold the notion of 'procedural fairness' has raised the ire of employers. While the attacks have focused on the Employment Court, it appears that the employers' goal is to abolish the Employment Tribunal too and to create an 'employment at will' framework (Anderson 1996:3; cf. below ch. 4).

Besides the issue of procedural fairness, there has been a focus on bargaining issues such as access for employee representatives, recognition of employee representatives, harsh and oppressive contracts, and home workers' contractual status. This focus is caused by the 'permissive nature' of the *Employment Contracts Act* which left bargaining guidelines 'incomplete, inconsistent and invisible' (Skiffington 1996:50). Thus, the notion of *fair* bargaining practices has constantly been challenged by both sides. For example, some employers have tried to avoid bargaining with the duly chosen bargaining agent and instead communicate directly with the employees. Although this practice has been restricted to some degree by several Employment Court and Court of Appeal decisions, there is still room for further interpretation (Kiely 1996:58).

New Zealand ER have been unstable in the 1990s with several turning points. In 1997–98, the Government conducted a review of the *Employment Contracts Act*, the *Holidays Act* and the statutory minimum wage. While the then Minister of Labour stated several misgivings about these policy areas, the former conservative government's legislative plans contained few drastic changes (*NZ Herald*, 27 July 1998:A3). Radical plans allowing the sale of statutory holiday entitlements for money were also abandoned, following a public outcry (Rasmussen & McIntosh 1998:129). ER were key issues in the 1999 general election, when the Labour and Alliance parties, which won the election, promised to repeal the *Employment Contracts Act*.

There have also been turning points in other aspects of ER. It was possible to bypass the employee protections under the *Employment Contracts Act* by employing workers as contractors. However, this use of notional contractors may be restricted in the future because of a Court of Appeal decision which deemed that ten home-care workers were employees. This decision created some media debate as it involved the Central Regional Health Authority as the employer and, in some cases, the workers were paid less than half the statutory minimum wage (*NZ Herald*, 28 August 1996:A13). In occupational health and safety, the courts have stepped up the approach to deter negligent employers, with recent cases resulting in large fines. The courts awarded part of the fines to the victims and this prompted talk about the re-introduction of lump sum accident compensation payments in another form (abolished by the National Party's accident compensation legislation) (Kiely 1996:69–75).The focus on Occupational Overuse Syndrome (OOS) incidents also increased since the first well publicised conviction of an insurance company (Rasmussen & Schwarz 1995:344).

Employers' associations

Boxall observes that 'Management can no longer be considered the reactive party in the ideological debate over the nature of the employment relationship and in the practical regulation of its terms' (1993:148). This was certainly true throughout the 1980s and 1990s, when there was increasing pressure by employer lobby groups on the Labour and National governments to enact radical labour market reforms. At the heart of their argument for labour market reforms was the notion that the traditional protection for unions and centralised collective bargaining was in fact diminishing the rights of both employers and employees, undermining business competitiveness and creating unemployment (Harbridge 1993).

Arguably one of the most influential of the employer lobby groups is the New Zealand Business Roundtable (NZBRT). Membership of the Roundtable is by invitation only and restricted to the chief executives of about 57 of New Zealand's largest companies. Some chief executives have declined membership because they oppose the Roundtable's policy position. As such its members have a consistent ideology (Kelsey 1997). Formed in the late 1970s, it began as an informal grouping of leading industrialists with common interests and the desire to influence government policy (Deeks et al. 1994). It became more active when Roger Douglas, the Minister of Finance in the 1984 Labour government, led the movement to introduce monetarist economic policies. According to Kelsey (1997:76): 'Throughout the structural adjustment program, the Roundtable used its resources, public profile and corporate power to fortify and accelerate the rate of change and to condemn any suggestion of retreat.'

However, the NZBRT has not been successful in every instance. As mentioned, the NZBRT, together with the NZEF and Treasury, were rebuffed in their attempt to abolish the specialist ER institutions during the debate on the *Employment Contracts Act* 1991. Instead the National government endorsed the formation of separate institutions—the Employment Tribunal and the Employment Court (Walsh & Ryan 1993). Since then the NZBRT, and to a lesser extent the Employers' Federation, have conducted a vigorous, but so far unsuccessful, campaign to overturn this policy (Howard 1995; Hunt 1996; Robertson 1996a & 1996b).

The NZ Employers' Federation (NZEF) and the NZ Manufacturers' Federation (NZMF) are more representative of employers' interests. A recent amalgamation between the Auckland Employers' Association and the Auckland Manufacturers' Association in 1997 has created a membership base of over 4000, making it, the Employers' and the Manufacturers' Association (Northern Region), the largest employers' association in New Zealand. These associations draw their membership from the private and public sectors and represent large, medium and small enterprises.

Under the pre-1991 ER system, the activities of the NZEF and NZMF reflected the more centralised approach (Deeks et al. 1994). By the late 1980s, the NZEF began to abandon its long-standing support for centralised wage bargaining and compulsory unionism, once these institutions had proved ineffective in holding down wages and preventing industrial disputes (Kelsey 1997). The NZEF agitated for a reform of the bargaining structures that would stem the rise of the cost of labour and reduce the unions' power in the bargaining process. However, employers' associations have had to adjust to the deregulated economic and employment environment. As Carroll & Tremewan (1993:195) stated:

For the Employers' Association, the changes brought about by the passing of the *Employment Contracts Act* were profound. The organisation can never return to the ways of the past: having to work in such a new environment posed a great threat to a number of staff; the competitive marketplace was an alien place for some; others are having to undertake work that they were never originally employed to do. [However] there will also be a need for employers' views to be presented collectively. This is an appropriate role for the Employers' Association to continue to undertake.

The post-*Employment Contracts Act* period has seen the employers' associations pursue several options, which are intended to strengthen service delivery to their members (Rasmussen & Schwarz 1995:345). For example, they have expanded their legal advice service and training courses which in turn has increased the number of members after stagnation in the early 1990s. The amalgamation between branches of the NZEF and the MF has also created a stronger lobbying position under New Zealand's novel election system where more political parties can influence government policy. Under the *Employment Contracts Act*, the NZEF has focused on its lobbying role and on developing coherent policy positions for its member organisations since it no longer has a bargaining role.

Employees and trade unions

The *Employment Contracts Act* was a direct attack on the unions' power base. The Act abolished the unions' monopoly position. It restricted the unions' ability to pursue multi-employer bargaining since strikes in favour of multi-employer employment contracts as well as secondary, supporting industrial action were deemed unlawful. The tax exemption of union funds was also abolished in 1991.

Thus, there was an immediate decline in union membership from 603 118 members in March 1991 to 428 160 in December 1992 (Harbridge & Honeybone 1995). In the period from May 1991 to December 1998, union membership fell by around 55% to 306 687 and union density declined from 41.5% to 17.7% (Crawford et al. 1999). After an initial reduction in their number, the number of unions was relatively stable.

Since the *Employment Contracts Act*, unions have found it difficult to organise at many work sites. As Boxall and Haynes (1997:586) have explained:

> The state no longer underwrites the union survival. It is an environment in which leading managers and the state share a common ideology: neither envisages a significant role for trade

unions. [In short] the neo-liberal ascendancy in New Zealand has all but eliminated state-dependent, arbitrationist unions.

By the mid-1990s, there were many enterprises in the private sector where there was no union presence. Also, as a result of a weakened union movement and legislative restraints on industrial action, strikes and lockouts have been at their lowest point for four decades.

On the other hand, since 1995 unions have begun to consolidate their position. There have been mergers creating 'super unions'. For example, the Engineers' Union not only recruited most of the members of the bankrupt and defunct Communication and Energy Workers Union, but it also merged with the Print, Packaging and Media Union in 1996 (Rasmussen & Schwarz 1996:206). This has created the largest private sector union—the Engineering, Printing and Manufacturing Union, with nearly 60 000 members. The Public Service Association (PSA) has also sustained a strong presence in the public sector, as have the teachers' unions. In addition there are smaller unions that are not only surviving but thriving. Thus, the number of unions increased from 67 to 83 in the 1993–98 period. According to Boxall and Haynes (1997), this increase reflected unions making *industrial* rather than *political* strategic choices.

Outcomes under the *Employment Contracts Act*

While the changes to workplace bargaining and the adjustment to employment conditions have been significant, it is questionable how much is attributable to the *Employment Contracts Act*. This question should be borne in mind when the following issues are considered: bargaining decentralisation, adjustments in employment conditions, changes in employment and unemployment, growth in productivity and the level of industrial disputes. There is an interconnection between these issues. For example, the rise in average weekly working hours has been related to the low productivity growth. Also there were several predictions regarding the detrimental effects of 'deregulation' on the so-called secondary labour market when the *Employment Contracts Act* was implemented. It is surprising, therefore, that there is still a lack of information about the outcomes in the secondary labour market (Rasmussen & Deeks 1997; McLaughlin & Rasmussen 1998). There can be no comprehensive understanding of the deregulation outcomes until this issue has been researched more thoroughly.

In the 1990s there was a massive shift from collectivism towards individualism—including a shift from nationwide arrangements to workplace arrangements. An outstanding feature was the shift from collective employment contracts (CECs) to individual employment contracts (IECs) after 1990. It has been estimated that collective contracts covered around 56–60% of the total employed workforce prior to May 1991 (Visser 1991). This was to some degree attributable to the notion of 'blanket coverage' whereby wages and conditions were applied to a particular industry or occupation (Deeks et al. 1994). The elimination of blanket coverage produced an immediate shift towards individual employment contracts, with 56.6% of the work force employed on IECs by February 1993 (Statistics NZ 1995). Statistics New Zealand's last economy-wide survey focusing on the distribution of collective and individual employment contracts was conducted in February 1993. It is possible, however, to estimate the current distribution by drawing from surveys of bargaining trends and from the two national databases of collective employment contracts (Rasmussen & Deeks 1997). The two databases cover around 20–24% of the workforce but there are probably a number of smaller CECs that are not covered by them (Harbridge & Crawford 1996; Industrial Relations Service 1997). Thus, we would estimate that more than a third of the workforce are covered by CECs.[1]

Average hourly earnings increased every year in the 1990s, though average *real* hourly earnings stagnated in the 1990–96 period. Since 1996, average hourly earnings have risen slightly faster than the consumer price index (Statistics NZ 1998). While contractual basic wages have risen, many total pay packages have become less generous: overtime payments are stipulated or triggered less often, penalty rates have become less widespread and less generous, and performance-based pay covers only a minority of employees on collective employment contracts (Harbridge & Crawford 1996; Industrial Relations Service 1996). Thus, there has been a shift favouring higher incomes with lower incomes being stagnant or declining (Campbell 1998; Statistics NZ 1999b).

The upward pressure on working time—well known from the UK—has also occurred with the 40-hour week becoming less prevalent under the *Employment Contracts Act*. The work force is split approximately into three sections, where about a third usually work less than 40 hours per week, another third usually work the traditional 40-hour week and a third work more than 40 hours per week (Rasmussen & Deeks 1997). While the debate about casualisation has focused on people working less than 40 hours per week and will be discussed later, many people seem to be increasing their hours of work. Of those people who usually work more than 40 hours (35.8% of all employees in 1998), a significant proportion usually work very long hours: a third (35.4%) work between 50 and 60 hours per week and a fourth (24.8%) work more than 60 hours per week on average (Statistics NZ 1999a:171).

There were significant adjustments in employment conditions in the early 1990s. Even apparently moderate employers obtained significant concessions in the areas of 'penalty' rates and overtime payments (Rasmussen & Deeks 1997). While large scale adjustments of employment conditions have slowed since 1993, employees have had little success in reversing the concessions obtained earlier by employers (McLaughlin & Rasmussen 1998).

Employment and unemployment

The strong economy of the early 1990s led to a growth in employment with more than 120 000 new jobs or an 8% increase in employment in the 1992–95 period (Statistics NZ 1999c). While employment growth remained strong, unemployment declined from 11.1% in March 1992 to 5.9% in December 1996. Then, unemployment rose again. The economic slowdown and rising unemployment started, therefore, before the so-called Asian economic crisis. Tight monetary policy and the associated high NZ dollar contributed significantly to this slowdown. The already weak economic activity level was further undermined by the direct and indirect effects of the Asian economic crisis. This increased worries over unemployment, rising from 5.9% in December 1996 to 7% in June 1999 (Statistics NZ 1999c:6).

Job losses are mainly in the manufacturing sector where the New Zealand government is committed under an Asia Pacific Economic Co-operation (APEC) agreement to eliminate tariffs by 2019 at the latest. The car assembly industry and the textile and clothing sector have been the hardest hit by the tariff reductions. For example, in 1985 the textile and clothing industry employed 30 939 people but by 1997 it only employed 16 710. The job losses in this industry affect 10% of the manufacturing work force in which 74% of employees are women and 32% are Maori, Pacific Islanders and Asians. All four NZ car assembly plants closed in 1998 after the government suddenly reduced tariffs to zero.

Following the Employment Taskforce report in 1995 and as part of a 1996 conservative coalition government agreement, the pre-1999 government began to take a more proactive approach to reducing the unemployment levels and creating new jobs. Streamlining employment services and introducing a range of employment programs, such as Taskforce Green and Job Link, were attempts to stem the growth in unemployment. However, these efforts did not succeed in reducing unemployment. There was also a continuous rise in the numbers in part-time employment and in self-employment (Statistics NZ 1996). This led to talk about 'McJobs' and casualisation (Rasmussen 1995). While part-time employment in itself cannot be interpreted as a clear indicator of casualisation there are indications that some part-time employment falls into this category (Statistics NZ 1997:61). Thus, there was a strong growth in part-time workers who were looking for not only more hours but ultimately a full-time job. The number of part-time workers who would prefer to work more hours increased by 58% between 1991 and 1998. In the same period, the number of part-time workers who were looking for full-time work increased by 48.5%. There was also a significant rise in the number of sub-contractors by over 27.1% in the 1991–98 period. Similarly, there has been a 28.5% increase in multiple job-holders in the 1991–98 period as more people raised their income by having more than one job (Statistics NZ 1999a). There is also anecdotal evidence that some employers are using more on-call arrangements and split shifts.

The productivity conundrum

The *Employment Contracts Act* was promoted as a way of creating a new and more productivity oriented ER culture to support the extensive restructuring of the economy (*NZ Herald*, 1 May 1991:10). 'By introducing voluntary unionism and changing bargaining pro-cedures it will increase productivity, enhance employment and encourage the sharing of benefits that flow from in creased output' (National Party 1990:27). The award system and compulsory union-ism were regarded as major blockages to more pro ductive work practices (e.g. Brook 1990 & 1991). It was assumed by many that the new Act would facilitate a lift in productivity levels.

It has been debated, therefore, why there has been such a poor productivity performance subsequent to the Act (see Table 3.1).[2] Some economists have pointed to measurement problems (e.g. Kerr 1996), with some taking the risky route of using surveys of managers' opinions about productivity increases as their evidence of satisfactory productivity growth (e.g. Savage 1996). While there are measurement problems (the shift to services and the increased focus on quality) it is inappropriate to rely on opinion surveys. However, there appears to be no single reason why the productivity performance has been so low (Easton 1996; 1997).

Why has the *Employment Contracts Act* not facilitated a surge

Table 3.1 Aggregate labour productivity (% p.a. change)

Years	Real GDP	Employment	Labour productivity
1978–84	2.0	0.1	1.9
1984–88	2.0	0.6	1.4
1988–92	–0.4	–2.2	1.9
1992–96	3.8	3.1	0.7

Source: Philpott (1996:3).

in productivity? There appear to be three explanatory factors. First, the earlier restrictions on productive work practices may have been less than previously assumed:

> More generally, it is possible that the various allegations of unions interfering with the market are not true. It may be that unions do not inhibit productivity gains or compress wage differentials to an extent that when they are weakened there are major increases in output, and wage dispersion. That is the experience in the case of the *Employment Contracts Act.* (Easton 1997:12)

Second, employers may not have used the productive opportunities created by the Act. The changes to employment conditions instituted by employers in the 1991–93 period could have hampered the introduction of new, productive work practices. There are some indications that low morale or negative 'psychological contracts' have made sustainable, productive workplace changes difficult to achieve (Rasmussen & Boxall 1995; Wevers 1995; Wevers International Ltd/Centre for Corporate Strategy 1996; Rasmussen & Jackson 1996). Relatively few enterprises are involved in full-scale workplace reform, there is a tendency for enterprises to pick and choose specific organisational changes instead of applying a holistic approach, and there are distinct preferences for task related participation (Mealings 1998; Rasmussen 1997; Ryan 1995).

Third, the Council of Trade Unions (CTU) has constantly criticised the assumed productivity enhancing effects of the *Employment Contracts Act.* The CTU has argued that inadequate investments in infrastructure, education and training, and the continuous restructuring of public services, together with the short-termism created by the *Employment Contracts Act,* would act as barriers to high, sustainable productivity growth (NZCTU 1996). The fragmentation of bargaining has increased the bargaining effort at the enterprise level and thereby increased transaction costs (Rasmussen & Boxall 1995). Likewise, the extensive legislative reforms—at least nine new comprehensive legislative packages in the 1990s—have added a further burden to enterprises already strained under the adjustment to the new economic environment.

Importantly, the current approach to industry training may not overcome the traditional problems in this area and facilitate a move towards a high-wage, high-skill economy. The industry training approach was radically altered by the *Industry Training Act* 1992. The 1993–96 economic upswing coincided with skill shortages. There are concerns that inadequate government funding, the unsystematic development of the Industry Training Organisations (ITOs), and tensions between the key public agencies are blocking widespread training efforts (Meyers 1996; OECD 1993; Rasmussen et al. 1996a). The traditional employer reluctance to invest in training has yet to be overcome and a 'training culture' has not yet been established (Janes & Rasmussen 1998).

Shifting from collective to individual disputes?

When examining the data on disputes, it is necessary to distinguish between collective disputes in terms of work stoppages (strikes and lockouts) and individual disputes in terms of claims before the Employment Tribunal. The number of recorded work stoppages was relatively stable in the 1991–96 period, fluctuating between 54 stoppages in 1992 and 69 stoppages in 1995 (Statistics NZ 1997:104). However, the picture is different when the impact of stoppages on working days and wages lost is considered. Lost working time was the highest in 1992 with 113 700 working days lost compared to only 23 800 days in 1993 and 24 600 days in 1997 (Statistics NZ 1999:180).

The level of lockouts has fluctuated strongly. Lockouts constituted between 4.2% and 11.1% of all stoppages in the 1991–94 period, but declined sharply in 1995 to constitute 2.9% of all stoppages (Statistics NZ 1999a:181). The decline from 1995 onwards is probably associated with the fact that, subsequent to a decision by the full bench of the Employment Court in June 1994 (Lamm 1994:334), partial lockouts were no longer considered lawful under the *Employment Contracts Act*. It has been mainly in manufacturing and in the public sector that work stoppages have occurred. The two industrial classifications—'manufacturing' and 'community, social and personal services' (some of which are in the public sector)—accounted for over 75% of all stoppages during 1992–95. In 1995 and 1996, the public sector lost more working days and more in wages than the private sector.

Since the introduction of the *Employment Contracts Act*, there has been a significant growth in claims brought to the Employment

Tribunal. In the year to June 1992, the Tribunal received 2332 applications. This had increased to 5144 cases in the year to June 1996 (Harbridge & Crawford 1997:47). The large majority of these applications were in respect of individual grievances alleging unjustified dismissal (Dumbleton 1996). Several explanations can be offered for this growth (Harbridge 1997). First, the Act significantly expanded coverage of the grievance procedures, with people on individual employment contracts gaining access to the Employment Tribunal and the Employment Court (Rasmussen et al. 1996b). As many of these people have the resources and education, they are more able and willing to take cases to the Tribunal.

Second, the growth in Tribunal cases has been influenced by the declining role of unions in settling disputes before they enter the legal grievance machinery, and the willingness of other employee representatives (mainly lawyers and consultants) to take claims to the Tribunal and Court on a contingency fee basis. In addition, before April 1997, there was the incentive effect of avoiding the 26-week stand-down period before unemployment benefits were payable. The stand-down period covers employees leaving their employment voluntarily, since employees who could prove in front of the Tribunal that they were unjustifiably dismissed could draw such benefits immediately. It has been alleged that, as a consequence, some claims have been based on flimsy grounds or on the basis of procedural irregularities in the dismissal process. In April 1997, as part of the implementation of the recommendations of the Employment Taskforce (Rasmussen & Schwarz 1995:344–5), the stand-down period was reduced to thirteen weeks. Since then the number of cases taken to the Employment Tribunal has increased only slightly.

It has become a frequent complaint of employers and unions that American-style litigation has become more accepted in New Zealand in recent years. The rise in individual grievance cases brought to the Employment Tribunal, and in occupational safety and health cases brought to the District Courts, as well as detailed attention paid by ER managers to procedural and contractual matters, all indicate the shift towards increased litigation over employment issues. It can be argued that the NZBRT and the NZEF have contributed to this trend, since their long campaign against the Employment Court (in particular the notion of procedural fairness) has convinced many employees that 'it is impossible to dismiss anybody'. We can also speculate that the large compensation payments made to employees mentioned in the media have been another contributing factor.

Thus, the non-prescriptive or 'enabling' nature of much of the *Employment Contracts Act* has placed too great an emphasis in the determination of lawful employment practices and on the development of legal precedents. This has given rise to more cases at the Employment Court and to numerous appeals at the Court of Appeal. It is a cumbersome, drawn out process which not only adds to the insecurity of employers and employees but also has significant costs both for the parties involved and for the society as a whole.

Return to collectivism?

The General Election in November 1999 resulted in a centre-left coalition government and this will lead to major changes in the legislative framework. Both parties in the coalition government—the Labour Party and the Alliance—have promised to repeal the *Employment Contract Act*. While the promised new legislation will not re-introduce compulsory unionism and the award system, it will strengthen collective bargaining and union activity in various ways (Hodgson 1999). It will re-introduce the right to strike in association with multi-employer collective contracts, it will make collective contract coverage a right for employees, and union access and union meetings will be prescribed by the Act. There will be a duty of 'good faith bargaining'—inspired by North American practices (Clark 1993)—to promote consensus employment relations. 'The duty to act in good faith will not imply a duty to settle a collective agreement' (Hodgson 1993:173). Also, the statutory minima will be strengthened in areas such as holiday and parental leave entitlements, hours of work (including breaks), health and safety protection and the minimum wage.

Conclusions

Given the economic, political and social pressures facing the post-1984 New Zealand governments, it was almost inevitable that the century-old arbitration and conciliation system would be amended. Employment structures, once intended to contain conflict and control wages and conditions, functioned less well in a much more open economy. However, most people under-estimated the *extent* or the *speed* of the changes to the context of ER and on the underlying legislation.

The deregulated employment environment in the 1990s also uncoupled the traditional tripartite arrangements between the NZEF, the CTU and the government. This meant that the employers' associations and the unions no longer enjoyed preferential treatment nor did they have the exclusive right to act as bargaining representatives for employers or employees.

The employment reforms of the 1990s shifted the power balance between employer and employee which resulted in a tougher employer approach to workplace bargaining. Therefore, it not surprising that the average real hourly wages have increased only slightly since 1991 and employees have often been faced with income pressure through cuts to penal rates and overtime payments. While restrictions on collective disputes reduced the number of strike actions and lockouts after 1992, the number of individual disputes at the Employment Tribunal rose strongly and more than 5000 applications have been received each year (Rasmussen & Lamm 1999).

The 1992–96 economic upswing led to significant employment growth and a sharp decrease in unemployment. However, unemployment rose after 1996. The impact of the Asian crisis on an already weak economy saw unemployment rise above 7% in 1999—equivalent to its 1990 level. The casualisation of work and the widespread use of contractors have also become matters of concern. The corollary for the ER reforms was a much needed rise in productivity. It was argued that by forfeiting the security of a regulated and protected working environment, the increased labour market flexibility would result in higher productivity levels. The ER reforms have yet to deliver on this crucial aspect.

The issues of low productivity, restraints on collective bargaining and protection of secondary labour market groups featured prominently in the 1999 general election. The Labour–Alliance coalition government promised a new legislative framework that would attempt to confront these problems, without returning to the 'old system' of awards and compulsory unionism.

4 Changing approaches to employment relations in Japan

Charles T. Tackney

This chapter explores current developments in the working rules of Japanese employment relations (ER) from the comparative perspective of the legal environment of the modern enterprise. It begins by reviewing historical and theoretical dimensions of research in the field. This review brings to light the enduring dispute about the existence and nature of the 'lifetime' employment system. The dispute is discussed against the background of case law recognition of the 'lifetime' employment system as a standard Japanese labour relations practice since the early 1960s.

Three elements provided the legal foundations for the post-1945 emergence of this institutionalised practice. First, there was the important role of case law in Japanese labour law. Second, employee participation with management was institutionalised within the collective bargaining agreement. Third, societal dimensions of the employment contract—a rejection of the 'at will' employer prerogative—were recognised by the judiciary in response to legal struggles from organised labour. Significantly, all three developments represented adaptations of German employment and labour law theory from the Weimar era.[1]

This chapter examines the stability of Japan's working rules in the light of this legal environment and concludes by reaffirming their importance in helping to establish post-1945 'Japanese management' practices.

The enduring opaqueness of Japanese employment relations

Early research on post-1945 Japanese industrial organisation included the works of Abegglen (1958) and Levine (1958); both researchers became influential in the field. Abegglen, through the simultaneous publication of his 1958 book in English and Japanese, is credited with the remarkable achievement of introducing and popularising the term 'lifetime' employment (*shusshin koyo*) in both English and Japanese. Around the same time, Levine (1958) offered the first systematic examination of Japan's IR system. He also documented the peculiar long-term ER practices that seemed to characterise many Japanese workplaces at this time.

In the decades since, researchers have been debating these early post-1945 insights. The presumed 'traditional' nature of lifetime employment was criticised by Gordon, who wrote that Abegglen 'would not have written anything like *The Japanese Factory* had he gone to Japan a decade or more earlier, for not until the early 1950s did Japanese employment patterns come to resemble those since described by sociologists, economists, and anthropologists' (1985:1). Despite this important temporal constraint, Gordon fundamentally affirmed the institutional reality of the 'lifetime' employment system and defined it as a settlement achieved from postwar struggles between management and labour.

Abegglen, Levine and Gordon are representative of a genre of scholars who recognise the critically important role played by institutions, institutional practices and, for want of a more specific term, culture in defining the working rules of Japanese ER. Other researchers in this group include: Cole (1971a, b, c; 1972; 1979), Dore (1973; 1986; 1989), Shimada (1983a; 1983b; 1989; 1992a; 1992b), Taira (1970) and Taira & Levine (1985).

Beginning in the 1980s, a very serious theoretical division arose among scholars about Japan's working rules. The work of two scholars exemplifies the depth of the theoretical attack made on institutionalists. Aoki developed the theory of the 'J-firm', a particular form of industrial organisation that he believes emerged and diffused within Japan in the post-1945 era (1986; 1987; 1988). Koike, in contrast, claimed that the comparatively unique dimensions of post-1945 Japanese ER were due to the functional white-collarisation of Japan's blue-collar workers (1983; 1987; 1988; 1991; 1995).

Aoki and Koike both refrain from a complete negation of the influence of Japanese history, culture and institutions in the development of the post-1945 working rules that govern Japanese industrial enterprises. Aoki, for example, recognised the dissolution of the *zaibatsu* industrial arrangements and the public distribution of share ownership in the Japanese firm—later to evolve into *keiretsu* arrangements.[2] He also recognised post-1945 industrial conflict between organised labour and management as an important factor in the emergence of the J-firm (for example, the Miike mining conflict of the early 1960s). Through such struggles, Japanese management learnt the high value that Japanese workers placed on

Table 4.1 Consecutive years of work (male and female workers)

Nation	Consecutive years of work
Japan[d]	10.9
Germany[b]	10.4
France[c]	10.1
Norway[a]	9.4
United Kingdom[c]	7.9
Canada[c]	7.8
Australia[c]	6.8
United States[c]	6.7

Notes: a 1989; b 1990; c 1991; d 1992.
Source: Economic Planning Agency (1994:299).

job security. Management, therefore, designed ER polices with this in mind.

Koike, in turn, claimed that some democratisation of the workplace occurred in the immediate aftermath of World War II. He advanced the theory that the generalised skilling of workers was a requisite step towards achieving the egalitarian dynamic that is a recognisable feature of post-1945 Japanese enterprises. His 'whitecollarisation' theory provides a basis for the study of how Japanese ER practices may be exported to other nations (Koike & Inoki 1991).

In both cases, the Aoike/Koike theory-building process has been associated with an explicit critique of 'lifetime' employment. Simply put, both scholars deny the reality of the 'lifetime' employment system. Aoki sees 'lifetime' employment as a misinterpretation of observed long-term employment patterns, which are better explained by his J-firm theory. Koike, in turn, has written that the 'lifetime' employment system is, at best, a 'myth', and that reports of its existence are based on 'flimsy' research (1988:266).

The view that the 'lifetime' employment system is a 'myth' now pervades the literature. A similar point of view appears in some official Japanese government policy analyses (Economic Planning Agency 1994:298). The Economic Planning Agency listed average consecutive work years for men and women in several industrialised nations (see Table 4.1).

The table shows that average employment tenure in Japan paralleled Germany and France, and was around four years longer than the US. The 1994 Economic Planning Agency then evaluated the Japanese employment system within the context of Japan's emerging economic problems. Thus, 'the prolonged economic recession and employment adjustments by companies are changing the basic conditions surrounding employment and some worry that it is becoming difficult to maintain the Japanese employment system, which has supported the country's employment stability for so many years' (Economic Planning Agency 1994:298). Will the system continue? Answering this question depends on a proper theoretical understanding of the system. Ironically, postwar legislation does not help explain the observed long-term employment patterns. Japan's postwar legislation was strongly influenced by US New Deal employment policies.[3]

The obstacles presented by theories of Japanese ER have been implicitly recognised by Nitta (1997), who set out to determine whether or not ER practices in Japan had changed 'in the economic fluctuations that have occurred since the collapse of the bubble economy' (1997:267). His review of macroeconomic data included employment adjustment, unemployment, labour participation, working hours and white-collar overemployment. He chose this route of analysis because, as he argued, 'it is hard to reach a common understanding of what precisely Japanese employment practices and labour relations were in the past . . . Defining even "life-time" employment" is a rather complicated business' (1997:267). The data suggested that while some changes had occurred, such as a reduction in working hours, the scale of these adjustments were less profound than those following the oil price shock era of the early 1970s. In assuming a modified 'J-firm' stance, Nitta recognised that cross-shareholding among firms is a factor in governance structures. Thus, ER changes ought to follow from modifications of the former. Yet, he noted, it is difficult to detect changes in either governance structures or ER practices. He concluded that Japanese employment practices had undergone no fundamental change (1997:282).

Theory, then, presents a major obstacle to research on current changes in Japanese employment practices. Although more than 40 years have passed since Abegglen and Levine first reported on long-term employment practices in Japan, the status of the 'lifetime' employment system itself remains the central theoretical issue in debates about ER in Japan.

'Lifetime' employment and the legal environment of the Japanese enterprise

Research findings have identified case law references to the continuation of 'lifetime' employment in Japan (Tackney 1995). A 1961 Yokohama regional court decision ruled on the legality of an employer dismissal case. The action was brought to court by a group of employees who had initially been hired by the firm on the proviso that their retirement age would be some years earlier than that of most other workers in the firm. The court ruling at first appeared to deny the claim made by the dismissed: 'The 15 applicants assert that . . . they established a contract . . . similar to the lifetime employment labour contract of the regular employees. However, there is no evidence to compel the credibility of this claim' (Hanrei jijo 1961:12). But despite this apparent rejection, the court went on to find that the mandatory retirement age of those dismissed was not the same as that of those hired under the 'lifetime' employment system of the firm. And, based upon this line of analysis, the court invalidated the dismissals.

This is the very first reference to 'lifetime' employment in Japanese case law. Since 1961, more than 100 cases have made explicit reference to this phrase—in local, regional and even Supreme Court cases.[4] The significance of case law reference to 'lifetime' employment is summarised in the following 1987 regional court decision:

> For this dismissal case, [dismissals] 'according to the inevitable circumstances of firm operations' (Labour Standards Law, Article19:1) should be made by management and labour on the basis of the overall factual conditions of the enterprise. However, the lifetime employment system is a principle of labour–management relations in our country. The premise is that the worker will have a continuing employment relationship until retirement age. While the so-called rationalisation dismissal is wholly necessitated by the need to sustain operations on the side of management, the actual outcome is a destruction of the worker's pattern of life. Accordingly, the following conditions must exist before one can say that 'inevitable circumstances of the operations' actually obtain . . . (Rodo hanrei 1987:45)

The court decision invalidated 35 of 38 dismissals in a machine tools firm. The decision indicates that Japanese courts play some role in the institutional norms linking 'lifetime' employment with the regulation of possible abuse by the employer of the dismissal prerogative (Rodo hanrei 1987). The court specified four minimum conditions necessary for the possibility of legally valid dismissals.

1. dire financial circumstances of the firm;
2. documentation of specific steps taken to avoid dismissals;
3. objective and clear dismissal standards; and
4. the necessity and details of the personnel rationalisation must be sincerely explained to the workers and an effort must be made through adequate deliberations to obtain worker consent. (Rodo hanrei 1987:45)

The court stated: 'If the preceding conditions do not exist, it cannot be said that the occasion is "according to inevitable circumstances of the operations" and dismissals when these conditions do not exist must be said to be invalid' (Rodo hanrei 1987:45). More recently, a 1997 Supreme Court decision stated that 'lifetime' employment was 'a given premise of our nation's labour circumstances' (Lex/DB case 1997).[5] This reflects the continuing legal recognition and 'institutional regulation' of 'lifetime' employment.

The above references to case law provide evidence that 'lifetime' employment has become an accepted institution of Japanese ER practice. It is an explicitly presumed practice in larger firms and a strong social model, reinforced by case law, in other employment circumstances throughout the country. In case law, even repeatedly renewed part-time employees are presumed to have a continuing employment relationship. This appearance of 'lifetime' employment in case law would seem at odds with the US New Deal origins of Japanese labour legislation and a Civil Code that permits labour contracts to be terminated by either party, given proper notice.

We can puzzle over why 'lifetime' employment appears in case law. But a more useful framing of the question takes this form: is legislation the sole source of law? Considering other institutional sources of jurisprudence is essential for a more informed understanding of Japanese ER. This understanding will enable us to establish an explanatory model for studying the current pressures on Japan's rules about jobs and work.

The legal environment of the Japanese firm

There are several distinctive features of the post-1945 Japanese legal system that serve as foundations for the institutional emergence of the 'lifetime' employment system. These features clearly distinguish the legal environment of Japanese firms from their US or German counterparts (see Figure 4.1).

The use of a comparative legal environment allows us to capture the significant legal differences that shape ER in a modern firm. A German firm is governed by legislated co-determination and works councils which include representatives from among workers and among management—thus the arrows move in both directions. Employees in Germany are protected from arbitrary dismissal by 'just cause' legislated obligations on the employer and through other protections afforded by works councils and collective bargaining agreements. In stark contrast, the US has no legal provision for employee participation in managerial prerogatives—hence the solid black line in Figure 4.1 between management and the union. In the case of Japan, employee participation in management issues has been institutionalised by collective bargaining agreements since 1946. Therefore, Figure 4.1 shows arrows moving in either direction between unions, management councils and management.

Figure 4.1 The legal environment of the Japanese enterprise

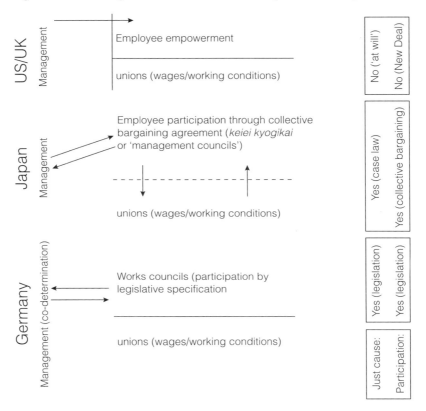

Three rules serve as key, antecedent foundations for the legal environment of the post-1945 Japanese firm:

1. the role of case law;
2. the recognition of an employee participation function; and
3. the employer's dismissal prerogative—tempered by the legal doctrines of just cause and abusive dismissal.

In this analysis, the differing parties and conflicting interests within the Japanese firm appear to have achieved a balance.

Case law

Japanese courts operate from the methodological premise that the judiciary can analyse, identify and abstract 'living law' from specific cases (Kettler & Tackney 1997). Accordingly, case law in Japan plays a very important role in deriving legal norms or 'working rules'. Given sufficient case accumulation on an issue, legal precedent in Japan approximates a legal norm. This process was particularly evident in the early post-1945 era, when occupation inspired legislation had to be interpreted to meet the realities of Japanese history and culture. The institutional role of the judiciary was instrumental in establishing legal norms that helped to shape the postwar development of employment practices.

Employee participation

A structurally distinctive feature of the post-1945 legal environment of the Japanese firm was the pervasive role of employee participation in unionised and, later, non-unionised settings; such processes were widely established by labour unions as part of the democratisation process. The first Central Labour Relations Commission (CLRC) saw such processes as a means of overcoming a crisis in capital presented by 'production control' actions, in which employees took over production of an enterprise (Kettler & Tackney 1997). In response to a formal government request, the CLRC issued a directive in 1946 that recommended the localisation of employee participation functions within collective bargaining agreements. Remarkably, this remains the last legal word on the matter to the present day.

This novel step was a careful adaptation of German works council and co-determination schemes. By avoiding legislative recourse, the CLRC pre-empted conservative influences that might have exerted pressure on any such proposed legislation in the Japanese parliament (*Diet*). This approach also insured closer linkages between market changes and the life of the industrial enterprise than could have been achieved through legislative control. Localisation of participation structures within collective bargaining agreements prevented the establishment of a 'ceiling' or 'limit' on the extent to which employees could exercise their voice in the management of the firm.

Employment participation groups, under various Japanese terms (such as management councils: *keiei kyogikai*), have been, and remain, a central feature of the Japanese enterprise (MOL 1995). More than 80% of unionised firms in Japan have established consultation processes and procedures. More than 70% of all Japanese firms having 5000 or more employees maintain formal consultation structures. Councils are found in 68% of firms with 1000 to 4999 employees and in 62% of firms with 300 to 999 employees (MOL 1995). Consultation topics determined by collective bargaining range from basic management strategies to employee welfare and company finance. The courts have established case law norms that require consultation between management and workers, particularly in the event of planned redundancy dismissals (*seiri kaiko*). This consultation process is often conducted through the management council. The function and strength of these consultation mechanisms varies. At times, consultation may amount to little more than a one-sided management presentation. It more often involves seeking informal feedback and the formal inclusion of workers' views in company policy. In a small percentage of Japanese firms, management proceeds according to explicit participatory consensus policy (see Tackney 1998).

Just cause and the legal doctrine of abusive dismissal

Post-1945 Japanese labour legislation is modelled on US labour law within a civil law legal system. Labour legislation and the Civil Code permit parties to cancel a contract with notice. Despite this, case law citations on 'lifetime' employment clearly invoke a widely recognised norm on dismissal restrictions (Gould 1984).

    'Just cause' is an adaptive appropriation of Weimar labour law. It appears in Japanese case law because the earliest post-1945 interpretations of the nature of the employment contract came from a judiciary trained before World War II. Their judicial training was German in academic focus (Yanagawa et al. 1950). Employers abuse of their dismissal prerogative induced the development of a Japanese legal doctrine early in the post-1945 era (Kettler & Tackney 1997). Ironically, it appears to have first been developed in reference to the dismissal of Japanese workers employed by the US Occupation forces. While 'at will' employment is recognised by legislation, Japanese courts have determined that it is possible to conceive of employers abusing their right to terminate a contract. This abuse of the dismissal prerogative is inherently associated with 'just cause', which relates to the recognition of reciprocal societal obligations in contract, when a firm contemplates the dismissal of workers.

Stability and strain within the Japanese legal environment

The legal environment typology can be used as a tool to explore contemporary areas of stability and strain within the lifetime employment system. First, let us consider the extent of the 'lifetime' employment system. Table 4.2 lists the percentage of the overall labour force employed as 'regular employees' (*seiki koyosha*).[6] A regular employee is defined as one employed on an indefinite term contract. The data in this table exclude those who are 'directors' (*yakuin*) of firms.

    The remarkable stability of the core male workforce throughout the 1990s needs to be contrasted with the steady decline in the

Table 4.2 Regular (*seiki*) employee participation rate by gender

Year	Combined %	Male %	Female %
1984	84.8	92.4	71.1
1985	83.8	92.8	68.1
1986	83.5	92.7	67.9
1987	82.6	92.4	66.0
1988	81.9	92.0	65.1
1989	81.0	91.4	64.1
1990	80.0	91.3	62.1
1991	80.3	91.6	62.9
1992	79.6	91.1	61.9
1993	79.3	90.7	61.7
1994	79.8	91.6	61.8
1995	79.2	91.2	61.0
1996	78.5	90.7	60.4
1997	76.9	89.6	58.4

Source: Nihon Rodo Kenkyu Kiko (1998).

proportion of women employed as regular employees. Given the broad social role of the 'lifetime' employment system, the significance of this decline is better understood from a comparative perspective. Abraham and Housemen studied long-term employment elasticities by sex in the Japanese and US workforces. While they found employment elasticities higher for female Japanese workers than for their male counterparts, their elasticities were still 'significantly less than those for either American men or American women' (1989:517).

The legal environment typology recognises the 'lifetime' employment system as a legally regulated institutional practice. Accordingly, the locus of strain between market pressures and employment policies within the Japanese firm ought to be manifest in the realm of employment law, not, as J-firm theory would suggest, through changes in shareholder governance structures. The next section explores the extent to which the 'lifetime' employment system has been contested during the economic recession of the 1990s.

Exploring the contested domain of the 'lifetime' employment system

As the New Year holiday approaches every year, three almanacs take up primary sales space in Japanese bookstores.[7] Each of the annuals maintains sections on economics and labour issues. *Imidas*, for example, contains a labour economics section by Hiroyuki Chuma of the Economics Department of Hitosubashi University. He begins the first section of the 1999 edition with the phrase 'lifetime employment system' and includes a discussion on 'the legal doctrine of abuse of the dismissal prerogative' (*kaikoken ranyo hori*). An informal check of prior volumes throughout the 1990s indicates that this is the first appearance of the abuse of dismissal prerogative doctrine in this almanac. The 1999 *Asahi* volume also lists the abuse of dismissal doctrine within the labour section. The unusual prominence given to this topic in the 1999 annuals suggests employer dismissal practices and the abuse of dismissal prerogative have become important topics.

A report from the Tokyo Labour Affairs Office (*Rosei jimusho*) documents domestic economic difficulties and provides evidence of strain in local employment relations (Labour Affairs Office 1998). The following examples of topics discussed in the report indicates some of the economic problems faced by Japan:

1. Company bankruptcies in the month of July 1998 exceeded that of the previous year by 36%—the worst month since the end of World War II. Hardest hit was the manufacturing sector, with a 64% increase in bankruptcies over the prior year. Overall, the 11 883 bankruptcies nationwide between January and July 1998 were at a pace to overtake the previous worst, 1984, which saw 12 063.

2. From January to May of 1998, personal bankruptcy filings nationwide increased by 38% over the prior year—an unprecedented rate. Two to three years ago, personal bankruptcies mainly impacted on middle-aged and older workers, victims of restructuring, and young women who overspent on entertainment expenses. In 1998, however, most categories in society were affected, including mid-level 'salarymen'.

3. In the 1998 summit between top officers of *Rengo* (the peak labour confederation) and *Nikkeiren* (the employer counterpart), *Rengo*'s chief stated that the worsening economic conditions compelled a *shunto* (annual spring labour offensive) focus on employment security in the coming year. In turn, *Rengo* would have to forgo any calls for a wage increase. This prompted a strong reaction from the President of *Zenkoku Ippan Roso* (National General Workers Union)—a federation for small and medium-sized unions within the *Rengo* umbrella—who stated, 'This may be good for big firms. But for those working in small and medium sized firms forgoing a wage increase is no guarantee of employment security. And the problems of insecure, unorganised workers are *Rengo*'s obligations, no less!'

Table 4.3 Labour Affairs Office (Tokyo metropolitan area): consultations

Year	Consultations	Number of items discussed
1956	4750	9186
1965	8582	14 393
1970	9576	13 618
1975	19 931	32 098
1980	24 683	42 393
1985	29 240	46 398
1990	30 747	50 474
1996	44 929	68 327
1997	48 875	77 571

Source: Labour Affairs Office (1998).

By 1993 the increased vulnerability of middle level management in Japan had spawned a new union structure: the Tokyo Managers Union, and regional affiliates. The President of this independent union, *Kiyotsugu Shitara*, published a text entitled, *I'll teach you 'how to fight' with your company* (*Kaisha to no tatakaikata oshiemasu*) (Shitara 1998). Originally founded with fourteen members, by 1998 the Tokyo branch membership had exceeded 700; new branches were also formed in Osaka and Nagoya. In addition, a non-managerial class union affiliate, the Network Union, was formed in 1998. Focused on younger workers, membership in the late 1990s was predominately female.

Against the background of these recent developments, data from the Labour Affairs Office show an increase in the number of enquiries it has received. As part of the Ministry of Labour and the Metropolitan Toyko Government, this office provides information and serves in a fact-finding capacity for those who seek advice about employment difficulties. Representatives from the Labour Affairs Office do not have legal grounds to compel corrective action. But, if circumstances warrant, they will visit employers in their fact-finding capacity and have the legal right to demand the provision of information. The lack of enforcement power should not lead the reader to presume this agency is ineffective or weak. Depending on the type of the employer, prompt relief may be obtained from a single phone call or inquiry by this government agency.

Table 4.3 lists the number of consultations and the number of issues involved in these consultations for selected years since 1956. Note the growth from 1970 to 1975—the oil shock era of restructuring. Note, too, the absolute increase in both figures over time. In one year alone (1997) there was a 48% increase in consultations at the Shinagawa Ward Office. Although an exact breakdown is not included in the report, most issues dealt with dismissals (15%), then wages and pay (10%), the non-payment of wages (9.8%) and the employment contract (6.7%). The data suggest that in contrast to the conclusions reached by Nitta, ER during the 1990s, in metropolitan Tokyo at least, were generating more unease than in any previous period in the post-1945 era.

Changes in legislation

This chapter has emphasised the central, norm-defining role played by non-legislative sources of law in Japanese ER. However, there have also been significant changes in legislation.

Revision of the Labour Standards Act 1947

The most notable change in legislation in the late 1990s was the formal revision of the *Labour Standards Act*. This was passed by the Japanese parliament (*Diet*) in 1998 and took effect in 1999.[8] This revision was the outcome of years of consultation and sustained labour opposition. It appears to have been motivated by a general push towards 'deregulation' in Japan (and other countries), with changes occurring in several areas of employment regulation. Three-year term contracts have become possible for certain professional positions, while other areas are still governed by the predominant regular employee status—indefinite contracts—or one-year contracts.

The legislative revision explicitly deals with one area of central interest for the legal environment typology. An amendment to Article 22 of the Act obliged the employer to deliver without delay a certificate stating the reason for any worker being dismissed. Yamakawa wrote: 'if a reason for discharge is clarified, it will be easy for the courts to determine whether the discharge is based on a just cause' (1998:9).

Case law norms defining the parameters for a 'just cause' dismissal are, in fact, very narrow. The new obligation upon employers to specify the grounds for exercising their dismissal prerogative appears to leave the employer open to more rapid accusations of abusive dismissal. The failure to provide a cause for the dismissal now becomes a potentially illegal action. This may result in the invalidation of dismissals by the courts through provisional dispositions.[9] In these respects, the outcome of the revision amounts to a re-regulation, not a deregulation, of employment law.

Equal employment opportunity law

Evidence of women being treated differently in Japanese workplaces was noted previously in the comparative decline of women workers as a percentage of regular employees. This trend must be considered against the general increase in the labour participation rate by Japanese women. Thus, while comparatively more women are entering the workforce, they are likely to be employed on a casual, contract or part-time basis.

The Equal Employment Opportunity Law (*Danjo koyo kikai kintoho*) (1985) aimed at having workers assessed on the basis of their ability, not their gender. The significance of this law remains in dispute (Sugeno 1992; Sano 1995). In practice, the law *prohibits* discriminatory treatment of women in areas related only to training, health/welfare, retirement, resignation and dismissal procedures. The following areas were considered *obligatory* for equal treatment: recruitment, employment, employment arrangements (location) and promotion. In the instance, 'obligatory' meant that violations were not expressly prohibited by law. Chuma explained that one large reason for this distinction was 'a lack of national consensus about changes induced or compelled by law in the personnel management methods of individual firms' (Chuma 1999:146).

In 1997, recruitment and hiring were shifted from 'obligatory' to 'prohibited' by a Diet proposal. After passage through the Diet, violations in these areas, too, became expressly prohibited. Firms failing to provide evidence that they intended to improve illegal procedures could potentially be subject to public disclosure.

One conclusion to be drawn from the continued controversy over the significance of the Equal Employment Opportunity Law in Japan concerns the role of law in the working rules of ER in Japan. That is, in the absence of compelling obligations (i.e. financial penalties) to behave otherwise, Japanese employers display no greater effort to change than their counterparts in other countries. As Sano wrote: 'One reason why the employment opportunity law has not been extensively practised is, according to some opinion, because there are no penalties for violations' (1995:63).

Conclusions

Despite long debate about the existence and nature of the 'lifetime' employment system, this chapter provides evidence that it has been recognised by case law since the early 1960s—the system was shown to be an institutionalised practice. The legal environment typology then framed a subsequent exploration of stability and strain within the rules of the current ER system.

An area for future concern is that the standard arguments for continuing the 'lifetime' employment institution, particularly from organised labour, centre on an insistence for 'employment security'. There may have been reasonable grounds for this claim during the relatively stable decades of the Japanese 'economic miracle'. Labour was then in comparatively short supply and unions rarely had to protect their members' employment security. In the new millennium the increasingly global nature of economic competition requires a better argument. In this new era, unions' insistence on employment security runs the risk of being perceived as anachronistic. The only apparent alternative then becomes a steady movement towards the kind of 'at will' employment practices found in the US, where there is much less employment security.

Yet, ironically, there is evidence of interest in the Japanese approach to employment relations from Merrill-Lynch, one of the world's most competitive multinational firms. Following the unprecedented 1998 bankruptcy of Yamaichi Shoken, a leading Japanese investment firm, some 7000 workers faced imminent dismissal. Efforts were made by management to find subsequent employment for these staff. Then, remarkably, Merrill-Lynch entered the picture. It bought a considerable number of the closed offices and, not content with plant and equipment, it also offered employment interviews to all the workers who had lost their jobs. Merrill-Lynch seized an opportunity to move quickly into the newly deregulated Japanese financial market and welcomed 2000 new employees to its new subsidiary in 1998. The corporate press release stated most of the new employees 'used to work for Yamaichi Securities'.[10]

The legal environment examined in this chapter suggests that employment security throughout the post-1945 era has been the consequence of ER rules that recognised the social dimension of the employment contract within a legal framework. These rules had implications for the nature of the post-1945 Japanese enterprise. Trust was enhanced and high levels of firm-specific employee commitment were provided in exchange for some degree of participation in the management and outcomes of the firm.[11]

At a national level, just cause dismissal standards are a legal recognition that employers have obligations to their workers due, in part, to the social relationship inherent in the employment contract— labour is not merely a commodity. The localisation of employee participation (*keiei kyogikai*) in the collective bargaining agreement is a long overlooked middle ground between the legislative approach of Germany and the New Deal prohibition still constraining the development of management councils in the US.

The world still has a great deal to learn from 'Japanese management' and Japanese ER. The future development of ER theory for the Japanese case depends on a broadening of empirical research. This analysis of the legal environment has attempted to make such a contribution. Japan faces a great challenge. No longer the 'late developer', learning better ways by studying the earlier paths of others, the future success of Japanese ER may well reside in recovering the 'working rules' of the post-1945 era that contributed to the nation's economic growth.

5 Changing approaches to employment relations in South Korea

Funkoo Park and Young-bum Park

Since 1987 South Korea has experienced the promotion of labour rights, reduced state intervention into union activities and the establishment of a system of collective bargaining to determine wages and working conditions in workplaces. The price of this transformation has been substantial. Consecutive wage rises, often surpassing the productivity gains, have become a heavy burden on the competitiveness of South Korea's companies. The Korean economy has also had to pay a high price due to the frequent strikes and work stoppages that occurred during this period.

Against this backdrop, discussions on the need for employment relations (ER) reform began and focused on two major issues. The first was to establish more co-operative and participatory ER practices. The second involved labour law reform, particularly in the area of expanding union rights and extending labour market flexibility. In May 1996 the Presidential Commission on Industrial Relations Reform was established. The Commission's immediate mandate was to formulate a recommendation for labour law reform based on a compromise between labour and management. Falling short of a compromise, especially on a list of critical issues, the government and the ruling party unilaterally passed the controversial legislation at the end of 1996. Discontent over the content of the Bill, as well as the procedures in passing the Bill, led to the calling of a nationwide strike. The government yielded to this pressure and political negotiation resumed. Having achieved a compromise among the political parties, new legislation was passed in March 1997. The issue of dismissals was a major difference between the 1996 and 1997 legislation. According to the 1996 legislation, this provision was supposed to go into effect from March 1997. The effective date was changed subsequently to March 1999.

In November 1997, even before the most controversial provision of the 1997 labour law amendment became effective, South Korea was hit by a severe financial crisis. The South Korean government decided to approach the International Monetary Fund (IMF) for a rescue plan.

As the IMF offered a relief fund, it demanded that further steps should be taken to improve labour market flexibility. President-elect Daejoong Kim established the Tripartite Committee for Industrial Relations and in January 1998 the Committee had agreed to allow dismissals in two instances: when they are unavoidable or during mergers and acquisitions (M&As). These changes were to be effective from April 1998, a year earlier than originally agreed.

Confrontations between unions and management over collective dismissals for managerial reasons have been escalating, with rising unemployment rates aggravated by the financial crisis. A year later, unemployment had risen by more than one million. Labourers and those already jobless were calling for job security guarantees.

This chapter examines the implications of such labour law amendments and the financial crisis for South Korea's ER practices. The first section contains a brief summary of the recent developments in South Korea's ER since 1987. The second section describes the nature of the debate surrounding the labour law reform. The third section examines developments and major issues in ER after the financial crisis. The implications for the future of ER in South Korea are outlined in the final section.

Developments in employment relations since 1987

1987 was a landmark year for political liberalisation in South Korea, and was also a turning point for its ER. The policies, the institutional framework and the practices encompassed in South Korean ER have undergone a significant change since then. From June 1987 to December 1987 the number of unions increased from 2725 to 7883 and union membership rose from one million to 1.9 million. During the same period the number of industrial disputes also increased (see Table 9.1).

Since 1987, unions have become a powerful institution in South Korea's labour–management relations, and collective bargaining has become an important institution for improving the working conditions of both union members and general workers. The major South Korean manufacturing firms in the auto, steel and ship-building industries, which were the engine of South Korea's remarkable economic growth, became unionised. Before 1987, unionisation was prevented through strong government intervention. After 1987 these newly organised unions in large firms became the power base for South Korea's new union movement. Large-scale industrial action

Table 5.1 Selected employment relations indicators in South
Korea

ER indicators	1985	1990	1995	1997	1998
GDP change rate (%)	6.5	9.5	8.9	5.0	−5.8
Unemployed ('000s)	622	454	419	566	1463
Rate of unemployment (%)	4.0	2.4	2.0	2.6	6.8
Nominal wage/change rate (%)	9.2	18.8	11.2	7.0	2.4
Real wage change rate (%)	6.7	9.5	6.4	−2.5	−9.3
Working hours per month	225.5	209.5	207	203	199.2

Source: Office of Statistics, Korea, *Monthly Statistics of Korea*, various issues.

continued after 1987 on issues related to union recognition, the
improvement of wages and working conditions, and issues concerning union security. Violence often accompanied the industrial action
and in some cases this promoted confrontation with police.

Another important development in South Korean unionism since
1987 was the rise of an independent union movement, separate from
the officially recognised Federation of Korean Trade Unions (FKTU).
Since 1987, there have been many attempts to organise a separate
independent national centre by union activists who do not follow
FKTU policy lines. The Cheonnohyup (Korean Council of Trade
Unions) was formed in January 1991. The Cheonnohyup and other
non-recognised unions formed the Minjunochong (Korean Confederation of Trade Unions or KCTU) in November 1995 (see below ch. 9).
Minjunochong affiliated unions are based in the large manufacturing
firms that were unionised after 1987, and are more aggressive and
militant than FKTU affiliated unions.

In the early 1990s, prior to the financial crisis, the number of
industrial disputes had declined substantially, dropping from 3749
in 1987 to 322 in 1990. In 1995 and 1996, less than 100 industrial
disputes were recorded. The large drop in the number of disputes
is due to a combination of factors. First, in 1989 the South Korean
economy suffered a recession which made workers and union leaders realise that their hard-line stance would not win support from
the general public. Second, employers and unions gained experience
in settling conflicts through dialogue. Both parties realised that
lockouts or strikes should be the last resort in the process of
collective negotiation. Third, the government, which remained on
the side-lines in major industrial disputes after 1987, made it clear
that law and order should be established at workplaces. More
unions and employers, as they encountered difficulties in their collective negotiations, began to follow the procedures outlined in the
labour laws.

After December 1997, disputes increased sharply as the threat of job losses mounted, with South Korea having implemented a serious reform program which aimed to overcome the financial crisis. There were 129 labour disputes recorded in 1998, a 65% increase compared to the 78 recorded in 1997. About 146 000 workers took part in the disputes, three times as many as the 44 000 who participated in 1996. The number of lost production days reached 1 452 000 in 1998, compared with 444 000 days in 1997.

In the 1990s the number of unions decreased compared with earlier annual increases. This does not necessarily mean that union influence on the collective negotiation process declined. The drop in union membership reflects the changes in South Korea's industrial structure. In that decade, under industrial restructuring, labour intensive manufacturing industries declined rapidly and employment in manufacturing declined significantly. Until recently South Korea's growth strategy in the manufacturing sector has been to promote large-scale industry for low cost competition. Even though South Korea is trying to move towards a high-value technology based economy, manufacturing industry still plays a key role in South Korea's industrial structure. Unions are very strong in manufacturing, particularly in large firms.

A neo-corporatist approach has been trialled in South Korea as part of the process of economic restructuring which started with the IMF rescue package. The newly installed national leadership of Daejoong Kim emphasised social agreement among the three ER parties to facilitate the quick and decisive implementation of structural reform measures. A Tripartite Commission was established in January 1998. It was this Tripartite Commission that fostered the process of structural reform and some additional amendments to labour laws by reaching the landmark agreement on 20 January 1998.

The second Tripartite Commission was established in June 1998, based on the social consensus that the current national crisis could only be overcome with the participation and co-operation of all the ER parties.

Debate over labour law amendment

Debates about labour law reform have been on the political agenda since the labour laws were amended in November 1987. The amendments helped improve ER in South Korea by making it easier for unions to organise workers and exercise their bargaining power. As a result, a larger proportion of disputes then occurred within, rather than outside, the legal framework.

In 1989, the opposition parties, who gained a majority in the

National Assembly in the 1988 general election, called for further amendments to strengthen labour rights. However, a presidential veto ensured that none of the proposed changes were enacted. In 1992 the government attempted to initiate another round of amendments to the labour laws, this time to check the rapidly expanding union movement and rising wages, but strong opposition from the unions forced the government to withdraw its attempts.

Another force for change had come from the International Labour Organisation (ILO), which South Korea joined in 1991. Since then, cases involving the labour rights of South Korean workers, such as violations of the principle of freedom of association, have been filed with the ILO against the South Korean government. In all the cases concerned, the ILO has recommended that South Korea's labour laws be revised in line with the ILO's principle of freedom of association.

With the inauguration of President Young-Sam Kim in early 1993, a civilian head of state, the labour law revisions promised during his presidential election campaign were expected. In August 1993, however, the government postponed his initiatives on labour law amendments until 1994, arguing that a debate on the subject would intensify labour–management confrontation and damage the South Korean economy, which was already in difficulty. This setback disappointed many union activists, especially those represented by the KCTU.

In 1996 South Korea joined the Organisation for Economic Cooperation and Development (OECD). In reviewing South Korea's application to be a member, some other OECD members found South Korea's labour laws to be of major concern. Some of the member countries strongly argued that Korea could not qualify as a member unless its government revised key laws concerning labour rights.

With all these concerns raised by the international community, as well as increasing pressure from the non-FKTU affiliated unions, in 1996 the Presidential Commission on Industrial Relations Reform was established with a view to proposing reform of labour law and ER practices. The Commission consisted of 30 members: five from labour (three from the FKTU, two from the KCTU), five from management and twenty members representing public interests.

Proposals for amendments were brought to the Commission's attention. Among them, two sets of the so-called three key issues concerning government intervention in union activities were:

• The prohibition of multiple trade unions, an issue which related to the legalisation of the KCTU and permitting multiple unions at workplaces;

- the prohibition of third party intervention in union activities;
- the prohibition of political activities by unions.

Management opposed lifting these restrictions, arguing that such action would further destabilise workplace ER.

The three major labour market flexibility measures which employers demanded be introduced were:

- The *Labour Standards Act* did not include criteria and procedures for determining dismissals. The merit of each collective dismissal was ruled on by the court which was a lengthy process. Hence, employers demanded the introduction of a provision on collective dismissals.
- The *dispatch* system was prohibited except for limited areas such as security or cleaning. The number and use of such temporary workers was growing despite the lack of legal provisions governing their employment.
- Management wished to introduce flexible overtime arrangements to respond to fluctuations in production demand without paying overtime premiums. Workers opposed these measures, concerned that they would lead to a deterioration in working conditions.

Through extensive talks and discussions, the Presidential Commission reached a consensus among the representatives from labour, management and the public on 101 out of 148 issues that were put on the table, but compromise could not be reached on some issues. In November 1996, the Presidential Commission submitted its interim report to the government with many key issues not having been resolved.

On 3 December 1996, the government (the Industrial Relations Reform Promotion Committee chaired by the Prime Minister) concluded the discussion and arrived at an amendment proposal based on the Commission's report, including some modifications of the Commission's proposals. Unions threatened strikes if the government pushed its proposals further. The government sent the amendment proposal to the National Assembly and, after modification of the government draft by the New Korea Party (South Korea's ruling party) passed the Bill.

Passage of the new labour law immediately provoked strikes. A general strike was called by both the FKTU and the KCTU just after the Bills were passed. During the first few days 200 000–300 000 workers participated. The government yielded to the pressure and resumed negotiations with the minority parties in the National Assembly. In March 1997, after a compromise was reached by the political parties, legislation was passed.[1]

The newly enacted labour laws were essentially similar to the administration drafted Bills, except for two additional clauses. The ruling party reflected the opinions of employers who have feared confusion among union representatives arising from conflicting directives from different labour federations. The new Bills also delayed authorisation of multiple unions in workplaces. With regard to dismissals for collective redundancy, the New Korea Party also tried to accommodate demands from labour in the Bills by postponing implementation of that provision to March 1999 instead of March 1997.

Employment relations since the financial crisis

Tripartite co-operation

When the IMF offered its financial package, the South Korean government and the IMF agreed that further steps should be taken to improve labour market flexibility. Recognising that this issue could not be decided without consultation with labour representatives, in January 1998, President-elect Kim established the second Tripartite Commission for Industrial Relations. Members included representatives from unions, management, the ruling political parties, members of the Cabinet and representatives from other organisations. From the start, the Commission faced severe opposition from the union representatives for its dismissal program; on 20 January 1998 the Commission agreed to allow dismissals in cases where they were unavoidable or during mergers and acquisitions. In the 1997 labour law revision, M&As were not considered a justifiable reason for collective dismissals. In addition, under the new agreement, dismissals for collective redundancy would be allowed a year earlier (i.e. starting from April 1998) than the originally scheduled time.

Additional points of the agreement were as follows:

* The government must establish a five trillion won (approximately US$4.4 billion as at January 2000) unemployment fund.
* Public servants would be permitted to form a labour consultation body in 1999. (Teachers would be permitted to form a labour union in July 1999.)
* Unions would be able to engage in political activities starting in the first half of 1998.
* A dispatch system would be permitted.

The industrial rights of public servants and teachers as well as the dispatch system were issues which were not agreed in the 1997 labour law revision.[2]

Some radical members of the KCTU voted against the 1998 agreement, despite their representatives' endorsement of the package, claiming it did not fully reflect the interests of labour. They did not go ahead with major strikes, which they had scheduled, even though there was increasing nationwide public anger and disappointment. Most people hailed the 1998 agreement, saying that it would contribute greatly to restoring the confidence of South Korea within the international community.

The establishment of the second labour–management–government Tripartite Commission was more controversial than the first one. At the start, the progressive KCTU boycotted the second Commission, claiming it lacked government measures to minimise lay-offs and to help the unemployed. South Korea's unemployment rate had reached a record high since the first Commission produced an agreement among the three parties on legalising lay-offs and restructuring businesses. The KCTU also called general strikes, claiming that workers were constitutionally guaranteed to stage collective action to protect workers' rights which were being ignored in the name of restructuring the national economy. The government decreed that the strikes could not be protected by labour laws and it would deal sternly with illegal strikes. Despite these warnings, many of the unions went ahead with a general strike.

The second Tripartite Commission was launched without the participation of the KCTU. As the nation's unemployment problem increased, the FKTU also refused to participate in the second Commission. Both union confederations accused the government of forcing sacrifices unilaterally on to workers in violation of the basic spirit of the landmark agreement which called for a sharing of the burden brought about by the economic crisis. On 23 July 1998, the head of the second Commission accepted most of the claims that unions had stated as preconditions for returning to the negotiating table. This move was welcomed by the union representatives but angered employer representatives. Under the agreements, unions would be given more say in the Tripartite Commission. Legal charges against union leaders involved in illegal strikes would be also minimised.

Through the second Tripartite Commission, teachers' unions were legalised. In February 1999, both the FKTU (with some conditions) and the KCTU withdrew from the Commission, claiming that the Commission was generally ignored in the process of restructuring the nation's economy. This was expected, as the government ministries concerned had not agreed on the role of the Commission.

Both union confederations claimed that the standard number of working hours should be reduced from 44 hours per week to 40 hours per week to create more jobs. In addition, the FKTU claimed that the system of employers paying the wages of full-time union officials should continue. In the 1997 labour law amendment paying wages to full-time union officials constituted an unfair labour practice and would be discontinued from the year 2002.

Unemployment, job protection and wage cuts

Unemployment increased substantially after the nation was hit by a severe foreign currency crisis. In November 1997, prior to the financial crisis, unemployment was 2.6%. Unemployment reached 8.5% by 1999, which meant that 1.8 million South Korean workers were unemployed. Approximately 74% of people defined as jobless had been forced to leave their workplace.

The government has been putting measures in place to cushion the impact of lay-offs occurring in the wake of the IMF's restructuring plan. It has spent a great deal of money on projects to help the unemployed. Labourers and the unemployed were calling for guarantees of job security, the suspension of unilateral moves by employers to dismiss workers in the name of structural reform and better financial measures for those dismissed. They argued that present government measures lacked guarantees for a minimum livelihood for the unemployed, as only a limited portion of employees were entitled to unemployment allowances. According to a survey by the Korea Labour Institute (March 1998), two out of five unemployed did not receive severance pay.

Confrontations between union and management concerning collective dismissals for economic reasons are demonstrated in a labour dispute which took place in June 1998 in the Hyundai Motor Co., South Korea's largest car manufacturer. Union leaders insisted that the lay-offs should be averted through wage cuts and work-sharing while management argued the lay-offs were the only available means to help the company overcome its current economic difficulties. After a long dispute, a compromise was reached to reduce the number of dismissed workers and to increase the offer of additional dismissal payments to laid-off workers above the then legal minimum.

In June 1998, for the first time in South Korea's history, five banks were closed. This signalled the beginning of the planned financial sector restructuring. The government also closed 55 private companies in financial trouble. Some 30 000 workers of public corporations, including Korea Telecom, Korea Electric Power Corp. and the Korean National Tourism Organization, would be dismissed in a 3-year period. In addition, 73 of 108 state-managed enterprises would be privatised. Some 30 000 (10%) of local public servants were dismissed by the end of 1998.

Tension between unions and the government concerning the nation's economic restructuring reached another peak in April 1999 as the Seoul Subway System union led a strike to contest the scheduled restructuring plan which would result in the dismissal of Seoul Subway workers. The strike ended without the union achieving any gains as no other unions joined the general strike called by the KCTU.

On the other hand, most companies involved in negotiating wage deals with their employees froze or cut wages. There were also substantial cuts in bonus payments and overtime payments. The impact was that real wages decreased by 9.3% in 1998.

Unfair labour practices by employers

The first Tripartite Commission agreed to take strong action against employer mistreatment of employees perpetrated under the guise of economic difficulty. These practices might include collective dismissals for business reasons and delaying payment of wages. The government repeatedly appealed to employers to refrain from unnecessary lay-offs, with a warning that those firing workers arbitrarily would be legally punished. In fact, the Labour Minister asked the prosecutor's office to undertake investigations of some 400 companies that had abused the economic situation and some of the companies were punished.

According to union representatives there has still not been enough such government action. Since the financial crisis, the two union confederations have often demanded that the government introduce measures to investigate and curtail employer use of unfair labour practices. When the union confederations decided to join or return to the second Tripartite commission in June 1998, the head of the Commission promised swift and drastic measures to end the maltreatment of employees on the pretext of 'economic difficulties'.

The amount of unpaid wages also increased dramatically because of the growing numbers of businesses declared bankrupt. According to the Labour Ministry, at the end of March 1998, there were huge amounts of unpaid wages to at least 79 000 workers. There was also a great deal of unpaid severance pay.

Conclusions

Swift and drastic economic restructuring was prescribed to overcome Korea's economic difficulties. There were loud voices of workers protesting about their situation in the economic crisis, with some unions in major industries threatening to call major strikes.

Attracting as much foreign investment as possible was the first crucial step towards remedying South Korea's crisis. Keeping industrial peace is one prerequisite for attracting foreign capital for the revival and survival of South Korean industries. An outbreak of strikes and subsequent social unrest would deter foreign investors, and reckless industrial action would precipitate national collapse.

Public unease intensified as there was no guaranteed minimum livelihood protection for many of the unemployed. The sense of uneasiness among the unemployed is precipitating exasperation and could possibly even induce organised violence.

South Korea's fate depends on whether the government can create specific and easily implemented measures to assist the survival of those workers and their families who are dismissed. In the process, organised labour should be consulted and given its due role as economic restructuring continues. Establishing a tripartite institution at the national level would be a reasonable option and may legitimise the reform process in the workers' view.

In 1996 the six-month period of debate over labour law reform via the Presidential Commission, and with the participation of the KCTU and FKTU, was seen as a step forward in recognising the need for KCTU participation in South Korea's ER framework. The KCTU was then an illegal organisation (it was finally legalised late in 1999). The parties involved had a chance to express their views on the issue. The reconciliation framework, established through the Presidential Industrial Relations Reform Commission, was disbanded however, as efforts to restore a tripartite national body to facilitate dialogue after the final revision of the law in 1997 did not lead to any meaningful outcomes.

This approach was tried again to achieve a compromise among the concerned parties to accommodate the conditions of the IMF rescue package concerning labour market flexibility; it produced effective results. We infer from the progress of the second Tripartite Commission in 1998 and 1999 that South Korea needs more time and experience for this kind of arrangement to be institutionalised.

At the workplace level, management has been experiencing difficulty introducing labour market flexibility measures, especially in large firms with strong unions, as there are few re-employment prospects for dismissed workers. In non-union sectors or smaller firms it was easier for employers to introduce more flexibility. Thus, a short-term outcome has been the further polarisation of working conditions between large and small firms.

To some extent institutionalising a system of collective dismissals for managerial reasons was much easier in the context of the IMF package. Unions as well as workers have had no alternative but to accept the principle of employment adjustment, a mandate required by the IMF and international investors.

Since the new labour law permits the existence of multiple unions at the national and industry level, some changes in the bargaining structure are expected. In the two months following the finalisation of the labour law revision in 1997, eight new industrial federations were organised: one is affiliated with the FKTU, five with the KCTU, and two are independent.

Some unions are promoting a structural shift from enterprise, to industrial unionism. To achieve this, unions are working to strengthen solidarity among unions belonging to the same federation by concentrating the wage-bargaining process into the same period, and by entrusting bargaining to their federations.

The provision prohibiting the payment of wages to full-time union officials will also be a factor in determining South Korea's future bargaining structure, if it is enforced as proposed. Most small unions would not survive financially without support from employers. Even large unions, those with about a thousand members, might face difficulties without the wages of their officials being paid by employers.

Following the agreements of the first Tripartite Commission, permitting political parties to participate in the political activities of unions will be influential in shaping South Korea's bargaining structure and its industrial relations framework. While the KCTU put up a candidate for the 1997 presidential election, the FKTU strengthened its ties with then President Kim by supporting him in the 1997 election. Having more say in the national political arena will give more power and authority to senior union leaders, which may influence the outcomes and the structure of enterprise-based bargaining.

The last, but perhaps most important, issue is that of transforming industrial relations to a climate of participation and co-operation. In recent years there have been moves in this direction in a number of work sites and some have been relatively successful.

In those firms where such efforts are still to be initiated, it may take time and be more difficult for management to induce more co-operation and participation from union leaders, particularly those most threatened by restructuring. On the other hand, unions did not devise an appropriate alternative strategy to deal with the threats to employment security due to South Korea's economic difficulties.

Appendix 5.1: Major points of the 1997 labour law amendment

The finalised amendment is far reaching in its coverage. It not only contains major issues of the debate discussed earlier in this chapter, but also other issues related to collective industrial relations and labour standards. Amendments were also made in the *Labour Relations Commission Act*. The *Act Concerning the Promotion of Worker Participation and Cooperation* was newly enacted based on the *Labour Management Committee Act*. The major revisions are briefly outlined below.

Trade Union and Labour Relations Adjustment Act

The *Trade Union Act* and the *Labour Dispute Adjustment Act* were merged and became the *Trade Union and Labour Relations Adjustment Act*.

Multiple unions
The most controversial issue concerning the presence of multiple unions in a workplace was resolved. The new law, by allowing multiple trade unions to be present in a workplace, enhances the basic labour rights of workers by granting them the right to join the trade union of their choice.

In order to avoid unnecessary confusion arising from conflict among trade unions over bargaining rights as the result of the changes to current negotiation practices, and to allow time for the introduction of the new practices, multiple trade unions at the enterprise level will be permitted from the year 2002. This allows the independent KCTU to gain legal status and will open avenues for multiple union organisations at the industry level.

Payment to full-time union officials
Payment to full-time union officers, which is prevalent in most trade unions in Korea, will constitute an unfair labour practice under the new labour law. In order to allow trade unions and employers to prepare for this particular provision it will come into effect in five years. To establish a foundation for the financial independence of trade unions, the regulation in the previous law which limited monthly union dues to less than two percent of monthly wages, has been lifted.

Third party intervention
The ban on third party intervention has also been lifted. Instead, the new law defines the scope of people or organisations from whom labour and management may seek assistance concerning collective bargaining as well as collective action. These definitions include

upper-level organisations of either labour or management and those reported to the Labour Minister for assistance by either labour or management.

In negotiations with management over wages and other conditions, trade unions are now able to seek professional help from a third party such as upper-level organisations or anyone who is registered with the Labour Minister.

Replacement of striking workers
Under the new law, employers are allowed to replace striking workers with workers in the same enterprise. This will allow employers to deploy non-union workers, union members not participating in the strike activities, or those who work in other factories within the same enterprise.

Payment during a strike
Employers are not obliged to pay wages during a strike and strikes demanding payment for the period of a strike are prohibited under the new law. This provision was made to eradicate the practice of unions demanding back pay for days on strike and will help establish the so called no work—no pay rule.

Union membership status of dismissed workers
When a dismissed worker files a petition with the Labour Relations Commission calling for relief from an unfair labour practice, they are not entitled to union membership until the decision of the Central Labour Relations Commission is finalised. Under the previous law, the union membership of dismissed workers was often an issue as the dismissed workers were allowed to retain their membership as long as their appeals were pending at the Supreme Court.

Political activities of trade unions
The new labour law abolishes the provision in the *Trade Union Act* prohibiting political activities by trade unions. Only cases where 'the main objectives of a trade union's activities lie in political movement' constitute a violation of the law. The political activities of trade unions, like those of other social organisations, are to be subject to the elections-related laws.

Banning industrial action inside workplaces
The provision banning industrial action outside workplaces was abolished. Instead, new provisions were added to prohibit the occupation of the production line and industrial action in maintenance facilities. This is to minimise losses caused by a strike. Prohibiting the occupation of workplaces is to avoid a situation where production facilities are paralysed and employees are prohibited from choosing to continue working.

Validity of wage agreements
A maximum term of two years applies to the validity of wage and collective agreements under the new provisions. Past practice was to sign the wage agreement and collective agreement separately, since the law mandated the duration of the wage agreement as a year.

Compulsory mediation prior to industrial action
The new labour law replaces the previous system of dispute reporting prior to collective action, with a system of mediation procedure incorporating a mandatory cooling-off period. Under the new system, industrial action should proceed only after 10 days of mediation provided by the Labour Relations Commission.

The Labour Standards Act

Dismissal for managerial reasons
The criteria and procedures of dismissal for managerial reasons approved by the 1989 Supreme Court ruling were written into the law. The criteria and procedures for dismissals are:

- urgent managerial reasons
- employer's prior efforts to avoid dismissal
- fair selection of workers to be dismissed and
- consultation with workers' representatives.

This provision will go into effect from 1999.

The system of flexible working hours
The new law introduces two types of flexible working hour system:

- a fortnightly flexible working hours system with a maximum of 48 hours a week to be worked based on company work rules;
- a monthly flexible working hours system up to 56 hours a week, based upon agreement with the union.

Working conditions for part-time workers
Before this amendment, the *Labour Standards Act* did not have provisions on working conditions for part-time workers. The amended law stipulates that working conditions for part-time workers should be determined in proportion to their working hours and to those of full-time workers. Part-time workers who work less than 15 hours per week are exempt from the provision of weekly and monthly paid holidays, severance pay, and paid annual vacations.

Complement to compulsory severance pay system
Employers have to pay severance pay with an average amount totalling the equivalent of more than 30 days for each year of consecutive service. Employers do not have to pay retirement allow-

ances immediately upon retirement, as they may pay in advance at the request of the worker concerned. Employers may also enrol in pension programs whereby workers can receive a lump sum payment on retirement or when they begin to draw their pensions.

The Labour Relations Commission Act

With the new labour law, considerable revision has been made to the *Labour Relations Commission Act*. In order to assure independence in the operation of the Commission, a set of provisions have been made including the procedures for selection of public representatives and the status of the Chair of the Commission. The Commission also underwent organisational restructuring.

To enhance the fairness of the Commission, public representatives are to be elected by a ballot of members, workers and employers, and from among those recommended by the Chair of the Commission, the trade union movement, and employer associations. To improve the expertise of the public representatives, they are either designated as adjudication members who deal with disputes over rights or mediation members who deal with interest disputes.

The Act Concerning the Promotion of Worker Participation and Cooperation

The previous *Labour–Management Council Act* has been changed and renamed the *Act Concerning the Promotion of Worker Participation and Cooperation*. This new law characterises the labour–management council as an employee representative organisation, and strengthens its role of employee participation.

Worker representation
The previous law stipulated that trade union representatives, recommended by a union, took worker's membership at the council in the unionised firms. Under the new law, worker's representatives at the council are designated by the union only in cases where the trade union is formed by a majority of workers. In other cases, worker's representatives are to be elected by workers.

Matters subject to the council's resolutions
Under the previous law, the council had two functions: overseeing labour–management consultation and receiving information from employers on management plans, production plans and results, manpower plans and other items pertinent to the firm's operation.

To strengthen worker participation, the new law introduced matters on which employers should seek the resolution of the council. These include:

- establishment of employee education and training plans and skill development schemes;
- the establishment and administration of welfare facilities;
- the establishment of employee welfare funds;
- matters not resolved by the Grievance Committee;
- the establishment of various labour–management cooperative committees.

In case these matters are not resolved by the Council, they should be referred to an arbitration procedure established by the council or by the Labour Relations Commission.

Appendix 5.2: Tripartite joint statement on fair burden sharing in the process of overcoming the economic crisis

Wage stabilisation and the enhancement of labour and management cooperation

Employers will endeavour to put an end to illegal dismissals and unfair labour practices to stabilise employment. Trade unions for their part will strive to improve a firm's competence and improve the productivity and the quality of goods. The government will accomplish industrial peace through impartial and strict supervision of union and management action to prevent taking advantage of the economic crisis.

Labour and management will consult sincerely with each other in wage negotiations and collective bargaining procedures and closely cooperate to resolve common issues through industrial and regional labour–management schemes.

The government will guarantee labour and management negotiation autonomy in wage and collective bargaining and improve support programmes for collective bargaining through the provision of information.

Labour and management will further their efforts to make the wage system more rational and the government will come up with a tax incentive scheme to reform the wage system to include a profit sharing system.

Labour and management will establish an organisation tentatively named the Centre for Labour–Management Cooperation and Support to monitor labour disputes at the company level. The Centre will work to eradicate unfair labour practices and to promote labour-management cooperation.

The government will guarantee the independence and management responsibility of government-invested, government-financed institutions and local public firms, and promote their management efficiencies. The government will strive to address and reflect the opinions of labour and management while making major policy decisions, such as setting the guidelines for budget assignments and privatisation.

The government will endeavour to implement, in close collaboration with labour and management, a complete monthly pay system in the taxi industry.

Trade unions will adhere to democratic principles in the election of officials and their daily operations as well as promote financial transparency.

Protection of basic labour rights

In February 1998, the government will submit to the National Assembly drafts of laws regarding the establishment of work councils for government employees to be introduced in January 1999. The government will guarantee government employees' rights to organise trade unions, taking into account nation-wide public opinions and the revision of the related laws.

Stage 1: Establishment of work councils
- Structure: Work councils will be established at the levels of the ministry, metro-city-province, and city-county-district.
- Function: Handle grievances and other labour disputes.

Schedule: Commencing in 1999

Stage 2: Organisation of trade unions
- Structure: The unions for central government employees will be organised at the national level, and the unions for local government employees will be organised at metro-city-province levels.
- Function: The rights of collective bargaining will be permitted regarding wages and working conditions but the right to conclude collective agreements and the right to act collectively will not be recognised.

Schedule: Implementation will be scheduled after taking into account the convergence of public opinion and arrangements in related laws

The government will proceed with modifying the related laws with a view to guaranteeing the right to organise the teachers' unions at the National Assembly in September 1998.

The political parties will grant permission to participate in the political activities of trade unions by revising the Elections Law and the *Political Funds Act* during the first half of 1998.

The government recognises the right of unemployed workers to maintain their union membership. It will also extend the mandatory prior notification period from 3 months to 6 months before the unilateral termination of collective agreements, whose effective period has been automatically extended in order to enhance the protection level. The government will submit a proposal to revise related laws to the National Assembly in February 1998.

The government will submit proposed revisions to the related laws delegating limited authority for labour affairs from local labour offices to local governments to the National Assembly in February 1998.

The government will set up arrangements to provide tax benefits to trade unions at the earliest moment possible to facilitate the financial independence of trade unions.

Enhancement of labour market flexibility

The government will proceed with revision of the Labour Standards Act at the National Assembly in February 1998 to amend the procedures regarding employment adjustments. The title of the article is: 'Limitations on Employment Adjustment of Workers for Managerial Reasons' and includes:

Conditions of dismissal
Dismissals should only be carried out in cases of urgent managerial need which include transfers, mergers and acquisitions of businesses to avoid managerial deterioration.

Efforts to avoid dismissal of workers
Employers should exert every effort to avoid the dismissal of workers.

Standards in selection of dismissal of workers
Rational and fair standards should be adopted in selecting workers to be dismissed. (Prohibition of discrimination on the basis of gender will be explicitly cited.)

Procedures for the dismissal of workers
An employer should inform the workers' representatives of the measures taken to avoid dismissal and of the criteria in selecting workers to be dismissed 60 days prior to dismissal and should consult with them. Notification to the labour administration office should be made prior to a dismissal.

Addition of an item specifying the employer's rehiring obligation of dismissed workers

Repeal of the suspension in the efficacy of Article 31 of the February 1998 Labour Standards Act

The government will submit to the National Assembly in February of 1998, a draft act for dispatched workers entitled the *Act on Dispatched Workers' Protection* which contains the following:

Work for dispatched workers

- Work that requires specialised knowledge, techniques, and experience, the scope of which will be determined by Presidential Decree.
- Employment of dispatched workers to serve as a replacement for temporary vacancies due to: maternity leave, illness, and injury of workers, or for temporary and irregular needs are permitted in principle except in cases prohibited by decree. (An employer should consult with the workers' representatives or the trade union representing the majority of all workers prior to employment.)

The dispatch period

Up to one year (extension to be permitted for up to an additional one year if mutually agreed upon.)

Measures for protecting dispatched workers

- Employers' obligation to avoid unfair discrimination between dispatched and regular workers.
- Prohibition of termination of dispatch contracts on the basis of religion, gender and social status.
- Prior notification of work conditions to dispatched workers.

Restrictions concerning dispatching workers

- Dispatching workers to establishments in the process of labour disputes for the purpose of influencing the collective activities are prohibited.
- Worker dispatches where workers have been dismissed for managerial reasons will be prohibited during a certain period determined by Presidential Decree.

Clarification of the employers' responsibilities regarding the dispatched workers

- Employers dispatching workers should assume the responsibilities regarding wages and work injury compensation.
- Employers using dispatched workers should assume the responsibilities regarding working hours, work leaves, and industrial safety and health.

6 Changing approaches to employment relations in Taiwan

Joseph S. Lee

Taiwan, an island with an area of 36 000 hectares, lies 190 km off the coast of southern China. Taiwan was an integral part of China. It was ceded to Japan in 1895 as a result of China's defeat in the Sino-Japanese war of 1894–95. Following the Japanese surrender at the end of World War II, Taiwan was returned to China and it has been the seat of the government of the Republic of China (ROC) since the communists took over mainland China in December 1949. Today the island has a total population of 21 million.

During the last fifteen years the economic, social and political environments in Taiwan have undergone significant changes. Taiwan's economy has shifted towards more technology intensive, service-producing industries. The regulatory environment has also become increasingly liberalised. Taiwanese society is no longer a closed and authoritarian society but increasingly a pluralistic, democratic and open one. Complementing the economic and political changes are changes in the social structure, value system and practices of employment relations (ER) in Taiwan's workplaces. The following discussion outlines changes in the economic and political arena, and then examines how these changes have affected ER.

As Taiwan's economy matures, the education and skill levels of its work force are increasing. Its unions are establishing their independence from the ruling party and are playing a larger role in improving the working conditions of their members. For management, changes in the economic environment have fostered an awareness of the importance of their employees and the vital role of human resources management (HRM) practices. The changing economic structure prompted the government to reform its *laissez-faire* labour policies and implement a more active and regulatory approach. Since the late 1990s, however, there have been signs that the government's ER policy approach is moving towards a more voluntary one, incorporating input from the private sector. The government has set goals but left it to employers and unions to determine the means for achieving these goals. For example, in 1997 the government asked the Chinese Federation of Labour (CFL) and the Chinese Management Association (CMA) to negotiate adjustments to the minimum wage rate. The intention was to replace an annual centralised government decision with a negotiated union–management agreement. The CFL and the CMA did come to a tentative agreement, deciding that the minimum wage for 1997 was to remain unchanged. Each association member, however, was to raise wages by at least 3% for all their employees. In effect the agreement excluded all foreign workers from receiving wage increases. The negotiated agreement was rejected by the members of the CMA and resulted in the government deciding to award a 3% wage increase to all workers.

The shift towards a more active and regulatory policy occurred in part through the democratisation of society. The government then had to be more receptive to voters' demands or risked being voted out of office. Changes in employment relations policy were also partly in response to pressure from the US. Taiwan has enjoyed a large trade surplus with the US since the early 1980s. Unionists and employer groups from the US saw the trade surplus as a result of workers in Taiwan not being protected by unions or government legislation, and a threat to their employment and trade opportunities. (See below, ch. 13, for reflections of such views in the Asia-Pacific Economic Co-operation forum.) The implication was that low labour standards in Taiwan meant that American and Taiwanese workers competed unequally, so Taiwanese imports into the US should be restricted. Unions and employer groups lobbied the US government to restrict Taiwan's access to the US market. To ensure continued access for Taiwanese products into the US market, during the second half of the 1980s the Taiwanese government passed several pieces of labour legislation. The most important one was the Fair Labour Standards Law 1984 (FLSL) which covers a range of employment issues. It was not until 1987, however, with the establishment of the Council of Labor Affairs, that the FLSL was seriously enforced.

The government has recognised that the internationalisation of the economy has reduced its ability to influence ER and so has made several attempts to redirect its labour policy. A more voluntarist approach has emerged, with unions and management encouraged to take a more active role in determining the terms and conditions of work.

Table 6.1 Production index by intensity of skill

Year	High-skill intensity	Medium-skill intensity	Low-skill intensity
1981	44.24	46.10	74.74
1982	44.38	45.65	76.51
1983	50.57	53.15	83.83
1984	56.56	61.10	91.72
1985	57.85	61.33	94.66
1986	66.26	72.48	105.70
1987	75.39	83.06	111.06
1988	82.48	87.90	106.46
1989	89.80	89.96	104.66
1990	92.13	91.86	96.64
1991	100.00	100.00	100.00
1992	109.38	104.75	95.87
1993	117.78	108.46	87.74
1994	127.66	116.33	86.62
1995	138.01	123.43	80.76

Note: 1991 = 100.
Source: Ministry of Economic Affairs, *Monthly Bulletin For Industry*, 1998.

Changes in economic structure

Since 1987 Taiwan's economy has been transformed from a newly industrialising economy into an industrialised market economy. Like other such economies, its growth rate has slowed. In 1987 the rate of economic growth in Taiwan was 12.7%; a decade later it had dropped to 6 to 7%. In the postwar period Taiwan's economic base has shifted from a reliance on agriculture, then to industry and then to services. In 1997 the share of GNP generated by the service sector was 52%. Taiwan is moving towards a post-industrial society (CEPD 1999). With the transformation in Taiwan's industrial structure, there has been a shift away from labour intensive industries to capital and technology intensive industries. As Table 6.1 indicates, before 1987 labour intensive, low-skilled industries expanded faster than skill intensive industries: their production index rose from 74.74 in 1981 to 111.06 in 1987. After 1987 the production index for labour intensive, low-skilled industries declined. By 1995 it had dropped to 80.76—a decline which was offset by the expansion in capital and technology intensive industries. The production index of these expanding industries rose from 75.39 in 1987 to 138.01 in 1995.

The change in economic structure is also illustrated by changes in the structure of exports. The share of labour intensive products as a percentage of Taiwan's total exports dropped from 43% in 1989 to 34% in 1998. The share of products requiring highly skilled labour increased from 24% to 41% in the same period (CEPD 1999:208). This switch to more capital and technology intensive industries, along with the increasing importance of the service sector, has significantly affected ER. HRM is now recognised as more important to a firm's success than when the economy was dominated by agricultural and labour intensive industries. Consequently, employers pay more attention to their ER policies and practices.

Another important development is the globalisation of Taiwan's economy. Since 1987 the government has taken several major steps in liberalising its economy. Prior to 1987, no citizen from Taiwan could visit mainland China, since the two areas were officially at war. In 1987 the government permitted visits to relatives on the mainland for humanitarian reasons. Many business people took the opportunity to relocate their labour intensive firms to China, as the cost of wages and land had become more expensive in Taiwan. Compared to Taiwan, mainland China has a growing industrial work force and lower wage costs. Labour intensive firms from Taiwan also relocated to South-East Asian countries—such as Thailand, Malaysia, Indonesia and the Philippines—to take advantage of their comparatively low labour costs.

A further contributing factor to the relocation of Taiwan's labour intensive firms abroad and the internationalisation of small and medium-sized firms is the liberalisation of Taiwan's financial market. Taiwan's citizens are now permitted to send US$5 million abroad without government approval. A recent survey indicates that 82% of large businesses and 58% of small and medium-sized businesses in Taiwan have invested abroad (Chung 1998:3–8).

The internationalisation of Taiwan's businesses has created ER problems in Taiwan that are more diverse and sophisticated than in the past. Employers can choose where to invest, in Taiwan or abroad, and so have achieved much more flexibility. A further impact of the internationalisation of Taiwan's economy has been a weakening of employees' bargaining power.

Changes in employment structure

Changes in economic structure affect employment. Employment opportunities have shifted from manufacturing to services. In 1987 the share of employment in manufacturing industries was about 43% of total employment but by 1998 this had dropped to around 38%. In the same period the share of employment in the service sector industries had risen from approximately 42 to 53% (see Table 6.2). With the shift in jobs away from agriculture to industry and from

Table 6.2 Employment distribution in Taiwan

Year	Agriculture	Manufacturing	Services	Total
1987	15.28	42.76	41.95	100
1988	13.73	42.47	43.80	100
1989	12.9	42.09	45.01	100
1990	12.85	40.83	46.32	100
1991	12.95	39.93	47.12	100
1992	12.34	39.01	48.06	100
1993	11.49	39.08	49.43	100
1994	10.92	39.22	49.86	100
1995	10.55	38.74	50.71	100
1996	10.12	37.49	52.39	100
1997	9.57	38.17	52.26	100
1998	8.85	37.92	53.23	100

Source: DGBAS (1999).

Table 6.3 Highest levels of educational qualifications of employees

Year	Illiteracy	Primary school	Junior high school	Senior high school	Junior college	College and above	Total (%)
1987	7.15	32.61	19.82	26.60	7.65	6.17	100
1988	6.20	31.38	19.83	27.87	8.15	6.56	100
1989	5.65	30.15	19.93	28.92	8.50	6.84	100
1990	5.12	28.77	20.90	29.86	9.15	7.19	100
1991	4.56	28.07	20.23	30.48	9.45	7.22	100
1992	4.16	26.59	23.39	31.17	10.24	7.45	100
1993	3.76	25.01	20.00	32.27	10.91	8.05	100
1994	3.53	23.97	20.18	32.73	11.39	8.19	100
1995	3.28	22.82	20.11	33.15	11.79	8.85	100
1996	2.95	21.24	19.40	34.14	12.81	9.46	100
1997	2.80	20.22	19.24	33.89	13.62	10.23	100
1998	2.56	18.81	19.14	34.60	14.08	10.82	100

Source: DGBAS (1999).

labour intensive to capital and technology intensive industries, the importance of the educational composition of the work force has increased. The share of the work force with primary education dropped from about 32% of the total work force in 1987 to 19% in 1998. In the same period the share of senior high school graduates rose from 27% to 35%, and college graduates rose from 6% to 11%. These changes indicate a decline in the labour force participation rates of young people, with more young people continuing their education. Between 1987 and 1998 the labour force

Table 6.4 Labour force participation rates

Year	Total	15–19 years	20–24 years	25–49 years	50–54 years	55–59 years	60–64 years	65 years and above
1987	60.93	32.09	69.21	76.15	66.12	58.50	41.82	10.59
1988	60.21	28.98	68.31	75.98	65.62	58.49	41.68	9.64
1989	60.12	27.62	67.83	76.03	65.54	58.07	41.98	10.34
1990	59.24	24.68	65.73	75.71	65.04	56.43	40.90	9.77
1991	59.11	22.86	65.42	76.01	65.64	56.29	41.84	9.93
1992	59.34	21.20	65.13	76.88	65.98	56.72	41.97	9.69
1993	58.82	19.44	63.69	77.13	65.80	56.06	41.61	9.83
1994	58.96	20.21	63.88	77.59	66.11	55.52	40.61	9.68
1995	58.71	19.46	62.95	77.67	65.79	55.75	41.06	9.79
1996	58.44	18.71	61.68	77.97	65.30	55.18	39.79	8.95
1997	58.33	17.94	60.91	78.07	65.09	54.75	40.10	8.76
1998	58.04	16.13	60.48	78.26	65.49	53.52	38.52	8.51

Source: DGBAS (1999).

participation rates of 15- to 19-year-olds dropped from 32% to 16% and for 20- to 24-year-olds in the same period dropped from 69% to 61% (see Table 6.4).

Changes in the political arena

The 1980s are also notable for important changes in the political arena. The most significant was the abolition in 1987 of martial law, which had been in effect since 1947. Subsequently, officials and legislators at all levels, including the president, were subject to direct election by Taiwan's citizens. Since 1995 the president has been elected directly by the people and not by the Assembly, as was the case in the past.

The repeal of martial law in 1987 paved the way for the legal recognition of activities such as the creation of additional political parties, street marches, peaceful street demonstrations and mass rallies in public places. By the late 1990s there were more than 60 new political parties in Taiwan, with the Democratic Progressive Party (DPP) and the New Party being the most influential. In recent years the DPP has controlled several major cities, including the capital, Taipei. In the 2000 presidential election the former mayor of Taipei, a DPP nominee, won the election and replaced the party which had ruled Taiwan for 55 years.

One implication of increasing democratisation is the necessity for the governing party to heed the demands of its citizens or face the possibility of being voted out of office. It is not surprising then that throughout the 1990s several pieces of social welfare legislation were introduced by the government. Important laws are the previously mentioned FLSL (1984) (although introduced much earlier), the *Health Insurance Act* 1994 and the extension in July 1998 of the FLSL to cover workers in all industries. An unemployment insurance program was implemented in January 1999. Under the DPP government, we can expect legislation more favourable to labour interests and that more welfare programs will be implemented.

The democracy movement has had an effect in workplaces, with moves towards greater industrial democracy and employee participation. The increases in social welfare, however, may create disincentives for Taiwanese employees to work.

Developments in employment relations

The number of union members has increased from 2.09 million members in 1987 to 2.92 million in 1998. This aggregate figure is somewhat misleading as the increase in membership has occurred in craft unions but not in industrial unions, and does not reflect a growing union strength. The membership of craft unions rose from 1.39 million in 1987 to 2.53 million in 1995 but fell to 2.24 million in 1998. The membership of industrial unions fell from 703 562 in 1987 to 575 606 in 1998, a fall of 127 956 members. A large percentage of craft union members are self-employed. These members join craft unions to be eligible to enrol in employment insurance programs and not for union activities. The current Labour Insurance Law demands that self-employed workers must join a craft union to benefit from an insurance program. Membership in a craft union allows the union to enrol them in the employment insurance program and the government subsidises 40% of their insurance premium, because their self-employed status means they do not have employers to pay part of their premium. In many instances, the families of self-employed workers also join craft unions. Taiwan's industrial union members constitute the majority of *bona fide* union members. Table 6.5 shows that industrial union membership reached its peak in 1990; since then both the number of unions and the number of individual members has declined.

The decline in union membership in industrial unions is partly attributed to the shift from manufacturing to the services sector. As in many other countries, workers in Taiwan's service sector, compared with those in manufacturing, appear disinclined to join unions. The liberalisation of Taiwan's economy and the increasing proportion of enterprises investing abroad are also important contributing factors

Table 6.5 Number of unions and union membership in Taiwan

	Number of unions			Number of union members			
Year	Total	Craft unions	Industrial unions	Total	Craft unions	Industrial unions	Union density*
1987	2510	1350	1160	2 099 813	1 396 251	703 562	25.66
1988	3041	1756	1285	2 260 585	1 594 070	666 515	27.41
1989	3315	1970	1345	2 419 664	1 721 546	698 118	28.84
1990	3524	2170	1354	2 756 620	2 057 248	699 372	32.73
1991	3654	2304	1350	2 941 766	2 249 187	692 579	34.33
1992	3657	2357	1300	3 058 414	2 389 331	669 083	34.89
1993	3689	2418	1271	3 172 116	2 521 030	651 086	35.75
1994	3706	2469	1237	3 277 833	2 640 738	637 095	36.10
1995	3704	2500	1204	3 135 875	2 537 396	598 479	34.05
1996	3700	2510	1190	3 048 270	2 460 711	587 559	32.74
1997	3714	2518	1196	2 952 883	2 363 886	588 997	31.31
1998	3732	2556	1176	2 921 400	2 345 754	575 606	30.59

Note: * % of work force belonging to unions.
Source: Council of Labour Affairs (COL) (1998a:45); Yearbook of Labour Statistics (September 1999).

to the shrinkage in employment in the manufacturing sector and thus the decline of industrial union membership.

The decline in union membership does not mean a decline in union strength. Union influence has been increasing. The growth of democracy has weakened the government's control over unions, allowing unions greater autonomy. This more independent union movement is concerned with members' welfare to a greater degree, as unions in the pre-martial law period largely functioned as an extension of the government.

Prior to 1987, unions were strictly controlled by the government, a situation which reflected the post-1945 period. During this period Chinese communists infiltrated workplaces in mainland China and gained control of unions. Through strikes they paralysed the functioning of the Nationalist Party government, which contributed to its downfall and subsequent retreat to Taiwan. Learning from this experience, once established in Taiwan, the Nationalist government controlled union activities. Until 1985 the government nominated union officials in many unions to prevent the infiltration of Chinese communists into Taiwan's workplaces (Lee 1988).

The threat from the Chinese communists was significantly less in the 1970s, nevertheless the government maintained control over the unions and their activities. This was due in part to the United Nation's recognition in 1971 of the People's Republic of China as the only legal government of China: the Republic of China lost its UN membership. As a result many countries severed their diplomatic relationship with Taiwan, recognising mainland China instead as the sole legal representative of China. The government in Taiwan used civil organisations, including unions, to maintain contact and conduct business with people overseas. The government encouraged workers to join unions to maintain contact with international union organisations, including the American Federation of Labor–Congress of Industrial Organizations (AFL-CIO) in the US. As AFL-CIO unions are generally anticommunist, the government in Taiwan believed it could convince the governments of these anticommunist countries to implement policies favourable to Taiwan.

Control of the unions also meant the government could use them to campaign for its candidates in political elections. The repealing of martial law also made it legal to form opposition parties. To obtain workers' votes, opposition parties have worked hard to maintain contact with workers by assisting in the establishment of their own unions, independent of the government and the CFL, and to nominate their own union officers. Leaders of the independent unions are more militant and have used strike action to achieve their goals. In 1988 and 1989 this new breed of union leaders used strikes to draw attention to the issues of year-end bonuses and overtime payments (Lee 1988). The independent unions during the late 1980s and early 1990s formed largely in response to local workplace issues and did not attempt to establish relations with other unions. They also tended to dissolve themselves when the disputes were settled. A Federation of Independent Unions formed in 1987 but its membership was small and the Federation did not invoke any collective action (Huang 1996:25). It was rare for unions to join other groups and engage in mass demonstrations. In the early 1990s, this first wave of independent unions retreated discouraged after losing several major strikes.

A new group of independent unions has emerged since 1995 in response to the downturn in Taiwan's economy. In 1995 and 1996 many firms in Taiwan closed and workers were laid off. The unemployment rate reached 2.6% in 1996 and 2.7% in 1998, comparatively not a high rate, but the highest unemployment rate in Taiwan since the 1985 energy crisis. To protest against company closures without adequate notice and the failure to pay severance pay or pensions to dismissed workers, many workers again formed independent unions. The most important examples during this period were in the Fu Chung Textile Company, Lien Fu Textiles, Tung Yuong Needles, Tung Lienn Electronics, Lou Min Electronics, Chung Hua Machinery, United Containers and at the Tai Tung San Hsia Plant. These cases all involved the closure of plant facilities and employer failure to pay severance pay or pensions as required under the FLSL.

This second wave of independent unions differs from the first wave because these unions formed federations, set common goals and established a support network. In April 1994 a regional federation for the independent unions was formed in Taipei County. By 1998 eight regional federations had formed outside the CFL framework, comprising 252 member unions and 142 593 individual members (*Labor*, 95, April 1998:8).

In addition to the regional federations a number of national independent industrial unions formed. These are largely unions formed in the national enterprises, including in the China Telephone and Telegraph Corporation, the China Petroleum Corporation, the Taiwan Railroad Company, the Taiwan Tobacco and Wine Monopoly Bureau, and the Taiwan Power Corporation. These industrial unions had been affiliated with the CFL but in March 1998 declared themselves independent. In May 1998 they formed the National Federation of Industrial Unions. Its membership totals 163 182 workers (*Labor*, 95, April, 1998:8). These unions left the CFL and elected new leaders because of government plans, announced in 1996, to privatise all public enterprises within five years. Fearing losses in jobs and benefits, employees moved to protect their interests. After joining the eight regional federations of independent unions, the public enterprise industrial unions, together with the regional federations, marched in the streets of Taipei on 1 May 1998. They demanded the government introduce anticorruption measures, amend the FLSL, introduce unemployment insurance programs and guarantee full employment.

The independent unions are illegal if they have not officially registered with the government, as is required under the Trade Union Law, or if a registered union exists in the same workplace, as dual unionism is illegal in Taiwan. While technically illegal, the government has taken no action against these unions, fearing a political backlash. But they have not been invited to participate in government sponsored union activities, such as honouring workers on Labour Day, nor been consulted on labour legislation and ER policy issues. The government has refrained from including these independent unions in official activities as that could be construed as legitimatisation.

The activities of the independent unions could have repercussions on the CFL and their member unions. Their actions have forced the CFL to take a more independent position from the government and to take a more active role in improving the welfare of their members by initiating bargaining activities with employers and negotiating better benefits for their members. A recent survey showed that CFL member unions in 1997 offered more services in job search assistance, job-related training and labour education than previously. The focus of the labour education programs is occupational safety and health, explaining workers' legal rights, and the function of unions (COL 1998a:8).

As mentioned above, the CFL recently worked with the two largest employer associations, representing employers in the industrial and commercial sectors, to negotiate the annual minimum wage increase. The CFL has also worked with management in resolving some of the problems encountered by management in complying with the FLSL, especially for businesses receiving coverage by the law for the first time in 1998. Interestingly, management claims that it is more productive to work with unions on these matters than with government officials.

Increasing government intervention in employment relations

Until 1980 the government adopted a *laissez-faire* approach to ER policy. Despite the many pieces of ER legislation, the government had not enforced them. This is partly because many of these laws were enacted in the 1930s or 1940s when the government was still on mainland China where economic conditions differed from those in Taiwan. Also the government wanted to provide a favourable investment climate by providing incentives for foreign investment in Taiwan. Thus, until the 1980s, wages and benefits in the private sector were mainly determined by market forces and not by institutional factors such as unions or minimum wage laws.

Demands for democratisation in the mid-1980s persuaded the government to demonstrate its commitment to improve conditions for workers. As a result the government abandoned its *laissez-faire* approach to ER policy and adopted a more active and regulative approach. The FLSL covers a range of ER issues, including individual labour contracts, wages, working hours, time off, leave of absence, child labour, women workers, retirement, compensation for occupational accidents, apprentices and work rules. In 1987 the Council of Labour Affairs was created for the express purpose of enforcing this law. In 1997 the Council of Labour Affairs announced that the coverage of the FLSL would be extended to workers in the service sector in addition to those in agriculture, mining, manufacturing, construction, utility, transport and public media industries. The extension of the coverage took place in three stages—in March, April and July 1998—and a total 1.09 million workers were added to the coverage (COL 1998b). This law has a profound impact on ER.

Codifying management's ER policies

The FLSL requires an employer with more than 30 employees to submit written work rules to the government agency for approval. When approved, a copy must be displayed on workplace bulletin boards. The intention of this measure is to force employers to codify their ER policies, reducing the arbitrary and capricious nature of previous practices. A 1991 study implied that approximately two-thirds of the 8000 manufacturing firms had written work rules for their employees (Lee 1995). A survey conducted by the Council of Labour Affairs of those industries covered by the FLSL showed that 99% of the firms surveyed had written contracts with their employees (COL 1997:2). Responding to these needs, many consulting firms have been established to help employers to draft employment contracts.

Limiting management flexibility

The FLSL includes many regulations on the management of ER rights. One example concerns overtime. The law stipulates that overtime cannot exceed 36 hours per month for men and 24 hours for women and that, prior to imposing overtime work, management must seek the approval of the union. If there is no union in the workplace, management must seek the approval of two-thirds of the work force. Women workers are prohibited from working after 10 pm unless it is a three-shift workplace and certain conditions have been fulfilled. The law does, however, create compliance problems. The requirement of one day off a week makes it difficult for many employers to comply. It is not generally practicable for employees in the logging and fishing industries to descend from mountain work sites or return to shore every seven days. Given the difficulty in complying with these regulations, employers have tended to ignore the provisions, and the government has tended to overlook these items when conducting inspections.

Changing employment patterns

The many regulations imposed by the FLSL have increased business operating costs and have restricted management's ability to maintain competitiveness. To avoid compliance with the FLSL, many employers are changing their current employment contracts into sub-contractor agreements. This occurred in the insurance industry after it was included in the FLSL's coverage. Employers in this industry argued it was not practicable to comply with the FLSL. The irregularity in hours worked by their sales force made it impossible to determine overtime hours. In attempting to address this problem, several insurance companies changed the employment status of their sales people to subcontractors. Employers thus avoided paying pensions, overtime premiums, severance pay and complying with other measures demanded by the FLSL. The situation is similar in the banking and financial sectors. Paradoxically, the FLSL has led to the deterioration of employment conditions in these industries.

The Council of Labour Affairs is fully aware of these problems and has tried to address some of them via executive orders. Recently it issued an order to remove the ceiling on overtime work. At the urging of academics, management and unionists, the Council of Labour Affairs has recently taken steps towards allowing union and management more scope to handle their own problems.

The Council is also promoting the establishment of a privately operated but government subsidised labour arbitration system, to reduce the government's role in ER. Differences of opinion within the legislature and the Council over the focus of the Council's role mean that very little progress has been made to implement this system.

Increasing the importance of human resources management (HRM)

The concept of HRM became fashionable in Taiwan in the 1990s. This trend was a reflection of the internationalisation of Taiwan's economy, the shift from labour intensive industries to capital and technology intensive industries and the increasing regulation of ER. All of these factors indicated the need for more formal and systematic ways of handling personnel matters. The move towards a more mature economy also meant the work force had to be better educated and trained. A greater number of firms were developing training programs to provide opportunities for continued improvements to workers' skills and establishing HRM departments for handling FLSL regulations. Aside from these factors, the following developments also help to explain the growing prominence of HRM.

Due to the rapid expansion in the number of social welfare programs there has been a reduction in work incentives. Successful economic programs have raised Taiwan's 1997 annual per capita income to more than US$13 000 and led the IMF to classify Taiwan as a high-income country. As Taiwan's citizens become more affluent, however, their demands for social welfare provisions are increasing. The government implemented the comprehensive health insurance and the unemployment insurance provision under the

Table 6.6 Work experience of different age groups

Characteristics	Under 30	30–44	45–54	Over 55
	Age (yrs)			
Average length of service for the first job (years)	2.23	5.74	9.90	19.80
Number who found jobs via formal channels of labour market information (%)	56.35	49.74	40.20	30.06
Job content is similar to the first job and current job (%)	61.89	39.30	37.11	19.45
Number who voluntarily left their first job (%)	90.45	85.22	74.86	52.19
Number of times job changed	2.25	3.08	3.12	2.69
Experienced unemployment (%)	29.22	40.31	29.53	14.05
The longest period of unemployment (weeks)	21.31	26.76	30.11	33.60
Expected age of retirement (years)	57.29	59.08	68.87	65.70
Age on entry to the labour market (years)	19.50	18.15	17.18	16.11
First job held in:				
Agriculture (%)	2.60	6.67	18.78	43.00
Manufacturing (%)	42.77	53.48	42.93	20.64
Services (%)	54.63	39.85	38.29	36.36

Source: DGBAS (1998).

Labor Insurance Law. The new President, Mr Chen, announced that he would implement the national pension program, a 40-hour work week, and monthly subsidies of NT$5000, which are not income tested, to all elderly people. The impact of such social welfare programs has been to reduce people's incentive to work. This is especially true for the youngest and oldest workers. Labour force participation rates for workers in the 60–64 year age group, however, dropped more rapidly between 1978 and 1987 but were relatively stable between 1987 and 1998 (see Table 6.4). The rise of social welfare programs and the growing affluence of society are not the only reasons for the decline in labour force participation rates in these age groups. As discussed earlier, the reduction in participation rates is caused by rising demand for a better educated workforce and the desire of young people to remain in school.

The mobility and commitment of young people to their work is also changing. Young people are entering the labour market later and leaving the labour market earlier than their parents did. Table 6.6 indicates workers 55 years of age or over first entered the labour market at the age of 16, while workers aged 45 to 54 years entered

Table 6.7 Percentage of the work force in fear of losing current job

Age	Percentage
15–24 years	11.41
25–49 years	11.52
50–64 years	9.19
Over 65 years	7.92

Source:　DGBAS (1998).

at the age of 17. Workers aged 30 years or younger, on average, did not enter the labour market until they were around the age of 20.

Younger workers also are more mobile between jobs than their parents were. Their average tenure in their first job was 2.23 years, while for workers in the 30–44 years group, the figure was 5.74 years. Older people, 55 years and over, averaged nearly 20 years. The difference in the length of tenure for different age groups is partly attributable to the characteristics of their first job. Forty-three per cent of older workers, 55 years and over, found their first job in agriculture. Only 20.64% entered industry and 36.36% the service sector. When the next generation entered the labour market, Taiwan was an industrial economy. Fifty-three per cent of 30- to 44-year-old workers found their first job in manufacturing. Fifty-five per cent of workers in their twenties entered the labour market in the service sector (see Table 6.6). Young workers are more mobile because the jobs they hold, such as service jobs, are more mobile than those held by older workers. On the other hand, young workers feel less secure about their jobs than the older generation, a contributing factor which explains their lower commitment.

As Taiwan has developed economically, and become more affluent and more democratic, the trend is for young workers to delay entering the labour market and retire from it earlier than their parents. They also tend to move between jobs more frequently. For this reason, issues such as the maintenance of a stable work force, motivating workers, and the provision of training to maintain skill levels are of immediate concern to Taiwan's employers. Employers need to pay more attention to HRM practices which motivate their workers and also comply with the increasing number of employment regulations.

The development of high-tech industries in Taiwan also highlights the need for HRM, since people are the most important asset of these industries. Lee and his associates found that all firms in the Hsin Chiu Science Park had HRM departments and that they have introduced innovative techniques for recruiting competent workers, reducing the rate of staff turnover (Lee et al. 1998), and for developing remuneration (compensation) strategies. HRM specialists in these firms designed appropriate programs for training and upgrading the skills of employees, allowing them to remain competitive in the international market.

HRM techniques adopted by management

High-tech firms are not the only industries introducing innovative HRM techniques; employers in other industries are also recognising the benefits. Sophisticated pay schemes, grievance procedures, training programs and new techniques of recruiting and selecting employees have been widely adopted by employers. End of year bonus payments and stock options are popular. Findings from one study indicate 98% of surveyed firms had introduced an end of year bonus program (DLA 1996). Bonuses on average were between one and three months of an employee's base monthly wages (COL 1998b:2). Stock options, while not a common practice in Taiwan (offered by only 15% of firms), are popular among high-tech firms (DLA 1996:43; Lee et al. 1998).

Training is an important tool, allowing workers to maintain skill levels and a work force to remain competitive. A growing number of employers in Taiwan are providing their employees with on-the-job training but, as training is expensive, employers recognise the importance of training the most appropriate employees. For this reason the development of competence tests has become a priority. Some tests have been developed in co-operation with overseas HRM consulting firms, such as DDI from Pittsburgh. The China Steel Corporation is one of the pioneers in this area and has developed its own competence study centre.

Grievance procedures is another area receiving attention in Taiwan. The procedures used in Western industrialised countries, in union and non-union contexts, allow employers to communicate with employees to settle complaints. In the past, grievance procedures were rare in Taiwan (Lee 1980). In the late 1990s a growing number of firms established formal grievance procedures to handle the rise in the number of labour disputes, which increased from 1803 cases in 1992 to 2659 in 1996. The Council of Labour Affairs has identified grievance procedures as useful in reducing the number of employee complaints and for the maintenance of industrial peace. To this end it has established a program encouraging employers to introduce grievance procedures. A recent survey showed that 16% of firms in Taiwan had these procedures in place while 6% were in the process of establishing them (COL 1997). Although the use of Western-style grievance procedures is still far from usual in Taiwan, their usefulness and importance are being recognised as more firms adopt them. Colleges and universities are also paying more attention to HRM practices. In recent years several universities have offered graduate programs in HRM, including MA and PhD degrees. HRM and labour relations courses have also been added to many graduate and undergraduate programs in business administration.

Conclusions

Since the mid-1980s, Taiwan's economic and political structures have changed rapidly. In the economic arena Taiwan has moved away from labour-intensive industries towards capital and technology intensive industries. It is also moving away from an economy dominated by industry to one dominated by services. The per capita income for Taiwan has risen swiftly. Taiwan has undergone democratisation. These economic and political changes have had a significant impact on the demographics and values of the work force and on ER.

Taiwan's unions are more independent and influential under the impact of these changes, despite a decline in union membership. Moves towards creating a more democratic society led the government to adopt a more interventionist approach in ER. The government's motivation for changing its labour policy is to attract workers' votes and to demonstrate it is concerned about the welfare of workers. But recently it has recognised the problems of interventionist approaches and is gradually switching towards voluntary approaches by permitting and encouraging employers and unions to agree on employment conditions. The changing domestic environment and the increasing internationalisation of Taiwan's economy have made ER much more challenging and varied. To cope with this new environment, employers in Taiwan are paying more attention to HRM. In short, a new ER system which is more HRM oriented is being formed. It would appear that aspects of Taiwan's ER systems and practices are converging towards those practised in some Western countries, but the shape and form of Taiwan's future patterns of ER are yet to be determined.

7 Changing approaches to employment relations in the People's Republic of China (PRC)

Ying Zhu and Malcolm Warner

The year 1976 marked the end of an era in the PRC—Mao Zedong died and the Gang of Four fell from power. After ten years of 'Cultural Revolution', the PRC faced tremendous tensions, both politically and economically. By the end of the period, over 100 million people suffered shortages of food and clothing. The national economy needed to be revitalised and to achieve this employees needed to be motivated. Deng Xiaoping's approach was to change the parameters of economic behaviour and employment. The old command economy was to be phased out and one more attuned to market forces was to be gradually introduced. Deng's famous phrase 'it does not matter if the cat is black or white but whether it catches mice' became a guiding economic principle.

Following the implementation of economic reforms and the 'Open Door' policy in the late 1970s, many institutions of the employment relations (ER) system were gradually restored and fused with a new pattern of ER. The All-China Federation of Trade Unions (ACFTU), which had been in abeyance during the Cultural Revolution, was reactivated in 1978. In the PRC, the majority of enterprises were either state owned enterprises (SOEs) or collectively owned enterprises (COEs), and these were responsible for producing approximately 80% of industrial production. Under Deng's new economic policy, foreign funded enterprises (FFEs) and domestic private enterprises were encouraged. Diversity of ownership did not occur immediately, but by the end of the 1980s the system had diversified. The emergence of new interest groups and the diversity in enterprise ownership accentuated conflicts of interest and, in order to cope with these challenges, the employment relations system required modification. The fact is that many changes have occurred, especially in the areas of state policy and ER in relation to domestic private enterprises and FFEs, as greater flexibility in labour and capital markets has been introduced.

Table 7.1 Old and new systems of Chinese employment relations

Old	New
Maoism	Dengism
Command economy	Price mechanisms
Technical efficiency	Allocative efficiency
Relatively 'red'	Relatively 'expert'
Economic cadres	Professional managers
State owned firms	Diverse ownership
Jobs for life	Labour contracts
Work assignment	Job choice
Egalitarian rewards	Performance based wages
In-house welfare state	Contributory social insurance
Company housing	Market priced accommodation
Strong union	Weak worker representation

Source: Warner (1995).

There are opportunities for reforming the old ER system and the adoption of a new pattern of ER. The following sections describe the concept and practices involved in reforming the previous ER system, and explore the transition towards a more institutionalised focus for ER.

The pre-reform industrial relations system

In 1949 in the PRC, the main characteristics of the ER system centred on jobs for life in state owned enterprises (SOEs) under a Party-state command economy, egalitarian rewards and an in-house welfare system (*danwei*) (see Table 7.1). The 'lifetime' employment system, labelled the 'iron rice bowl', was a definitive element of the socialist system, and was adopted from the Soviet Union (see Kaple 1994; Warner 1995). It continued the tradition of the 'golden rice bowl' (*jin fanwan*), introduced by the Japanese in Manchuria (Warner 1995:17). Under this system job security could extend inter-generationally, as the children of retiring employees could inherit a job (Zhu 1995). In 1956, a nationally standardised wage system based on the Soviet model was introduced. The system consisted of eight grades, covering the majority of manual workers. Technical workers had fifteen grades and party cadres had 25 (Zhu & Campbell 1996). The gap between the grades was small in order to achieve 'egalitarianism' (*pingjun zhuyi*). Employment status, position and wages were defined as the 'three old irons': the iron rice bowl (*tie fanwan*), the iron chair or position (*tie jiaoyi*) and iron wages (*tie gongzi*) (Li 1992). In addition, work units could offer permanent employees a cradle to grave, enterprise based welfare system, which was more comprehensive than in the conventional Eastern European model (see Granick 1990; Kaple 1994). A large number of SOEs could be referred to as 'mini welfare states', as their functions extended well beyond production to include subsidised housing, leisure activities and facilities and social security benefits. In the PRC these firms have survived into the 1990s but are slowly undergoing transformation (see Ng & Warner 1998).

The management practices adopted after 1949 were institutionalised and ranged from collective leadership to one-man management (Leung 1988; Child 1994; Ng & Warner 1998). The model of management adopted was a hybrid of Soviet-style 'Taylorist' management practices and indigenous thought and was called the PRC's new 'industrial management mechanism' (Kaple 1994:58–9). In most enterprises, leadership comprised a 'dual system' of both Party and management control. In some cases the leader of the Party was also the general manager of the enterprise. At enterprise level the basic institutional structure comprised three committees—the Party committee, the Workers' Congress and the union. In the late 1990s it was not uncommon for a capable manager to be appointed Party secretary as a formality.

In the early period of transformation the concept of human resource management (HRM) was unknown. Each work unit comprised a personnel administrative department responsible for recruiting and allocating new workers, arranging training and promotion, and managing personnel files (Warner 1997a). Personnel files are important records for individuals. A file could also include records of an individual's behaviour and would be transferred with the individual should he or she change work units. The information recorded in the file could be an important measure in deciding to promote or punish a worker.

From 1949 the 'red' unions, formerly underground organisations under the nationalist regime, became official and the ACFTU, formed in 1925, was revitalised (Lee 1986:xi, f2). The traditional role of the ACFTU was as a 'transmission belt' between the Party and the 'masses'. Its role was enhanced until 1966, when it went into abeyance during the Cultural Revolution (Warner 1995). Unions were tightly integrated into party structures and indeed even into management structures, and the key union personnel owed their appointment to their links to these structures (Zhu & Campbell 1996). The main functions of unions were largely administrative rather than as representatives of workers. Their role included activities such as ideological work, mobilisation in support of Party campaigns, the promotion of enterprise economic goals, the supervision of the allocation of welfare benefits (such as housing) and some responsibility for training (Ng & Warner 1998). The union carried out the day-to-day tasks of the representation in the enterprise; these varied over the period from 1949. Most matters arising in Workers' Congress discussions related to production rather than welfare issues.

A socialist ER system with Chinese characteristics was gradually introduced from 1949 but in 1966, with the beginning of the Cultural Revolution, the functions of the ER system were fundamentally abolished. During the period of the Cultural Revolution, factories reduced the production of consumer goods and concentrated on the production of military weapons. Party leaders and managers were punished as 'counter-revolutionary' bourgeoisie. Even unions were banned. The PRC's production losses during this period amounted to more than RM500 billion (Zhu 1992). This was a huge amount, approximately US$60 billion at 2000 exchange rates.

In 1976, following Mao's death and the Gang of Four's removal from power, the PRC faced tremendous pressure, both politically and economically. The increase in population which had occurred during the Cultural Revolution, combined with a reduction in the production of consumables, resulted in shortages of food and clothing. In urban areas, wages had not risen for more than ten years. Mao's successor, Hua Guo-feng, introduced the Four Modernisations—of industry, agriculture, defence and science and technology—which became the new national goal until the year 2000. Political and ideological struggles continued among the party leadership, between the extreme left wing led by Hua and the reformists led by Deng Xiaoping. Hua insisted on the 'principle of two principles'—everything that Mao said was truth and everything that Mao did was right. Deng, however, believed that Mao had made a tremendous contribution to the new PRC but recognised he had made a great mistake in the Cultural Revolution. According to Deng, the ratio of Mao's mistakes to his contribution was 3:7. For the Party and the people, the principle was 'seeking truth from facts' (*shishi qiushi*) and 'liberation of thought' (*jiefang sixiang*). The outcome of the struggle was that Deng's ideology gained the support of the Party and the people. His economic reform initiative and Open Door policy were formally adopted at the Third Plenary Session of the Chinese Communist Party's (CCP) Eleventh Central Committee in December 1978 as the central Party policy (Korzec 1992).

Reforming the employment relations system

In the post-1978 period, the previous arguments about reforming ER had been replaced by arguments about new policies for the reform

Table 7.2 Unions in the PRC

	Number
Total ACFTU membership	104.00m
Male membership	59.00m
Female membership	41.00m
Minority membership	4.00m
Basic union committees	0.60m
Workshop union committees	0.94m
Small group cells	6.13m
Firms with Workers' Congresses	0.30m
Workers' representatives in Workers' Congresses	12.40m
ACFTU national unions	16
ACFTU provincial unions	30
ACFTU chairpersons	1
Vice-chairpersons	9
Secretariats	10
Praesidium members	25
ACFTU executive Committee members	241

Source: Ng and Warner (1998:44–7, 88). Data as in 1995–96.

of wages, employment, welfare and management (Warner 1986; Yamashita 1989; Granick 1990; Child 1994). These debates linked to the broader economic issues of factor-allocation, such as the allocation of labour and capital, and structural impediments to reform. In the 1980s, the reform initiatives were defined as the breaking of the 'three irons' and the 'establishment of three new systems'. The three new systems include the establishment of a labour contract system, a floating wage system and a manager engagement system (Yuan 1990). In the 1990s, the formation of the tripartite system was seen as the central task of reforming ER.

The formation of the tripartite system in the early 1990s occurred with assistance from the International Labour Organisation (ILO) in order to implement ILO standards (see Unger & Chan 1995:43). Eventually a new Labour Law was introduced, along with the principle and practice of collective negotiation and collective agreement (CNCA, a Chinese version of collective bargaining). The tripartite relationship comprises, at the national level, the Labour Ministry, the Chinese Enterprise Directors' Association (CEDA) representing employers and the ACFTU representing workers (see Table 7.2). At provincial, city and county levels, equivalent labour bureaux, enterprise directors' associations and unions form the regional and local tripartite system. They are engaged in designing legislation and regulations, negotiating the articles of the CNCA, and mediating disputes. Two important Chinese terms which reflect

tripartism as it operates in the PRC need to be clarified. These terms
are 'relations' (*guanxi*) and 'corporatism(ist)' (*shituan zhuyi*).
Guanxi is an important force in Chinese society (Warner 1997b)
and understanding this concept and practice is essential to an understanding of how tripartite relations have emerged in China's
contemporary ER. *Guanxi* is deep-rooted in Chinese society and has
shaped the hierarchical structures within society. In the current
political and economic structure, relations between the three parties
appear to be even more complicated as the government has different
relationships with publicly owned enterprises, domestically owned
private enterprises and foreign enterprises. For the State, public
ownership is still acknowledged as an unshakeable basic economic
principle underpinning the socialist market economy (Li 1998:13)
and so relations with publicly owned firms are stronger. In domestically owned private enterprises and FFEs the relationship with the
State is more distant.

Unions are controlled by the State and are an important channel
for 'guiding' the masses, but unions also require support from below
to enhance their own status as a representative organ. The relationship between the State and unions in the area of negotiations is
paternal. Unions, however, are becoming increasingly assertive in
requesting participation in the internal bargaining process for the
drafting of administrative directives and in the drafting of new
legislation relating to workers' interests (Unger & Chan 1995:41).
The ACFTU—the main Chinese trade union confederation—was
heavily involved in negotiations preceding the 1994 Labour Law.
The relationship between the unions and management at both the
national and enterprise level is mixed, as demonstrated by the
opposing views on legislation between the ACFTU and CEDA and
the intermediary role played by the Labour Ministry.

'Corporatism' (*shituan zhuyi*) was borrowed from the Soviet
Union and introduced after 1949 (see Chan 1993; Unger & Chan
1995). It was believed that corporatism would bring a harmony of
interests to prevail in a socialist state with corporatist sectoral
agencies such as the ACFTU serving as 'transmission belts' but with
limited autonomy. Following the reform and the relaxation of direct
Party-state controls, it was necessary to introduce additional mechanisms to fill the vacuum. Consequently, a large number of new
associations have been created to serve as corporatist intermediaries
and agents, such as CEDA. These new associations are becoming
more aware of their own organisational interests and are engaged
in more grassroots oriented strategies in order to obtain more space,
support and bargaining power. A transformation in the corporatist
framework from 'state corporatism' to 'societal corporatism' (*shihui
shituan zhuyi*) is akin to a complete transformation in Chinese

society. The following sections illustrate the gradual changes of ER under economic reform.

During the pre-reform period, the reward system was often geared to ensuring greater 'egalitarianism'. Deng's ideological position shifted policy to the restoration of the principle of 'distribution according to work' and to link individual performance, skills and position to income as a way of stimulating employee motivation. New wage systems were introduced, including a piece-wage system, a bonus system, a structural wage system, a 'floating wage system' (Li 1992) and a 'post plus skills wage system' (Warner 1997a). The new wages policy was designed to break the policy of 'iron wages'. This was an important step because the economic reform process required greater efficiency in factor-allocation, with labour flexibility as a priority. A nascent labour market was high on the reformers' agenda. At the time, labour mobility was low and dismissals for poor performance were rare. Jobs were allocated to school and university graduates by the local labour bureaus and job choice was almost non-existent.

Despite these practices, the mid-1980s found many young school-leavers unable to obtain the guaranteed employment opportunities their parents had enjoyed, often finding themselves among the ranks of the temporarily unemployed. The practice of 'inheriting' jobs was diminishing. Young people were often required to reside in rural areas for several years to receive education from peasants. When they returned to the cities many of them found that they could not secure work. Officially this situation was described as waiting to be employed (*daiye*) rather than unemployment (*shiye*) (Feng 1982). Mao had pronounced unemployment to be inadmissible because it could not be admitted that a socialist society suffered from unemployment and this notion continued. The limits of the definition of '*daiye*' were expanded to include workers laid off from factories during the late 1980s and 1990s (Geng 1992).

Unemployment or *shiye* refers to people who have not been employed for several years. An unemployment benefit is available for eligible unemployed (Lim et al. 1996; Chen 1997). Despite the insecurity, a growing number of unemployed are creating self-employment or small business opportunities (Zhu 1995). As opportunities in the protected state environment with 'jobs for life' decline, a growing number of young people are also taking this route. Added to this is the pressure and demand for jobs from the rapidly increasing volume of migrants from rural areas, estimated at 100 million.

The lifetime employment system, or 'iron rice bowl', still existed in SOEs and COEs in the early 1990s (Warner 1997a). As a result the familiar problems closely associated with this system—including overstaffing, a mismatch in skills and the stagnation of productivity—also continued (Zhu & Campbell 1996). The government initiated attempts to break the 'iron rice bowl' by implementing temporary regulations in 1986. These regulations dealt with such practices as early retirement, enterprise powers to dismiss employees, and the supplement and gradual replacement of permanent employment with a 'contract' system (White 1987; Han & Morishima 1992; Hu & Li 1993; Walder 1996; ILO 1996). It will take time for all these changes to reach fruition, but since 1992 reform of the employment system has accelerated (Bell et al. 1993; Sziraczki & Twiggy 1995; Lim et al. 1996).

In some regions all employees in all enterprises have been drafted into, at least in theory, a modified version of the contract system (Zhu & Campbell 1996). In 1993 the Shenzhen Special Economic Zone (SEZ) was completed and an 'All Employees Contract System' (AECS) was introduced, covering staff and workers in all enterprises (Zhu & Campbell 1996). Under this system there were both individual and collective contracts. The latter formed a type of framework agreement but did not quite resemble a Western-style collective bargaining contract (see Ng & Warner 1998). Most SOEs, joint ventures (JVs) and FFEs have implemented a system of individual contracts. Collective contracts are found in larger SOEs and a minority of larger JVs. Workers with ten or more years' service may enjoy an indefinite contract.

A major policy concern is non-wage benefits, including the social insurance system (see Leung 1988; Kaple 1994). This system represents a major financial burden for enterprises, a barrier to the introduction of performance-based pay and an impediment to labour mobility. A social insurance system was first implemented by the FFEs, with 25% of wages covering all kinds of insurance costs (Zhu & Campbell 1996). In SOEs and COEs, the introduction of the contract system has involved some alteration to the welfare system. The provisional regulations of 1986 stipulated that a separate labour insurance scheme be set up for contract workers in the state sector (Dong 1996). Since then, the policy on social insurance has been revised several times and it is proposed that institutional and industrial workers pay 1% of their monthly salary for medical insurance, and 3% for unemployment insurance. Work units are to add a further 20% as a retirement provision and 10% for medical care (Goodall & Warner 1997:581). More generally, but also more tentatively, the authorities have begun experiments selling public housing to individual employees and raising rents as a means of encouraging a housing market. In 1998, Zhu Rongji, who later became Premier, announced the extension of the housing reform to national level.

To improve the management system at enterprise level, economic reform policy has focused on decentralising economic decision-making powers to managers. In SOEs, previous ideological constraints were broken when the rights of ownership and management were separated (Li 1992; Lu & Perry 1997). The results are varied, but it appears managers have enjoyed an increase in power (Zhu & Campbell 1996). In addition, in order to break the 'iron position' the managers' engagement system was introduced. Different types of engagement have been practised at different enterprises according to their size, the sector and the relationship between firms and the authorities. In the early 1980s, two systems dominated: the manager's responsibility system and the leasing management or property management responsibility system (Zhu 1995:40; Li 1998:13–16). Large and medium-sized SOEs have implemented the entrusted management system, whereby managers sign a contract with the authority, agreeing to achieve a certain level of economic performance within a fixed period (normally between three and five years). Individual managers and workers can be rewarded with bonuses if they satisfy the contract's requirements each year. The term, the 'managers' responsibility' system, borrows from the 'farmer's responsibility' system of the rural reforms. Small SOEs have introduced the leasing management system whereby the firm is run according to a rental agreement, with the authority and individual managers paying the rental fee. The remaining profits go to the manager as individual income (Zhu 1995:40).

Economic reform policies are premised on reducing Party influence in the enterprise and the encouragement of a separation between politics and the management of an enterprise. Political networks have formed a readily accessible structure for informal bargaining and personal connections, which are generating problems ranging from unpredictability to corruption (Zhu & Campbell 1996:41). Management is still largely integrated into political networks (especially after June 1989) but has also increased its power in the enterprise, particularly at the expense of workers.

The conventional structure based on 'three old committees' has been replaced by 'three new committees'—the board of directors, the shareholders' committee and a monitoring committee. The monitoring committee involves supervision of management by investors externally and workers internally (Chen 1997). This step can be seen as part of a campaign by the authorities to promote so-called supervision and democratic management. In fact, the important forces for 'democratic management'—trade unions and Workers' Congresses—are still playing the roles of 'transmission belts' and 'rubber-stamps' (Goodall & Warner 1997:584). In recent years, a new term called 'scientific management' has been used widely (Huang 1996:49), but does not specifically refer to Taylorist practices. It emphasises several issues related to management reform including production, planning, quality, equipment, statistics and technology. Practitioners of scientific management have attempted to develop a framework to allow both the old 'three committees' and the new 'three committees' to function effectively (Huang 1996:50–1). The State retains a presence, but as the chaperone of the new tripartite system of relations. It is the apex of the triangle, with the employers and unions forming the base.

Human resources

With the reforms of the PRC's employment system in the mid-1980s came a new set of terminology describing HRM practices. Around this time several Western management schools, mainly from the US and the UK, set up joint teaching arrangements with Chinese universities to introduce Western management subjects (see Warner 1992). The translation of the term HRM into Chinese is *renli ziyuan guanli*, which literally means 'labour force resources management', but it is often understood as 'Personnel Management' or *renshi guanli* (Warner 1995; 1997a:38). Having said this, it still differs from the initial concept of HRM as understood in Western countries (see Poole 1997:281). The term HRM, and the practices associated with it, are commonplace in large joint venture companies. Even in these firms, management seems to be more introverted, focusing on firm-specific issues such as wages, welfare and promotion rather than on strategic concerns such as long-term development.

According to a recent survey (Benson & Zhu 1999), three models of HRM appear to exist in Chinese enterprises:

1. traditional industrial relations (IR) and personnel management;
2. more internationally oriented HRM; and
3. 'HRM with Chinese characteristics'.

The first model is a minimalist approach where enterprises have not attempted to adopt an HRM approach to the management of labour. They are either relatively large enterprises with a surplus labour problem or have much closer ties with the government in terms of contributing to local development. They have placed little emphasis on human resources and the traditional SOEs' management approach dominates their current operations. The pursuit of flexibility is essentially to reduce costs. Therefore, it is still based on the traditional IR/personnel management systems.

The second model represents an attempt to adopt the HRM paradigm. These enterprises have fewer constraints than the first group in their attempts to reform labour management. They tend to have little connection with the traditional SOE system (e.g. FFEs or newly established domestic private enterprises). These conditions have enabled them to adopt a more flexible HRM approach. They recognise that business survival and success in the market place relies on the quality of their human resources. Hence, these enterprises adopt a more internationally oriented HRM system, in other words, the model of Western/Japanese ER.

The third model is a transitional stage between the old and the new forms of labour management. These enterprises have the latest technology and they realise that quality is the key factor in determining their success. However, unlike the first group, they have little support from government. On the other hand, they are different from the small SOEs which are more easily able to adopt a flexible approach. They are facing substantial competition from both domestic and foreign firms. The lack of capital and the burden of surplus labour inhibits their ability to transform their ER practices. For these firms, substantial managerial reforms, including those of human resources, are crucial for their future success.

At the time of writing, there is not a homogeneous model of ER in Chinese enterprises. Individual enterprises are reforming their ER systems differently on the basis of their existing conditions and the impact of economic reform.

The debate about the 'third way of gradualism'

The 'third way of gradualism' is a phrase that has often been used as 'code' for explaining contemporary Chinese economic relations. On the one hand it differentiates Chinese practices from the old Stalinist central planning system, without on the other hand conceding a tendency towards ultimate convergence with Western/Asian capitalism and globalisation—hence, the description of the reforms in general as 'market socialism' but 'with Chinese characteristics'. The PRC has not had experience or a blueprint for a so-called socialist market economy. The philosophy of 'crossing the river by feeling the stones' reflects the pragmatism which distinguishes it from counterparts in the former Soviet Union and Eastern Europe.

The PRC is beginning to see the emergence of a more market-oriented, although not necessarily adversarial, tripartism, which differs from that developed in some Western countries. There are two peak corporatist confederations, the ACFTU and CEDA, which not only have a responsibility to represent their members' interests, but also have an obligation towards the State to maintain political 'harmony'. This practice defines the 'Chinese characteristics' associated with corporatism in the PRC.

Conclusions

The theme of this chapter has been to examine the emergence of the Chinese ER system, including IR and HRM, from pre-reform to the present. Since 1978, the command economy has become more market oriented, and it is within this context that we have analysed how ER and related practices have been adopted from Western practices (see Table 7.1). The impact of Deng's reforms has been that ER practices have developed into a nascent tripartite system.

Frequently the term 'with Chinese characteristics' is used with the expression 'market socialism' and this, we would argue, is fully consistent with the cross-cultural 'absorption' of exogenous forms and practices with indigenous ones. Concepts, terminology and practices have been taken over and adopted into the Chinese cultural context but in the process have been changed. In particular ER concepts have evolved that have characteristics distinct from their Western equivalents. It is clear that the specific national and cultural space in which ER take root shapes the idiosyncratic forms eventually found in the Chinese exemplifications of these concepts, terminology and practices. As such these concepts cannot be fully comprehended without an understanding of the complex institutional framework that has emerged in Chinese industry since the introduction of the economic reforms and how that framework has been implemented. Outside observers need to understand local cultural norms and values as exemplified in their economic and industrial contexts in order to understand the ongoing developments in the workplace. The gradualist transition in the PRC also requires the replacement of traditional methods of social control by developing a 'civil society' progressively with a multi-channel framework for negotiations between the State and the people. This is crucial for determining the outcome of further reform in the PRC (see Warner 1999; Warner 2000).

8 Changing approaches to employment relations in Indonesia

Sutanto Suwarno and Jan Elliott

During the period of colonial rule in Indonesia, it was the emergence of the nationalist movement which seemed to induce a growth of unions and the rise of worker militancy in the 1910s and 1920s (Ingleson 1986). Thus the character of the trade union movement was strongly influenced by internal political developments. Workers joined unions in the expectation that they could alleviate their working conditions and/or improve welfare services. Continuing industrial unrest in the first quarter of the 20th century culminated in 1926 with the repression of the union movement as a whole and the exile of many of its leaders. When the Japanese Army occupied Indonesia (1942–45) the labour movement was suppressed (Soepomo 1974) and workers were subjected to great economic hardships.

When Indonesia proclaimed independence in 1945, unions were assumed to have an important role in economic, governmental and political activity. During the revolution fought against the returning Dutch (1945–49), the prime union activity was once more the struggle for national recognition. Unions looked on themselves as an arm of the revolution and often played a paramilitary role. After the revolution there was a dramatic increase in union activity in the early years of the 1950s. By 1957 there were at least twelve labour federations, most with political affiliation. In addition, there were regional and local groupings and a large number of unaffiliated independent unions. The most influential, and the largest, strongest and most carefully organised federation was the communist party affiliated SOBSI (Sentral Organisasi Buruh Seluruh Indonesia—All Indonesian Central Organisation of Trade Unions) (Richardson 1958). Political party affiliation continued to characterise the labour movement in the 1950s and into the 1960s.

The development of employment relations (ER) and a union movement in Indonesia before and after independence, until the

129

advent of the Suharto government in the mid-1960s, was mainly one of action taken on an ad hoc basis. Such action was usually in the context of specific issues rather than more general collective bargaining. Unionism could be characterised as paternalistic. Constant political tension and upheaval meant that it was difficult to create a better standard of living for workers.

This chapter examines contemporary ER practices in Indonesia. The administrative structures of Indonesia have been moving towards decentralisation, especially in development planning which emphasises regional differences. However, many of the practices of the current government are still centralised. The Ministry of Manpower (Depnaker) is responsible for employment protection, labour placement, training and productivity improvement. In the area of ER, the Ministry is responsible for deciding the level of the minimum wage, based on the governors' recommendations. The mechanism is taken through a tripartite body, both at the provincial and district levels. Thus in the context of ER, the central government decides the policy that applies to its 27 provinces.

The first section examines the concept of Pancasila, which underlies the present ER system. The second section discusses the development of unionism and ER under the Suharto government, and examines the current national situation of Indonesia's unions. It is argued that to some extent the current system does not fit with the practice of ER as envisaged under the Pancasila industrial relations (PIR) concept.

The concept of Pancasila industrial relations (PIR)

Apart from the work of the present authors, there has been little research to analyse PIR. There was, however, a partial study based on secondary data conducted by Manning (1993), and preliminary studies by Thamrin (1995), Tjandraningsih (1995) and Hadiz (1997a), which examined the impact of strikes in the Jabotabek area and ER under the Suharto government.

In 1974 the Suharto government, with the financial and technical support of the Friedrich Ebert Stiftung, a German Foundation concerned with labour issues, held a national seminar attended by university staff and workers' and employers' organisations in order to initiate an ER system. This seminar discussed ER in the context of achieving socioeconomic development. As a result, a system was designed based on sociocultural and traditional values—the PIR system. The 1974 seminar produced the following recommendations: to develop an approach to ER appropriate for local conditions and national economic development; to formulate the principles of the system; and to conduct activities in promoting such a system to the wider community by holding seminars, workshops and public discussions to elaborate upon the primary concepts of the system. At the time it was argued that ER was a sub-system of the existing social and economic development process of the community (Prawironoto 1974). ER was but one of the numerous sub-divisions of the economic and social system dealing with social relationships within the workplace.

The PIR system emphasises partnership between workers, management and the government. The government has argued that the spirit and values of Pancasila, the state ideology, should be applied in the workplace as in other aspects of life. The justification is that continuing national development requires a stable yet dynamic situation for sustainable economic growth. This in turn requires a level of national stability which to some extent depends on industrial sector activities. In this regard, industrial peace is a major contribution towards stability in the production process. Such peace can only be achieved by workplace ER which ensures harmonious and dynamic ways of life (Ministry of Manpower 1985).

In 1981, a national workshop on the implementation of PIR recommended that at least eight laws and six ordinances were no longer compatible with the ER system and therefore needed to be reformulated. PIR does not recognise industrial disputes. Hence, when friction occurs because of differences of opinion and interpretations, a mechanism has been devised to settle such grievances. If a case continues after it has been through the mediation process, a final decision may be sought from the Minister of Manpower.

PIR recognises workers' and employers' organisations and sets out their responsibilities. There should be an equilibrium between the rights and obligations of both parties, and this equilibrium should not be achieved through a balance of power, but through social justice and fairness. Within the framework, unions play an important role in shaping ER processes. Industrial conflicts have been mainly due to the dissatisfaction of workers on specific issues—such as wages, welfare facilities and the setting up of a union—while employers have complained of low productivity. Employers argue that they are not against an improvement in workers' income and other welfare services, but that this has to be in line with productivity.

The primary objective of PIR is to ensure an ideal society. This objective can be achieved only through peace and stability, discipline, a dedicated work force, increasing productivity, and a commitment to improve workers' welfare and human dignity. There is no legal obligation on the part of workers and employers to comply with the commitment, but the government encourages its implementation.

Employment relations under the Suharto government

In 1973 the government amalgamated unions into a single labour federation called the FBSI (Federasi Buruh Seluruh Indonesia—All-Indonesia Labour Federation). The FBSI was made up of SBLPs (Serikat Buruh Lapangan Pekerjaan) which had an analogous structure to the FBSI. Sectoral *basis*, or enterprise level units, were in turn affiliated to the SBLPs. Later the basis became known as PUKs (Perwakilan Unit Kerja) (Hadiz 1997b:94). In early 1974 there were 21 SBLPs registered, but only half were active. Among the active SBLPs were the Textile and Garment Union, Rubber and Leather Union, Transportation Union, and the Oil, Gas and Mining Union; these industrial sectors involved more than half the workforce at that time. The programs of the FBSI included the education of workers, the promotion of income generating projects and the promotion of collective agreements to achieve better standards of living.

At the Second FBSI Congress in 1985, the Minister of Manpower, Admiral Sudomo, intervened and restructured the FBSI into a unitary union called the SPSI (Serikat Pekerja Seluruh Indonesia—All-Indonesia Workers' Union). This effectively eliminated the existing unions (SBLPs) and changed them into nine departmental units, such as: the department of agriculture and plantations; the department of textile and garments; and the department of trade, banking and insurance services. The objectives of the SPSI were to unify and foster a sense of collective purpose among workers, to protect and maintain workers' interests and rights, and to improve social welfare and working conditions (Shamad 1995:86–90). The intervention went further when in 1986 the Minister of Manpower issued a regulation restricting the ability of workers' organisations to obtain legal recognition from the government unless they were affiliated to a national union, which in turn had to be present in at least twenty provinces and have a membership of at least fifteen plant level unions in each province. In 1995 the SPSI changed its name to *Federasi* SPSI (FSPSI) to better denote its federation status. Table 8.1 indicates the number of enterprise level units (PUKs) affiliated to the FSPSI and its total membership.

According to Sudono—FBSI president from 1973 to 1985—the SPSI period meant a setback of ten years. Because the size of the labour force entering the industrial sector doubled during this period, more positive action should have been undertaken to reformulate the role of SPSI.

Table 8.1 **Plant level units (PUK) affiliated to FSPSI and total membership**

Year	PUK	Membership
1992	9 436	1 067 914
1993	10 014	1 291 672
1994	10 559	1 482 676
1995	12 739	2 113 640
1996	12 747	2 136 739

Source: Ministry of Manpower (1997a).

In 1992 an independent trade union, the SBSI (Serikat Buruh Sejahtera Indonesia—the Indonesian Prosperous Workers' Union) was founded as a rival to the existing SPSI, and to challenge the government to provide wider opportunities for workers to organise by their own choice. However, the effect of the 1986 regulation meant that the SBSI failed to obtain official recognition from the government as, rather than being a federation, it appeared to be a single national union without affiliates at national, provincial and district levels. The 1986 regulation also excluded SBM (Serikat Buruh Merdeka), an independent union committed to human rights issues. Neither group could prove membership at the workplace level, although SBSI claimed to have at least 500 000 members. In 1993, the government recognised these organisations as being mass organisations, but having nothing to do with trade unionism.

The refusal to recognise unions which were not affiliated to SPSI continued until 1994, when the then Minister of Manpower issued a regulation to set up unions at the enterprise level. These unions—Serikat Pekerja Tingkat Perusahaan (SPTP)—were not necessarily affiliated to SPSI but no more than one could be set up in each plant. According to available data, currently there are approximately 1200 SPTPs.

During interviews with labour activists at an SBSI branch office in Tangerang, activists stated that although police and military repression no longer took place, they were still under surveillance. In discussions with Dr Muchtar Pakpahan (the leader of the SBSI) and other SBSI activists it became clear that the aim was not merely to change the structure of unions, rather the prime objective of the SBSI was to totally reform the national political setting. Observation of SBSI activities showed that although the organisation appeared in many ways to be relatively powerless, in some instances SBSI activists were able to assist workers. In one case, for example, eight workers had been laid off because they did not work on New Year's Day. At first they tried to obtain assistance from the local Ministry of Manpower, but direct assistance was not forthcoming. SBSI activists met with the workers in front of the Ministry office and offered their help in negotiating a resolution to the problem. After several meetings between SBSI activists and the personnel manager, an agreement was reached which led to the eight workers being reinstated. (As the personnel manager appeared concerned by the presence of our research team, the success of this negotiation may be partly attributable to our presence.)

In an interview with *Mantra Magazine* in 1995, Dr Pakpahan said that the SBSI aimed to create an independent and strong union, self-financed and controlled by its members rather than by the government. During interviews with SBSI participants at the 1997 International Labour Organisation (ILO) Conference in Geneva, activists stated that they wanted to open dialogue with the national and local authorities and those concerned with labour matters to clarify the objectives of the organisation. They also said that given that the SBSI had achieved international recognition from many union movements around the world, it should also be supported by national leaders. International trade unionists questioned the FSPSI's lack of affiliation to any single international trade union movement (Silaban 1997; Simanungkalit 1997).

Public sector employment in Indonesia is separated from that of the private sector. There are no unions in the public sector, which employs over five million workers. In 1972, the government set up the Indonesian Civil Servants' Corps (KORPRI). Members are *pegawai negeri* (civil servants), and include those working in state owned enterprises (e.g. plantation, forestry, banking, transportation and communication workers). Law No. 8 (1974), concerning the basic provisions for public sector employees, guarantees the terms and conditions of employment in this sector. There is, however, no freedom for employees in this sector to form their own union. Whether government employees like it or not, they are directed to accept KORPRI as their organisation for dealing with grievances. Other professional organisations exist—for instance, the PGRI (Teachers' Association) is responsible for the well-being of teachers—but the KORPRI director, responsible for ER, assists in solving employment problems in the public sector. A mechanism for dispute settlement is not available, and often employees are left feeling frustrated as no attempt has been made to provide ER machinery in the public sector. The government has been content to rely on the capacity of personnel directors to handle day-to-day activities.

As part of its reform program on laws and regulations, the government submitted the manpower Bill to parliament in early 1997. This included a draft on the PIR system to be regulated by law—a recommendation which had come from a workshop held sixteen years earlier in December 1981. Based on the new manpower

Bill, laws which are not compatible with the PIR system are to be reformed. A provision on labour protection, including the right to organise, was also drafted. However, there is no differentiation between laws on industrial tribunals, labour protection, ER, unions and manpower planning, as all the laws have been reformed into a single draft.

The draft was rejected by a chairman of FSPSI, W. Bhoka (despite the fact that he was a member of the tripartite body involved in its formulation) as well as by the leaders of eleven non-governmental organisations (NGOs) dealing with labour matters. Bhoka argued that the tripartite meeting had only drafted 57 out of the 159 articles. He wondered where the other 102 articles had come from (*Republika* 1997; *Media Indonesia* 1997). The NGOs, led by Teten Masduki, Director of the Indonesian Legal Aid Institute (Yayasan Lembaga Bantuan Hukum Indonesia, YLBHI) urged the government to take into consideration international labour standards as stipulated in the International Labour Organisation (ILO) conventions and recommendations. The Bill was said to protect highly skilled labour, support low labour costs, ignore workers' rights (especially the right to conduct a strike outside the workplace), and to ignore international labour standards; these were reasons for its rejection. There was also opposition to the Bill from the international trade union movement. A spokesman for the six international trade union groups which visited Jakarta in August 1997 to take part in a conference on union rights in Indonesia—which was sponsored by the International Confederation of Free Trade Unions (ICFTU) and YLBHI—maintained that the manpower Bill had not sufficiently adopted the basic principles of labour protection. He urged the government and members of parliament to correct the Bill so as to meet basic minimum standards as required by international labour conventions (*Kompas* 1997).

Parliament discussed the controversial manpower Bill from June to September 1997. The Bill was enacted as Employment Law No. 25 of 1997, and replaced earlier laws and ordinances. As a result of the intensive discussion which surrounded the presentation of the Bill, 70% of its substance was changed to accommodate public opinion. Rangkuti, the Chairman of Commission VI of the Parliament, announced that the law was to be valid from October 1998. A subsequent revision delayed the date of enactment of Law No. 25 until October 2000 (Ford forthcoming). Rangkuti further requested that the government draft laws on unions and dispute settlement procedures as recommended by the new law (*Kompas* 1997).

Critics of the current legislation argue that it will intensify rather than settle labour unrest, as the government still seems intent on curbing the capacity of workers to organise in the hope that this will, in turn, curb unrest and create industrial harmony (Hadiz 1997a). There are also complaints from business leaders that the government's policy of periodically raising the minimum wage is unsound, given the huge burden that businesses have to bear in the form of bureaucratic levies. These levies, many of which are illegal and therefore comprise what is popularly known as 'invisible costs', comprise up to 30% of a manufacturing firm's total production cost (Hadiz 1997a). Schwarz (1997) points out that corruption, bribery and collusion have become a way of life in Indonesia, which automatically affects the minimum wage level. Further, there are no regulations that cover those workers already earning in excess of the minimum wage level. This becomes a burden, because workers who are paid above the minimum wage level also seek opportunities to increase their wages. In some workplaces, although negotiations on wage increases to reach the UMR (minimum regional wage) had led to an agreement, workers with over three years' experience have gone on strike demanding an increment equal to that received by those being brought up to UMR level.

Deyo (1989) has pointed out that in other countries of the region it is employees in labour intensive industries, the so-called hyper-proletariat, who are most exploited. They are least able and hence least likely to resist exploitation. This is partly attributed to the relatively weak bargaining power of workers in these predominantly non-unionised industries; many of the workers are migrants, and female, and have little attachment to urban work and residence. In Indonesia, however, the characteristics of workers in these relatively low wage industries are not consistent with this exploited labour picture. The national labour force statistics (Sakernas) for 1990 show that first, the low wage industries in these locations did not employ a significantly higher proportion of females. Second, because of the rapid expansion of education in Indonesia in the 1980s, younger workers were better educated than those elsewhere and hence were more likely to be aware of their rights. Both these factors have probably contributed to increased industrial unrest in low wage industries.

An examination of annual wage rates reveals that the level in all 26 provinces increased by an average of 20% in 1995, more than compensating for inflation which was less than 10%. This is, how-ever, only an improvement for workers who receive the minimum subsistence wage, which is no more than a third of the total labour force in the manufacturing sector. This justifies the claim of Bokha (1995) that the welfare of workers had not improved at the same pace as the nation's rising prosperity. Many analysts attribute this to the country's weak and mostly ineffective trade union movement (Sijabat 1995).

In 1997, the ILO Committee of Experts on the application of ILO standards noted with concern the allegations of anti-union measures submitted to the Committee on Freedom of Association. Discussion of these issues involving Indonesia have taken place in 1979, 1991, 1993, 1994, 1995, 1997 and 1998. The ILO Committee of Experts on the application of ILO standards and the Committee on Freedom of Association used forceful language to express their concern over the persistent and continuing violation of union rights in Indonesia. They were concerned with the seriousness of allegations regarding the murder, disappearance, arrest and detention of union leaders and workers. Etty, a worker delegate from the Netherlands, was critical of the Suharto government's denial over the years that there were any problems with the relevant legislation, and its rejection of new legislation on the grounds that it was not necessary as the law afforded good protection against anti-union discrimination. Etty noted that additional information supplied by experts, workers and employers was ignored. Although it was no longer compulsory for workers to obtain permission from their employer to set up a union, the Committee of Experts and the conference committee considered that the revised Indonesian legislation still did not provide adequate protection against acts of interference by the employer (ILO 1997). Nonetheless the government refused to take any further action.

The Committee of Experts reported that, despite the acceptance by the government of a direct contact mission in November 1993, and a subsequent technical assistance mission, the few changes made by the government did not go beyond mere cosmetics. It was alleged that the government, through the police, the army and unidentified employers' groups, regularly put pressure on workers who wanted to form unions. If they did not comply, dismissal followed. On several occasions local union offices were ransacked and files taken or destroyed (ILO 1997). The arrest and imprisonment of Dr Muchtar Pakpahan (in 1994 and again in 1997) was a result of such systematic anti-union policies. None of the FSPSI officers were affected by such actions. Only SBSI activists at the plant level were targeted. The allegations being made by these ILO committees were with respect to the application of articles 1, 2 and 3 of Convention No. 98 on the right to organise and bargain collectively for workers, which Indonesia ratified in 1957 but which have been more or less ignored in terms of implementation.

It was hoped that the FSPSI Congress in 1995 would help to improve workers' standard of living. In his address to the Congress, President Suharto emphasised the importance of empowering workers, and improving their skills and productivity to compete within the global economy. The Congress recommended that the union formally revert to its old format as a federation of unions while its leadership pledged to strengthen the workers' position *vis à vis* management. These high ideals were proposed despite the record of the ineffectiveness of the FSPSI in representing workers' interests. Available data reveals that out of 10 000 disputes between 1990 and 1995, only 2% were mediated by the unions affiliated to the FSPSI. With the absence of the FSPSI at the plant level, the government encouraged the development of an enterprise-based union (SPTP)—which need not necessarily be affiliated to the FSPSI, but with the power to negotiate collective agreements with management. There should be only a single union in each plant, which was in conflict with the ILO Convention. But these unions tended to be more democratic and independent in the sense that less intervention was made by the government. The relevant regulation was actually an adoption of the Serikat Buruh Lapangan Pekerjaan concept introduced in the early 1970s. Nevertheless, the presence of police and military personnel at union meetings and other activities was so widespread that it was considered to be a fact of union life. Although the government maintained that workers were free to set up their own unions, as in the case of the SPTP, if such unions expressed their intention to join the SBSI their existence was immediately forbidden (Etty 1997).

Moreover, based on the official state doctrine of the dual function of the army, whereby the army maintains an active role in the economic activities of the State, retired military personnel continued to take positions in the government backed union central organisation, the FSPSI, and its sectoral unions. After denying this practice for many years, the government has recently argued that retired army personnel had the right to take employment, become members of a union and be elected to union office. The real situation was, however, that these army pensioners were selected for these functions by a special army department in view of the government's preoccupation with security (Etty 1997).

A year after he retired as former FSPSI general chairman, Imam Sudarwo, argued that the government's one union policy should be reconsidered, allowing workers the freedom to establish their own unions. He also stated that the government had been half-hearted in dealing with companies which violated labour laws. However, while Sudarwo was still in charge, no effort was made to encourage the development of more independent unions. It would appear that officials are less prepared to criticise while still in power.

The PIR concept in practice

Although in practice strikes and/or demonstrations occur, there is no place for such conflict in PIR. To overcome this shortcoming, the government, together with other tripartite constituents, needs to provide adequate measures to protect any party which is in a weak position. The deficiencies of PIR have been criticised, as has the government's inaction in response to repeated requests by the ILO to strengthen its legislation against anti-union discrimination (Etty 1990:8). Instead, the government by way of a general denial of allegations of anti-union discrimination has referred to the PIR system. Some researchers have deemed such a bland defence as unacceptable (see Etty 1990). Manning (1993) maintains that the Indonesian ER system framework is a convenient way of giving a national tag to the regional and international trend towards tripartite and bipartite systems and the emphasis on employer and union co-operation. It is possible that ER can be developed through tripartism (Marshall 1992, cited in Manning 1993), but such co-operation can only come from positions of relatively equal strength. Given a weak and heavily government-controlled union movement, genuine tripartite co-operation is unlikely to occur.

Before the 1997–98 'Asian economic crisis', the Indonesian economy grew steadily (over 7% in 1995). Still, for many workers their direct prosperity hardly improved. Although there were less labour protests in 1995 than in the previous three years, workers were no longer protesting at the lack of normative rights such as minimum wages, but were seeking instead to strengthen the quality of co-operatives and other bastions of welfare services (Sijabat 1995). During the 1990s there was an increasing number of strikes. Some were for seemingly minor reasons, including dissatisfaction with union leaders; however, the majority—81%—were concerned with wages and welfare issues.

With the restriction of the union movement to a single federation, which has not been able to cope with the increasing number of protests and unrest, the industrial harmony envisaged by PIR seems impracticable in the current context. Despite the condemnation of international unions and the intervention by European governments and the NGOs, there has been no response by the authorities. In the future action must be taken to provide the opportunity for dialogue between all the parties involved in the labour process, at the national and regional levels, as well as at the workplace level.

The ILO Committee on Standards Application expressed a negative attitude towards PIR. The information and statistics supplied by the government showing increasing numbers of collective agreements and unions at plant level did not demonstrate either the real nature of the union movement or the success of collective bargaining. The Committee argued it was necessary to take into account the content of these agreements to verify that they actually covered improvements in working conditions and wages. Esguerra, a worker representative from Colombia, stated that in spite of the declarations of goodwill made by government representatives, the workers were very concerned at the persistence of anti-union policies in Indonesia. He emphasised that restrictions on the right of freedom of association and collective bargaining were unacceptable and questioned the positive view of PIR described by government representatives (ILO 1997).

According to Etty, given that the role of the government is too centralised and there is a general lack of opportunity for workers to organise into a union of their own choice, Indonesian PIR is impracticable. He argues that the SPTP could have become a reality only if the government had not interfered during the initial stage of development. The goal of freedom of association in Indonesia and reform of the unions could occur only through a partnership effort between the government and the unions. But it will not be possible without the full support of the government. When asked if local institutions, such as Paguyuban (association) gatherings could support such a development, Etty maintained that the union movement is a global movement advancing free collective agreement for the benefit of workers. Hence in his opinion, given that it is not able to negotiate collective agreements, Paguyuban could not support the ER in Indonesia. Nevertheless, he agreed that such a gathering should be encouraged to suit the local conditions (Etty 1997).

Conclusions

The Indonesian Reformation Government (May 1998 to October 1999), led by President Habibe, took moderate steps towards eliminating some ER problems. For instance, on 5 June 1998 the government ratified the key ILO conventions on Freedom of Association and protection of the Right to Organise. This was a positive step towards a fair platform for ER which would be more acceptable internationally. New laws on unions and for an Industrial Relations Tribunal were drafted (for details of the draft laws see Ford forthcoming) and through the abolition of the one union policy the new government provided wider opportunities for unionists to establish free and independent organisations. The ratification and subsequent implementation of Convention No. 87 resulted in a significant increase in union activity.

SBSI was legally accepted as a union and became an affiliate of the ICFTU. At the 1998 International Labour Organisation Conference in Geneva, attended by delegates from the employers' association, APINDO, and the Ministry of Manpower, the SBSI was the sole representative Indonesian workers' organisation. However, at several informal meetings held with international trade unionists during the conference, the Minister of Manpower, Fahmi Idras, confirmed that the government would tolerate international union activities only if they supported the development of the ER system, and if they were not merely directed to the individual unionist. Nonetheless, Dr Pakpahan was given the chance to speak at the plenary session, to deliver a public speech and to communicate with international trade unionists. There was significant intervention on the part of the international trade union movement led by the ICFTU, and the SBSI gained international support from such organisations as the International Metal Workers' Federation (IMF), Canadian Auto Workers (CAW) and the Australian Council of Trade Unions (ACTU). The leaders of these organisations had visited Indonesia in 1997 to investigate how far freedom of association and the right of workers to organise were guaranteed. Such direct involvement of foreign based unions/federations was indicative of widespread international concern about ER in Indonesia.

Although the PIR principles are not endorsed by the international union movement, local factors and local conditions should be considered before making a definitive judgment. An ER system based on Pancasila principles seeks to avoid class struggle as workers are seen as partners in the production process. While there is scope for additional national dialogue to facilitate improvements in ER, such discussions should encourage the input of Asian-based workers' organisations, and not be determined by influential Western oriented sociopolitical concepts proposed by specific Western pressure groups pursuing workers' rights. There is an indication that the development of SPTPs is leading to a lessening of outside interference, as they tend to be more independent compared to the FSPSI. To maximise their impact among workers, the development of SPTPs should be integrated into the informal traditional organisations.

PART III

Perspectives on unions

9 Challenges facing unions in South Korea

Changwon Lee

With the popularity of high-performance models of work organisation, the traditional power of collective action by unions has been
weakened in most industrialised market economies (Appelbaum &
Batt 1994; Kochan & Osterman 1994; Locke, Kochan & Piore 1995).
The emphasis on high-performance and efficient companies draws
attention to the participatory role of unions. Collective bargaining
at the industry level has been decentralised in many countries
reflecting national employment relations (ER) policies and corporate
governance structures.

The case of South Korea presents a contrast because unions
appear to have grown in strength. In terms of power in collective
bargaining, unions to an extent gained the upper hand over management. They have begun to ask for a full range of labour rights such
as shortened working hours and greater job security. In addition,
unions have achieved increases in wage levels to the point where
the national strategy of labour-intensive industrialisation has been
jeopardised.

Nevertheless, there has been a debate about trends of union
development. After the short-term rapid expansion in unionism in
South Korea from 1987, union membership and industrial disputes
decreased in the 1990s. Although the influence of the union movement after 1987 has had a significant impact on ER, unionism in
Korea has suffered due to the recent paradigmatic shift which has
occurred in ER. If we review the reforms in ER in South Korea,
and the challenges arising from the post-1997 financial crisis, it is
arguable that there has been a retreat by unions. Their primary
strategy has been to survive the reforms initiated by management
and government.

An alternative view is that there has been a transformation of the
union movement (Park 1996; Kim 1995). According to this view,
the union movement in South Korea is strengthening itself to prepare

for a 'second leap'. The establishment and institutionalisation of a second national union centre, the Minjunochong—Korean Confederation of Trade Unions (KCTU) has heralded an era of multiple unionism. Such developments are seen as evidence that South Korea's union movement is undergoing a resurgence. It is further argued that the 1996 general strike, which succeeded in changing revisions to the labour related laws, is the most important signal indicating increasing power of the unions. Considering that the gains made by South Korea's union movement have occurred through struggle, the alternative view suggests it is premature to predict that the union movement will decline in South Korea.

In this chapter I argue that the union movement has declined as a result of the changing nature of labour markets—in particular, the globalisation of labour. In identifying the features characterising the transformation of the unions, I focus on the interplay between labour, management and the government which has occurred in the face of recent economic changes. I examine why the union movement has been able to maintain its institutional power despite the challenges.

The union movement in South Korea

The union movement in South Korea had largely been inactive before 1987, due mainly to the government's repressive labour policies which emphasised a developmental, state sponsored, export oriented and labour-intensive model of industrialisation (Deyo 1989; Johnson 1987; Choi 1988). The government directly controlled the process of unionisation, wage increases and other major labour issues. Collective action by unions was minimised by the government and management. Major industrial growth in South Korea had been achieved through the expansion of the work force rather than by a growth in labour productivity (OECD 1994). As a result management had not taken collective bargaining seriously as a means of enhancing worker performance. Management also regarded the government's intervention in micro-level ER as necessary to maintain a quiescent work force (Amsden 1989:324–5).

Prior to 1987, the Federation of Korean Trade Unions (FKTU) had been the single national representative of the repressed union movement. Established in 1960, it acted as a united body for unions. In 1961 it was reorganised as a national centre for industry based unions. During the military regime of Park Jung Hee, the government decided unions in South Korea were to be organised on an industry basis. Before 1980, the FKTU comprised seventeen industry based unions. The repressive policies of the government and the docility of the FKTU contributed to the pre-1987 period being characterised by gradual increases in union membership and few industrial disputes.

The political upheaval of 1979, sparked by the assassination of Park Jung Hee, provided the unions with a short-term opportunity to expand membership. In particular, unionism emerged in previously non-union sectors. The subsequent military regime, led by Chun Doo Whan, moved once again to repress the unions. In 1980, at the beginning of Chun's regime, union membership had declined by 12.6% compared to that in 1979. Union membership fared no better in subsequent years, and continued to decline with the renewal of repressive government control (Park & Park 1989). The decline in the number of disputes during this period—407 cases in 1980, 186 in 1981 and 88 in 1982 indicate the extent of the repression.

The short-term increase in the number of unions around 1980 brought about two important changes which affected the development of the union movement. The first was that the illegal and informal but independent unions began to organise at the enterprise level. This paved the way for the rise of alternative unions at the national level (Kang 1996). The second related change was the transformation from unions organising on an industry basis to enterprise-based unions. This transformation took place in 1980 under the orders and guidance of the Chun military regime with the intention of exercising greater control over the unions. The enterprise union system continues and has had a significant influence on the development of the union movement.

Between 1987 and 1989: the peak

Union membership contracted during the first half of the 1980s but had an opportunity to expand with the 1987 Democratisation Declaration. The number of unions increased by 125% from mid-1987 to number 6142 in 1988. During the same period, union membership increased by 70%, reaching 1 707 456 members. Unionisation reached a peak in 1989 with 18.6% of all employees unionised (see Table 9.1). The expansion in membership and the number of unions was accompanied by an increase in the number of disputes. The unions differed considerably from those of earlier periods and could be seen as a new type of union movement.

The union movement expanded its presence to a greater number of industries and regions. This was achieved at a time when the unions experienced repression as they adopted a strategy of pursuing their demands despite the political upheaval. First, as in the case of 1979, the growth of the union movement took place in conjunction with an unstable political situation (Kim 1994). As a result, a period

Table 9.1 Major employment relations trends

	Union membership and density			Industrial disputes		
	Actual union membership ('000s)	Potential union membership[a] ('000s)	Density (%)	Strikes & lockouts	Workers involved ('000s)	Working days lost ('000s)
1970	473	3746	12.6	4	1	9
1975	750	4751	15.8	52	10	14
1980	948	6464	14.7	407	49	61
1985	1004	8104	15.4	265	29	64
1986	1036	8433	12.3	276	47	72
1987	1267	9191	13.8	3749	1262	6947
1988	1707	9910	17.8	1873	294	5401
1989	1932	10 389	18.6	1616	409	6351
1990	1887	10 059	17.2	322	134	4487
1991	1803	11 349	15.9	234	175	3271
1992	1735	11 568	15.0	235	105	1528
1993	1667	11 751	14.2	144	109	1308
1994	1659	12 297	13.5	121	104	1484
1995	1615	12 736	12.7	88	50	393
1996	1599	13 043	12.2	85	79	893
1997	1484	13 228	11.2	78	44	445

Note: a. Number of paid workers.
Source: KLIa; KLIb.

of labour quiescence in the mid-1990s is understandable, given the political stability of the period. The second important implication is that the growing activity of the unions after 1987 was relatively spontaneous and in reaction to particular events. But, during the 1990s when gains had been made in the areas of basic pay, it was difficult for the two types of unions to share a common approach (Lee 1995).

Unlike the previous union movement which was dominated by workers, particularly female workers, in light industries and small companies, the post-1987 union movement was dominated by male workers in heavy industries. This shift in industry focus occurred because of the development of heavy industries in South Korea in the late 1970s and early 1980s. Consequently, the following period is characterised by fragmentation. Figures indicate that the union movement in the 1990s has concentrated in large companies (see Table 9.2). The growing gaps in wages and bargaining power between workers in large and small companies has become a barrier tending to prevent workers from uniting the union movement.

Unions organising white-collar workers, including service workers, emerged after 1987 and became one of the rapidly growing

Table 9.2 Industrial disputes by size of establishment[a]

	Less than 100	100–299	300–999	More than 1000
1987	1 379 (36.8)[b]	1 480 (39.5)	629 (16.8)	259 (6.9)
1988	717 (38.3)	706 (37.7)	289 (15.4)	161 (8.6)
1989	570 (35.3)	645 (39.9)	249 (15.4)	152 (9.4)
1990	85 (26.4)	124 (38.5)	63 (19.6)	50 (15.5)
1991	44 (18.8)	79 (33.8)	62 (26.5)	49 (20.9)
1992	61 (26.0)	82 (34.9)	57 (24.2)	35 (14.9)
1993	26 (18.1)	51 (25.4)	36 (21.5)	31 (21.5)
1994	32 (26.4)	37 (30.6)	24 (19.8)	28 (31.8)
1995	21 (23.9)	27 (30.7)	28 (23.1)	12 (13.6)
1996	13 (15.3)	25 (29.4)	23 (27.1)	24 (28.2)
1997	19 (24.4)	26 (33.3)	19 (24.4)	14 (17.9)
1998	27 (20.9)	35 (27.1)	34 (26.4)	33 (25.6)

Note: a. Size in terms of employee numbers.
 b. Numbers in parentheses are percentages in total cases.
Source: KLIa.

sectors of the union activity in the 1990s. Increased employment in service industries has been coupled with a deterioration in working conditions. Another important factor fostering the development of a white-collar unionism may be the influence of the student movement of the 1980s, which was active in opposing the military regimes. After graduating from university and securing employment in the white-collar sector, former student activists are, directly and indirectly, participating in unions. White-collar unions formed the so-called democratic national union centre, the KCTU, in the 1990s.

The union movement in the 1990s

Unions have undergone a dramatic change in the 1990s. The rapid expansion of unionism after 1987 renders the labour quiescence of the mid-1990s, in the absence of political upheaval or state repression of the union movement, somewhat puzzling. As Table 9.1 indicates, union membership, union density and the number of industrial disputes fell after 1990.

What are the characteristics of unionism? With the degree of state repression declining, the growth of unionism is no longer strictly regulated. The decline in the union movement can be traced to its own internal situation. From 1987 union activity has been concentrated in large companies and so the focus of union activities has shifted to economic strategies such as wage negotiation (Lee 1995). Despite government policies controlling wages, during the 1990s leading public and private sector companies were unable to comply with the level of wage increases suggested by the State because unions demanded higher increases (Park 1996). As a result, the wages gap between workers in large and small companies has widened (Korea MOLa). The impact of a growing wages gap has undermined unions in small companies as well as the centralised union movement.

Declines in unionism are linked to the growth in other social movements. Emerging democratic civil movements have grown rapidly, and their focus on social reform has challenged unions (Park 1996). The union movement has thus been forced to concentrate on the negotiation of wages in an attempt to create a separate identity from the democratic movement. In addition, moral support for the unions nationally, which was strong in the late 1980s, has declined as a result of the unions concentrating on a narrow strategy of wage bargaining instead of broader social reform issues. In this context, the emergence of an alternative union movement, KCTU, and its institutionalisation in the 1990s, grew because of its strong commitment to the democratisation of industrial relations. Although the KCTU has also suffered from a lack of united effort on social reform, its impact in introducing multiple unionism has been significant.

Unions have been most active in large companies, pursuing a strategy focused on wage bargaining. In pursuing this strategy the unions appear to have lost the political character they gained from their participation in the democratic movement. The growing gap in bargaining power based on company size, the concentration on wage negotiations, and the replacement of the union movement by the emerging social movements have had a negative impact on the union movement. Historically, the centralisation of authority in national unions has been critical to the development of a strong union movement (Pontusson 1992:7–10)[1] but divisions between 'old' and 'new' unionism has prevented unity.

South Korea's union movement has been affected by the financial crisis. The economic adjustment program monitored by the International Monetary Fund (IMF) has pursued a strategy of labour market flexibility and targeted large private companies and the public sector—areas where the union movement flourished in the 1990s.

Recent changes in the economic context

The South Korean government has pursued a globalisation policy, so labour and management have been subject to pressures from the international community to reform their practices. These include the growing demand for labour market flexibility, an increase in outsourcing, a growing part-time work force and greater employment instability stemming from collective dismissals (ILO 1996; Bridges 1994; Frank & Cook 1995; Heckscher 1995). These changes have undermined the position of unions. Union members have also become a minority in many companies because of increases in the employment of non-standard workers. Workers' interests are represented less by unions and more by broadly representative bodies such as labour-management councils, which play a similar role but generally co-operate more with management. The major concern with this shift in representation for workers is that enterprise based unions and industry based unions may be at risk because the diversity in the range and interests of workers within a company may hinder their strength.

Rapid technological innovation and increases in unemployment induced by industrial and technological changes are evident in many countries (Craver 1993). There have been widespread redundancies (Barner 1994; Tomasko 1990). Consequently, collective bargaining aimed at increasing wages has been replaced by demands focusing on employment security, with workers considering the availability of employment as a higher priority. Accordingly, wage levels for workers, except for a limited number of professional workers, remained static or deteriorated.

The post-1997 financial crisis indicates it is impossible for South Korea's unions to avoid growing pressures to become industrially competitive in a globalised world economy.[2]

The changing environment for unions

This section examines the contextual changes affecting the union movement in South Korea from two perspectives: employment relations and labour markets. Although changes at both levels are interconnected, I will treat these aspects separately.

Employment relations

One of the important changes in ER in South Korea since the 1980s is the trend towards deregulation. The government has directly intervened by fostering autonomous collective bargaining between labour and management. In contrast to the guided policies prior to 1987, wage negotiations have proceeded based upon informal deals between labour and management. The government has generally acted with restraint in disputes by emphasising its role only as mediator. Although the relatively passive role of the government possibly encouraged confrontation between labour and management in the

Table 9.3 Labour shortages

Employees	1991[a] (%)	1993[a] (%)	1995[a] (%)	1997[a] (%)
Total employees	5.5	3.6	3.7	2.4
By type of workers				
Office workers	1.3	1.8	1.9	1.2
Production	9.1	6.0	5.8	3.9
Skilled	7.3	5.1	5.4	3.3
Unskilled	20.1	14.5	11.4	12.6
By size of firm				
Less than 30 employees	7.9	4.4	5.8	3.7
30–99 employees	7.2	5.0	4.0	2.9
100–299 employees	6.5	4.2	4.2	2.7
300–499 employees	4.9	2.2	2.2	1.4
More than 499 employees	2.3	1.7	1.4	0.8

Note: a. Labor shortage rate = unfilled vacancies/current employees.
Source: MOL.

1990s, both ER parties realised they could settle labour issues without government assistance. The political character of ER has been transformed into an economic one based on wage negotiations. As a result, the number of general or long-term strikes has declined.

The second change in ER is that related to the weakened bargaining power of unions compared to the growing role of employer associations. After 1987, these associations strengthened their strategies against unions. In the past, employers settled ER issues individually, with direct assistance from the government. Since the 1980s with the need for co-ordinated efforts, employer associations have acted collectively. In contrast to the emergence of alternative unions, the older national union federations are divided and have suffered from intra-movement conflicts. In addition, the KCTU, which includes many enterprise unions in large companies, cannot effectively represent the general interests of union members because union leaders in large companies have pursued enterprise-based issues such as wage negotiations. The old style of unionism represented by the FKTU, long dependent on the support received from consecutive governments, has not adjusted its strategies to operate effectively in the new context. As a result, the collective voice of unions against management has been weakened.

Labour markets

In the 1980s, the South Korean economy shifted from a position of labour surplus to one of labour shortage. In the 1990s the collective bargaining power of workers over wage increases has been closely related to labour shortages in manufacturing (see Table 9.3). Labour shortages, while still severe, have shown some improvement since the mid-1990s. The shortage of production workers is typically severe, with small companies the most adversely affected. Labour shortages contributed to unemployment remaining below 3% until 1997 and to a rise in wages (Korea NSO 1999).

In 1990, the proportion of production workers in the total workforce was 69% but dropped to 64% in 1995. Considering the growth of manufacturing firms during this period, the decrease in the work force reflects growth in the capital intensity of production (Park 1996). In large companies economic growth has been high, but their share of employment as a proportion of total employment has decreased despite increases in their share of national output. The proportion of employment in large companies (more than 300 employees) has decreased from approximately 35% in 1990 to around 28% in 1995 (KLIb). These changes indicate that unions in large companies, that led the union movement in the past, are facing threats arising from the intensification of capital.

Another important change in the employment structure is the ageing of the work force. The number of young workers continues to decline with the economically active population in the 15–19 years age group decreasing from 639 000 in 1990 to 441 000 in 1995. During the same period there was an 8% increase in the number of economically active people in the 40–54 year age group (Korea NSO 1996). The impact of the ageing work force on the union movement will be evident in the future. Given that the most active union members in South Korea have been under 40 years, labour militancy may decline. The ageing work force may intensify conflicts of interest between young workers and the growing number of older workers. This may detract from union solidarity. Job security has declined with the replacement of seniority based promotion with merit based promotion and by the dismissal of older workers. Younger workers to some extent support the new system, as it provides opportunities for more rapid promotion.[3]

The most important change in the labour market is the trend towards de-industrialisation. The reduction in employment in the manufacturing sector has been coupled with an increase in overseas investments and hiring by South Korean companies. According to the Bank of Korea, there were only 338 cases of overseas investment valued at less than US$1 billion in 1990—a figure which had increased in 1995 to 1285 cases valued at more than US$3 billion. In a similar context, overseas employment by South Korean companies increased rapidly in the mid-1990s. The overseas work force in one of South Korea's largest companies, the Daewoo group, expanded to represent half its total number of employees. Other large Korean companies have also increased the proportion of overseas employees. Like the large companies, small companies have also attempted to move production overseas in order to utilise cheap labour. The possibility of de-industrialisation in South Korea is forcing the government and unions to accept labour market flexibility which employers are keenly promoting.

The new union movement and employment relations trends

In 1996, the union movement in South Korea gained momentum. Although unions have long faced serious constraints, the gains in power of the Minjunochong appeared to be a sign of resurgence. Minjunochong gained members from large companies and the white-collar sector while the FKTU suffered losses.

There is, however, a dark side to the new unionism. The wage focused bargaining strategies adopted in large companies have reached a stalemate because of the widening gap between the large and small sectors. White-collar union organisation is limited because most white-collar workers have a relatively weak consciousness of being 'workers'. Despite such weaknesses, the institutionalisation of the KCTU is important for understanding the status of South Korea's union movement and to answer the question: does the current state of South Korea's union movement represent retreat or resurgence.

The characteristics of the new union movement

The FKTU was long the only legal national union confederation in South Korea. Since 1987 there were several attempts to organise an alternative national union centre which is ideologically distinct from the FKTU. Cheonnohyup (Korean Council of Trade Unions) was established in 1991 and, even though it lacked legal status, it organised more than 300 000 members. In 1995, Cheonnohyup, together with other non-authorised unions, formed the KCTU (Minjunochong) (Park 1996).

According to the KCTU's platform, the ideologies of the new union movement can be summarised as follows:

1. to pursue union activities independently of management and the State and to adhere to democratic rules;
2. to promote the general issue of social reform; and
3. to replace the current enterprise basis for organising unions with a national centre based on industrial unions.

The leaders of the new union movement are critical of the FKTU style. As a result, there has been some conflict between the KCTU and the FKTU. However, the new union movement has yet to achieve its proposed goals.

Under the pre-1997 legal framework, the KCTU was not recognised by the State. Despite this it played a major role in ER. In 1996 the KCTU claimed that its membership amounted to 400 000 workers which was small when compared to the FKTU with 1 200 000 members. But it has not been ignored by employer associations and the government because its membership is drawn from big conglomerates and the public sector.

Employment relations reform in 1996–97

In early 1996, with growing concerns from the International Labour Organisation (ILO) and the Organisation for Economic Cooperation and Development (OECD), the traditional tripartite actors—the FKTU, employer associations and the government—agreed it was time to discuss legal recognition of the KCTU. Consequently, the government initiated ER reforms, including the recognition of multiple unionism from 1996, and so the KCTU was invited to join the Presidential Commission on Industrial Relations Reform. It comprised representatives from the union movement, employer associations and public representatives, and it held a series of public hearings and meetings with expert panels over a period of six months. The leaders of the KCTU joined the Commission with the expectation that they would at last receive legal recognition in return for accepting some restrictions proposed by management.

The Commission's activity was aimed at building a new ER framework balancing the contrasting demands of, on the one hand, Korea's need for competitive companies and, on the other, the need to maintain the quality of workers' lives. The Commission reached consensus on several issues, but failed to agree on the major issues dividing labour and management (see above ch. 5).

Despite objections from the opposition parties and the unions, the proposed recognition of multiple unionism was postponed until the year 2000. The ruling party modfied the proposal without proper discussions with other interests, but considered the declining competitiveness of companies and the growing discontent from the FKTU. The sudden delay in recognising multiple unionism jeopardised the spirit of the Commission and evoked an anti-government atmosphere both within and outside the union movement.

After the amendment of industrial relations laws, the KCTU, which was dealt a serious blow with the delayed legalisation, organised a general strike in late December 1996. Contrary to the government's expectation, the FKTU also joined the strike, although compared to the KCTU's level of involvement, its actions were limited. The government and the ruling party were surprised by the intensity of the general strike and the participation of the FKTU in its first general strike. The FKTU participated despite the relative advantage it would gain from the delay in recognising plural unionism.

In early 1997, the KCTU was given institutional recognition (with full legal recognition to be implemented in November 1999). Unions also achieved the postponement of legal collective dismissals, so the general strike was halted. The strike provided unions with the opportunity to rediscover their potential power and union members gained an awareness of their collective strength.

Challenges since the financial crisis

The 1997 ER reform was significant in dealing with the impact of the globalisation of the labour market. On the one hand, the reforms aimed to incorporate the demands for a flexible labour market while, on the other hand, protecting basic labour standards and the social rights of unions. Despite some conflicts, unions and management agreed on the strategy of reforming ER incrementally until the year 2002.

With the impact of the financial crisis in late November 1997, the spirit and strategy of ER reform has encountered a fundamental challenge. More drastic and rapid reform has been a key demand of the structural adjustment program. As a result, ER have become more unstable and struggles and conflicts around the issue of economic reform have increased. In 1998 the newly elected leader, Kim Dae-Jung, established a Tripartite Commission with representatives from the three groups—unions, management and government—to examine measures for overcoming the economic crisis.

The economic adjustment program, pursued by the new government under the IMF's monitoring, has been painful, especially for unions and workers. In January 1998, the Tripartite Commission announced its first Joint Statement, identifying the goal of economic reform and the principle of fair burden sharing. In February 1998, the Commission agreed upon an agenda and declared its Social Agreement to the public.[4]

The most contentious issue in the agenda for social reform is the revision of the Employment Adjustment Laws. Unlike the labour law reforms of 1997 which delayed collective dismissals for up to two years, under the revision collective dismissals were permitted immediately following the amendment of the law. The legalisation of the agreed issues was completed after the announcement of the Social Agreement.

By the late 1990s, many of the issues agreed on by the Commission had been implemented. Unions, however, consistently claimed corporate structural adjustment had been delayed. Large private companies and the public sector had been the centre of debate regarding what constitutes reasonable levels of employment adjustment—in particular, what constitutes collective dismissals for managerial reasons. Furthermore, reform of the taxation system in favour of wage earners had been delayed because of the sharp contraction in the tax base. By withholding the imposition of a comprehensive tax on capital gains in the financial sector, the government had been criticised that its will to reform was weak. In response to such criticisms, the government began conducting tax reforms in 1999 that were more favourable to workers.

After the adoption of the Social Agreement, the KCTU faced strong criticism from its rank and file membership over its acceptance of collective dismissals. As a result, the KCTU leadership which participated in the Tripartite Commission has been replaced. The new KCTU leadership opposed collective dismissals on the grounds that they are illegal. They argue that far too many collective dismissals have been undertaken and that they have increased after the Tripartite Commission announced its Social Agreement. The KCTU argued this had jeopardised the spirit of fair burden sharing and it called a general strike on 15 July 1998. About 150 000 members participated.

There has also been growing conflict over the government's privatisation plan. As part of its structural adjustment program, the government plans to reduce the number of public companies from 24 to 13. This involves plans to retrench about 29 000 workers (20% of the total work force) employed in public companies by the year 2000. The unions and workers in question have protested against the government's unilateral decision, calling for discussion of the principles and procedures of privatisation and employment adjustment in the Tripartite Commission. The unions' criticism focuses on the government's emphasis on balancing the budget by selling public companies rather than addressing ways to reduce inefficiency in these companies.

In August 1998 the Tripartite Commission reconvened and the three parties discussed the next stage for economic reform. However, there appeared to be diminished trust amongst the parties and in late 1999 the KCTU withdrew from its participation in the Tripartite Commission. The government has attempted to activate the Social Agreement by re-examining the employment adjustment strategy. Tentatively, some collective dismissals have been regarded as illegal and unreasonable. The Hyundai Motor Company case, where 1500 workers were dismissed, was at the centre of this debate. The unions have consistently argued that firms should reduce working hours rather than lay-off workers. They suggest a maximum of 40 hours per week.

In 1999, most workplaces agreed on maintaining reduced wage levels. However, unions and management expected to pay wage increases in 2000, as the GDP growth rates for 1999 were as high as 10.2%. By the year 2000 a pattern of concession bargaining had emerged.

Conclusions

The changing ER context in the 1990s shaped the contours of the union movement. The protests of the unions against the repression had a limited role in establishing the national strategy on globalisation. Nevertheless, compared to its previous position, the union movement has achieved success in terms of its influence on national decision-making processes. Most of its achievements have been acquired through protest.

The impact of the 1990s' economic crisis on the union movement was negative. As participants in the Tripartite Commission, however, unions have been critical to the implementation of the structural adjustment program. Has a form of social corporatism developed, incorporating unions in the process of national restructuring?[5] If so, the unions have experimented with corporatism to survive the adversity of the 1990s.

The union movement has been active in the 1990s partly because of the adverse context and partly because its organising efforts have been conducted over a relatively short period. This evidence often leads to the conclusion that South Korea's union movement flourished in the 1990s. But the apparent resurgence of South Korea's unions has been their strategy for surviving a harsh period.

The unions have been reincorporated into the more general framework of social movements as they were in the democratic movement prior to 1987. South Korea's unions are the focus of attention, nationally and internationally, as they confront the challenges of globalisation.

10 Challenges facing unions in Australia

Bill Mansfield[1]

Introduction

For much of the 20th century Australian unions had the luxury of not having to critically re-assess either their strategies or their performance in meeting the needs of their members. However, with declining union membership and anti-union actions by conservative governments and some employers, the next decade represents a vital stage in determining the future of unionism in Australia. This chapter highlights the factors that underpin the need for unions in Australia to reflect on their methods and set new strategies for maintaining and representing their membership in a global, deregulated marketplace.

For most of the 20th century Australian employment relations were adversarial; management tended to regard ER as either of marginal importance or as an issue generally to be left to specialists. Regulation occurred through an industry based award system, which at times could be somewhat inflexible in catering to the needs of individual enterprises. Wage bargaining was largely undertaken in industry level negotiations or through the Industrial Relations Commission arbitration process for national and industry level adjustments.

The shift to a global economy

Australia's political economy, which was the context for its ER, was regulated by high levels of protective tariffs, fixed exchange rates, controls on currency movements and a regulated financial system. In addition, in the three decades following World War II, as the European and Asian economies were reconstructing, there was little external pressure to change the traditional ways of operating.

In acknowledging the way in which the Australian economy operated in the years after 1945 there were some admirable outcomes. In general there was a gradual rise in living standards throughout the period. Unemployment was low in comparison to today's levels and the benefits of the economic growth were shared reasonably equitably. There was less evidence of vast wealth being accumulated by some people from speculation and corporate takeovers. Australia accepted migrants in large numbers: not only did such a program give the migrants themselves opportunities, but it also benefited Australian society and continues to do so. These were the days that led Australia to be dubbed 'The Lucky Country'.

The 1950s and 1960s also marked the high point in union membership. In 1960 union membership represented around 55% of the work force. For example, on leaving full-time education in 1958, I joined the telecommunications provider, the Post Master General's Department, along with around 500 other 'young men of British nationality'. Like nearly all of my fellow trainees, I joined the union a couple of days later.

Contemporary Australian society is not what it was in 1958. The financial system and economy are well along the path of deregulation and trade liberalisation. There is now a global marketplace for some goods and services that will increasingly ignore national borders. There are bipartisan commitments from national leaders to deliver an international trading system free of protection within the next twenty years. Many employers recognise the importance of the contribution of employees, both individually and collectively, to high value-added, high quality enterprises, and they seek greater flexibility from their work force. The industrial relations system is largely based on individual enterprises, not industries; and within this system the Industrial Relations Commission plays a much less significant role. Many of these changes were achieved in the 1990s before the change of government in 1996. Most of the changes were introduced with the support of the union movement through the various versions of the Accord agreement between the Australian Council of Trade Unions (ACTU) and the Labor governments from 1983–96 (see above ch. 2).

Unions' strategic reactions to challenges

The major initiatives of the Hawke/Keating Labor federal governments were designed to alter the orientation of the economy towards an international perspective and to make it more competitive. In addition to the broader economic reforms, major changes have been made to the union movement and its broad policy approach:

- A major process of union amalgamation has been undertaken.
- Workplace reforms involving multiskilling and best practice, plus reforms to vocational training, have been supported.
- Wage fixing has been changed from an industry to an enterprise process.
- A more constructive culture has been encouraged to replace an adversarial approach.
- The number of strikes and disputes has been substantially reduced.

All these changes have taken place with the support and, at times, leadership from unions and Australia's peak union organisation, the ACTU.

Trends in union membership

The next decade is critical for unions in Australia. Unions are facing federal and some state governments which are legislating to minimise the influence of the union movement with the aim of reducing it to an insignificant force in Australia. There is a clear need for an effective response to a serious decline in membership, or else acknowledgment that the significance of unions will be reduced to the state of unions in the US and France with memberships of less than 10% of the work force. This task of reversing membership decline is the union movement's first and most fundamental challenge.

Since the start of the 1980s, the number of union members in Australia has been in decline, not only as a reduced percentage of an expanding work force but also as a decline in absolute terms (see Table 10.1).

In addition to a decline in absolute and proportionate terms, there has also been a significant change in the public sector/private sector, casual/permanent mix in relation to union membership. Table 10.2 shows that there has been a significant decline in public sector membership and also a major decline in membership among casual and permanent employees.

The situation confronting unions in Australia is similar to that confronting unions in a range of other developed economies, but it is more pronounced. In Japan and South Korea, for example, the number of union members has been falling as a proportion of the work force for some time, although not by the levels experienced in Australia.

As the figures for Japan and South Korea illustrate (see Table 10.3), work force growth, combined with slow or negative growth in union membership numbers, can result in a fall in the percentage of the unionised work force. In Australia's case the work force has

Table 10.1 Union membership and density: ABS members survey

Year	Number of members (m)	Union density (%)
1976	2.51	51.0
1982	2.57	49.5
1986	2.59	45.6
1988	2.54	41.6
1990	2.66	40.5
1992	2.51	39.6
1993	2.38	37.6
1994	2.28	35.0
1995	2.25	32.7
1996	2.19	31.1
1997	2.11	30.3

Source: Peetz (1998:6).

Table 10.2 Union density by gender, sector and employment status: ABS members survey

Year	Males	Females	Public	Private	Casual	Permanent
1976	54.3	41.8	–	–	–	–
1982	53.4	43.2	72.9	38.6	–	–
1986	50.1	39.1	70.6	34.5	21.0	50.8
1988	46.3	35.0	67.7	31.5	19.7	46.6
1990	45.0	34.6	66.8	30.8	18.8	45.7
1992	43.4	34.8	67.1	29.4	17.2	46.0
1993	40.9	33.5	64.4	27.5	15.9	43.7
1994	39.1	22.9	62.3	26.0	14.7	41.3
1995	35.7	29.1	56.4	25.1	13.9	39.4
1996	33.5	28.1	55.4	24.0	13.1	37.4
1997	33.0	26.9	54.7	23.3	13.8	36.0

Source: Peetz (1998:6).

Table 10.3 Union membership: Japan and South Korea

Year	Japan	% of work force	Korea	% of work force
1975	12 590 000	34.4	750 000	15.8
1985	12 417 000	28.9	1 004 000	12.4
1995	12 614 000	23.8	1 615 000	12.7

Source: Bamber & Lansbury (1998:253–79).

grown relatively strongly in the period 1985–95 and so the decline in union membership as a proportion of the total work force has been accentuated. The reasons for the decline are numerous and include: the changing composition of the work force, fewer large employers in traditional industries, greater numbers of small to medium-size enterprises, a smaller public sector and greater numbers of workers in part-time and casual employment. Despite these reasons, there is no reason to accept as inevitable the decline of union membership numbers in Australia.

Union initiatives to overcome the decline in union density

There are exceptions to the decline in union density. Some examples highlighted below are unions representing nurses, engineers and scientists, and retail workers. Several unions have demonstrated that with the right combination of activities they can increase with an expanding work force:

1. The Association of Professional Engineers, Scientists and Managers, Australia (APESMA), as its name suggests, represents engineers, scientists, professionals and managers. It has over 20 000 members and is growing at the rate of approximately 5% each year. Some of its features include:
   the provision of individually tailored advice on remuneration matters;
   • with Deakin University, the sponsorship of Australia's largest MBA program through distance learning mode;
   • national certification as a 'Quality Organisation'.
2. The Shop Distributive and Allied Employees Association (SDA) represents shop assistants. With the expansion in the retail work force its membership is growing each year. It provides good quality industrial services to its members plus a range of non-industrial services. Its communications with its membership are of a high standard.
3. Unions representing nurses in the health sector are also expanding with increases in their work force. Again, good quality industrial services, close contact with membership views, good communications and the positive public profile of their senior officials on health issues have contributed to their retention of membership numbers and loyalty.

The unions that are coping best are those which have the capacity to deliver quality services to members consistently throughout the country. These unions also are capable of taking a strategic approach to the issues, confronting them and planning for the future, not simply reacting to tomorrow's 'crisis'. Such unions put a premium on recruiting delegates and officials who are highly motivated and competent. Part of the success story of these unions is member access to leading edge technology—APESMA uses the Internet for membership communications—and properly equipping their organisations with modern systems appropriate to meeting membership needs.

National initiatives that have been taken include the establishment of a recruitment institute known as Organising Works. An initiative of the ACTU and a range of affiliate unions, Organising Works has operated since 1994 to recruit and train younger union officials as workplace organisers. Many of the recruits have been university graduates. Since 1994 there have been over 250 trainees taken on by Organising Works and placed with unions throughout Australia. The recruits have attracted tens of thousands of new members to their unions. They are also playing a role in changing the culture of the union movement away from one that relies on full-time union officers delivering services to members to effective membership activity at enterprise level to represent their interests to their employers.

In the past few years unions have also expanded their non-industrial services to include benefits such as discount purchasing, free legal advice, cheap travel, low-cost home loans and discounted medical and dental services.

There is potential in this area for the development of additional services, capitalising on the ability of the union movement to access over two million workers and their families. Areas where there is potential include access to more affordable finance and provision of information technology/access to the Internet at lower prices. However, while these additional services are of value, the empirical evidence suggests they are not sufficient to attract and retain large numbers of new members.

Most employees join unions for the 'industrial' services they can provide—services such as assistance in obtaining wage increases, advice on occupational health and safety, better superannuation, improved job security and collective protection when there is a problem with the employer. The services of most importance are to secure wage increases and to improve living standards and job security.

Workplace unionism

Unions need to structure themselves to deliver services to members effectively, with an emphasis on having an effective presence at the enterprise level. This requires the continuing rebuilding of enterprise-based structures of local representatives with relevant, good quality assistance to enable them to represent the interests of their members at enterprise level. There also needs to be an acceptance of the authority to negotiate with the employer being delegated to members at the workplace rather than held tightly by central councils of elected officials. While award standards will remain paramount and overall union principles should be maintained, there will be a continuation of the trend towards more flexible outcomes at workplace level.

The need for these changes has been recognised by decisions at the ACTU Congress and national union councils. What has to be achieved now is the effective implementation of the changes.

Wage improvements for union members

One critical area where members measure the performance of unions is in their ability to deliver wages increases and improve living standards.

Bargaining has continued to grow, despite an apparent slow down in the number of agreements certified in the first two quarters of 1997. In 1997, 5090 collective agreements covering 732 000 workers were certified. In the first nine months of 1998, 4403 agreements were certified covering 602 700 employees. It is estimated that around 1.4 million workers are covered by a federal enterprise agreement at any one time, with 1.2 million employees having their wages set by an agreement. Manufacturing and construction account for more than half the agreements made during 1997 and the first half of 1998. Manufacturing, education, government administration and defence, retail trade, and cultural and recreational services are the key industries in terms of numbers of workers covered (ACTU 1999:73).

During 1997/98 wage increases measured by average weekly earnings were 4.1% up on 1996/97. Average weekly earnings growth has outstripped growth in annual award rates of pay.

The difficulty for union leaders when engaged in enterprise bargaining should not be underestimated when compared to bargaining at industry level. Australia has around 800 000 individual enterprises. In the year ending in September 1998, unions finalised 5460 agreements (see Table 10.4) at the federal level, each of which will have to be re-negotiated every two years or so. At the state level there are several thousand more agreements; informal agreements would cover many additional enterprises. However, this leaves a large number of employees whose wage entitlements are influenced only by award safety net increases.

Although the number of agreements is much smaller than the number of enterprises, the proportion of employees covered is probably around 75% of those employed under federal awards. The

Table 10.4 Collective agreements: Year to September, 1997 and 1998

Industry group	No. of agreements certified		No. of employees covered	
	Year to September 1997	Year to September 1998	Year to September 1997	Year to September 1998
Non-metals manufacturing	711	635	65 728	51 212
Metals manufacturing	646	723	66 896	59 716
Infrastructure	2022	2532	111 560	114 707
Other	607	1206	242 799	502 857
Government administration	316	364	37 007	143 050
All industries	**4302**	**5460**	**523 990**	**871 542**

Source: ACTU Living Wage (1999:74).

reason for this outcome is that many of the individual agreements are with very large enterprises.

As a provider of services to members, it is not acceptable for unions to regard those not covered by agreements as irrelevant or unimportant. Even if workers are employed predominantly in the small to medium-size business sector, this is where the employment growth is occurring. If unions cannot service that sector, unions are consigning themselves to a smaller and smaller part of the work force. The union movement has to develop approaches that enable members in small to medium-size enterprises to be involved in enterprise bargaining.

There are other approaches which are being considered and introduced by a range of unions to improve their performance in the area of wage bargaining. These approaches include: the improved use of computer technology, greater scope for direct membership involvement in bargaining, and better servicing of membership information needs during the bargaining process. One way of improving the outcomes of wage bargaining which is being introduced by some unions is the co-ordination of industry-wide claims within a nominated period of the year. This represents one response to the many difficulties experienced in trying to undertake separate bargaining for members in thousands of individual enterprises. It is hoped that this initiative will result in better outcomes in enterprise bargaining for greater numbers of members.

The campaign for a living wage

An increasingly important activity for unions in Australia is the campaign for a decent living wage as a minimum rate that can be paid to an adult worker. In January 1999 the level of the Living Wage for workers under federal awards was A$373.40 per week. The annual union claim for an increase seeks to ensure that workers on minimum wage rates do not fall behind general community standards and that workers on wages above the minimum rates award, whose wages have not been increased through enterprise bargaining, obtain some of the benefits of economic growth.

Industrially weaker groups are not well served by bargaining and continue to rely on award provisions for wage adjustments. These workers tend to be concentrated among certain groups and include: women, part-time workers, labour hire workers, young workers and workers in small and medium-size enterprises.

The Australian initiatives in the area of the Living Wage are being echoed in the UK and the US where national governments have legislated for minimum wage rates for workers. In the UK, the Blair Labour government established the Low Pay Commission (LPC) to facilitate the introduction of a national minimum wage. In its report to the Government the LPC stated in part:

> Poverty wages cannot encourage people to move from benefits to work. Such wage levels encourage feelings of detachment and alienation. We were struck by a comment made to us in Northern Ireland, and echoed in other visits, that the low paid were often on 'the margins of degradation'. We hope that our recommendations will play some part in giving workless households and those in low-paid employment more opportunities to participate fully in the economic and social life of society. The introduction of a statutory floor for wage levels must encourage feelings of belonging not to the margins, but to the mainstream of society. (UK Low Pay Commission: 1998:160)

This is what the Australian Living Wage Case is all about—assisting to ensure that all workers and their families can participate in and 'belong to' Australian society.

Improving union structures

Another major challenge is to ensure that the union structures put in place in recent years are effective in servicing the needs of members. Since the mid-1980s the union movement has been restructuring to achieve fewer but larger unions. The process of substantial union amalgamations is almost complete. At the time of writing, twenty large unions represent over 95% of members under federal Awards.

There is no doubt that the restructuring of the union movement in Australia was necessary. For example, in the 1960s in the telecommunications and postal area there were over twenty craft based unions representing around 70 000 employees. This resulted in waste, duplication and general ineffectiveness. There are now four unions in the area and the potential exists for much higher standards of service.

Small unions can be uneconomic. Through economies of scale, larger unions can better service the needs of their members. However, if unions do amalgamate, but despite their increase in size neglect to deliver better services and resources, members will not consider the larger union better meets their needs.

Australian unions have historically been a mixture of craft and industrial organisations. The original unions were mostly craft organisations based on the British craft model of unionisation. Over time, through amalgamations and extensions of union constitutions, several of the traditional craft unions have broadened to adopt an industry base.

Australian unions did not adopt the enterprise model common in other parts of Asia. In Japan in 1996 the 12.5 million union members were represented by nearly 71 000 unions. Unions in South Korea are organised usually at a plant or enterprise level but can also be organised by region or occupation—the local unions make up federations, regional councils and national centres, but only the local union has the right to negotiate. There are over 6500 unions registered in South Korea.

The Australian experience of amalgamations is similar to that of unions in other developed economies. Other countries also see greater consolidation and amalgamations as part of the response to improving services and meeting the challenge of falling membership. In Germany, the Deutscher Gewerkschaftsbund (DGB) is moving to reduce the number of its industrial unions from twelve to five. In Sweden there are proposals for additional mergers of unions to form larger organisations.

The Australian experience with union amalgamations tends to suggest that a number of issues need to be addressed more closely if members are to benefit. These issues include:

- the means by which groups of members can identify their interests in a larger organisation, including maintaining familiar union names at least during a transition period;
- clear strategies to deliver better services to members in areas such as communications, bargaining advice, occupational health and safety and membership participation;
- serious efforts to achieve economies and improve standards in areas such as office accommodation, technology and administration;

- attention to the means by which the officers of the various groups work constructively together.

These matters need to be regarded as important and deserving of substantial attention from the union leadership. If they are not dealt with in a serious manner, the potential gains from the amalgamation may not be achieved.

Following the amalgamation of unions, union members should clearly see an improvement in the quality of service from their organisation. In some cases the need for a noticeable improvement in services following the amalgamation has not been high enough on the agenda.

Sometimes the amalgamation has been achieved but unions have been left with top heavy structures, as all the former officials have to be accommodated in the new organisation. At times, also, political or personality differences have inhibited the integration of amalgamating unions.

Legislation affecting unions

Since its election in 1996, the Federal conservative coalition government has taken a confrontationist stance towards the union movement and has enacted a range of legislation designed to reduce the ability of unions to operate effectively.

Some conservative state governments—for example, the Western Australian government—have also enacted a range of anti-union legislation.

At the federal level the effect of the legislation to vary the *Workplace Relations Act* has been significant, although it is not the key reason for the decline in union membership. The legislation includes provisions which:

1. reduced the role of awards of the Industrial Relations Commission to twenty allowable matters with only a narrow range of disputes subject to arbitration;
2. outlawed provisions between employers and unions that promoted closed shops or preference to union members;
3. restricted the right of union officers to enter workplaces to communicate with members or promote union membership;
4. encouraged individual bargaining and collective agreements that bypass union structures;
5. increased sanctions for industrial action and the withdrawal of protected industrial action where the dispute involved more than one employer or was in support of a union whose members were involved in protected action;

6. encouraged the formation of new unions, including enterprise unions and the break up of existing unions.

The current Federal conservative government has also taken a partisan role in disputes between employers and unions representing their members. In the 1998 dispute between the Maritime Union of Australia (MUA) and Patrick Stevedores (see ch. 2) there was considerable evidence not only of government support for the employer, but also of a conspiracy between some ministers and the employer to de-unionise the waterfront by sacking existing employees and recruiting non-union labour.

The Howard government has effectively rejected a constructive tripartite approach to employment relations and economic development in favour of a strategy that is based on confrontation, marginalisation and removal of unions, representing employees, from policy development and planning for the future.

Conclusions

In an environment of continuing economic change, high unemployment levels and pressure from governments and employers for further reductions in working conditions, the pressure on union and ACTU resources will continue.

The problems confronting the union movement did not begin with the legislative changes introduced since 1996. The major challenge facing the union movement is to increase its membership in line with the growing but changing workforce. Therefore unions should concentrate on the most important issues, including:

• Improving the delivery of services to members, particularly industrial services. Union members have to be assured that when they request assistance from the union, whether at the enterprise level or through a full-time officer, help is provided in an effective and timely manner. Typical areas of concern where members seek assistance include: wage bargaining, job security, occupational health and safety, workers compensation, harassment/discrimination and general entitlements in awards and agreements. Unions have to ensure that their job delegates and full-time staff provide quality advice to members in response to their needs. Whilst there is no clear evidence on the quality of service provided by most unions in response to member requests, there are grounds for concern that in too many instances matters raised with the union have not been dealt with to the satisfaction of the member. One means of improving the quality of service from the union is to regularly survey the membership on issues related to their satisfaction with the union's response to their concerns and act to improve the level of service where it is seen to be inadequate.

- Effectively representing members engaged in enterprise bargaining and obtaining consistent improvements in living standards. Enterprise bargaining is the means by which work conditions are improved above the minimum standards set out in awards of the Commission. Unions have to put in place a program which enables members at enterprise level to develop new enterprise agreements effectively and on a regular basis. With nearly one million separate enterprises in Australia, the task of organising and undertaking enterprise bargaining is immense. The problems confronting unions with many small enterprises in their membership area, often with part-time and casual staff, are particularly acute. Unions need to be prepared to facilitate bargaining between job delegates and management by providing good quality supporting evidence for wage bargaining and the assistance of capable full-time officers where required. Many unions need to develop better systems to alert them when an enterprise agreement is about to come up for renewal so union officers can communicate with and if necessary mobilise members regarding the terms of any new agreement. Above all the union must be proactive in providing advice and assistance to members during the bargaining process to demonstrate its relevance and value in regard to securing improvements in wages and working conditions. If it does not provide advice and assistance of value, members will legitimately question whether they should continue to belong.

- Ensuring that their organisations operate effectively and in ways which facilitate participation from members. Unions need to operate efficiently in servicing the needs of their members and also facilitate their active participation in the decision-making and operation of the union. Areas where members come into contact with the union include telephone contact with the office, access to the union outside normal working hours, communication to the members' home and work addresses and systems for payment of membership dues. Too often the standards in these areas do not reflect the levels members deserve; examples include non-answering of telephones, no facility for leaving a recorded message and poor quality printed communications.

- Maintaining the broad role of the union movement to work together with progressive organisations to represent the interests of employees in areas such as economic growth and development, environmental protection, Aboriginal land rights, an Australian republic, the advancement of women and promoting multiculturalism. The union movement is one of many organisations which seeks to act in a progressive way to improve the lives of working people and also to represent the needs of disadvantaged groups. Unions need to work closely with groups such as the Australian Council of Social Services (ACOSS) in the area of social welfare, those representing Aboriginals and Torres Strait Islanders, the women's movement and those promoting multiculturalism. In some of these areas the close links which should exist have become more distant and less effective over time. In addition, unions should actively participate in the general debates about economic growth and development policies to influence the direction of development and to achieve better outcomes in terms of more permanent full-time employment and better opportunities for creating and maintaining competitive and sustainable industries in Australia.

If unions can meet these fundamental challenges they will survive and grow. If they cannot, the future is at best questionable.

PART IV

Perspectives on companies

11 Employment relations at a large South Korean firm: the LG Group

Young-Kee Kim

Like many other nations that have experienced much industrial change and development, South Korea in recent years experienced considerable turmoil in its employment relations (ER). As a result many South Korean companies have suffered labour unrest, with the LG Group being no exception. In 1989 alone, member companies of the LG Group experienced a total of 23 separate strikes. This resulted in US$740 million in lost production and LG fell behind Samsung in the consumer electronics business. In the light of these experiences, the executive leadership of the LG Group resolved to try to change to dispute-free employment relations.

After 1990 the company experienced a relatively stable and peaceful period in ER, with a minimal number of strikes occurring; however, despite this period of relative harmony, the approach to avoiding and settling disputes was essentially passive and unsystematic. The LG Group has come to realise that such an approach is neither effective nor efficient in view of the turbulent economic times that lie ahead. Therefore, the company is committed to pursuing a more active and systematic ER strategy. To increase competitiveness and employee satisfaction, the new approach should lead not only to a peaceful relationship between labour and management but also an active relationship of co-operation.

This chapter briefly summarises the history of employment relations at LG and examines survey results that helped to uncover significant and underlying problems in the employment relationship. A description of the LG Group's new ER strategy follows, including details of the company's plans for implementation. To conclude, a case study of ER at LG Electronics illustrates the lessons learnt at LG, and shows how one Korean company is attempting to construct more co-operative ER.

Employment relations at the LG Group

The history of ER in LG can be divided into the following distinct stages:

Pre-1987: Paternalistic employment relations

Achieving and sustaining high rates of economic growth were the main priority of both the government and the LG Group in the period prior to 1987, with the government actively intervening to restrict wage increases and union activity. Thus, in the case of the LG Group, where 'harmony' between management and employees was valued as the most important component of management ideology, unions were recognised at only fifteen of the LG Group's 49 companies, with no large-scale strikes occurring during this period. During this time, management concentrated its efforts on suppressing union activities (and the formation of new union groups), while at the same time attempting to enlist the loyalty and commitment of employees through pursuing 'paternalistic' management policies and strategies.

1987–89: Hostile employment relations

During the late 1980s South Korean society went through a stage of rapid and dramatic 'democratisation'. The government ceased its active intervention in the suppression of union activity, through the Korean Central Intelligence Agency (KCIA) and the police. In June 1987 the then presidential candidate, Roh Tae-Woo, declared a program of democratic reforms and there was a massive increase in union organisation and strike activity nationally. The member companies of the LG Group did not escape this labour unrest. During 1989, for example, unions at seven LG companies engaged in serious and lengthy strike activity which resulted in production losses of US$740 million. Surprised, and unprepared to deal with such a volatile situation, some LG managers attempted to minimise the extent and the impact of these organisational confrontations by using force and even by trying to bribe union officials. Management also attempted to deal with the new employment relations context by preparing conflict-resolution programs.

1990–97: Stable employment relations

Since 1990 the LG Group has pursued a strategy of creating harmonious relations with its various unions to prevent the occurrence of disputes. Specifically, industrial relations departments in individual LG member companies have actively worked towards improving industrial relations (IR) and human resources management (HRM) systems by developing effective two-way communication channels between management and labour. As a result of these efforts, the LG Group has experienced few significant disputes during this period. However, despite efforts to create peaceful relations by opening up and maintaining new lines of communication, the labour–management relationship in most LG firms still tends to lack the voluntary and proactive participation of labour. It has become clear that the most important task is to create a spirit of mutual trust, respect and active co-operation between the parties.

Post-1997: The financial crisis—changes in labour market policies and massive dismissals

The economic slowdown and restructuring of industry impacted negatively on South Korean workers, with unemployment reaching 7.9% or 1.7 million in December 1998. As a result of the financial crisis, ER policies in South Korea focused on extending labour market flexibility to facilitate economic restructuring and on expanding the social safety net to protect unemployed workers. These environmental changes forced the LG firms to enhance the efficiency of personnel management; they also opted for shedding workers and reducing employee welfare benefits. Following the financial crisis, LG managers introduced new ER practices to determine pay based on an employee's ability and performance. In 1998, LG completely restructured its work force and dismissed 14 000 employees, or 11.6% of the total number of LG employees. On average, 14.9% of wage and fringe benefits were cut from employees' pay. In the process of restructuring, management received support from the union. Management and the union shared the same view on the seriousness of the financial crisis and the need for restructuring. In the process of cutting its workforce in all its organisations, LG has emphasised improving the ability and performance of its employees.

The future: Leap 2005

A review of the LG Group's history, taking into account the lessons learnt over the many years since the company was first founded, and a careful scanning and analysis of environmental changes, led to the LG Group announcing its new strategy, *Leap 2005: LG's Second Management Revolution*. The central objective of Leap 2005 is for each of the member firms of the LG Group to become one of the most successful and best managed companies in its particular field by the year 2005. To accomplish this goal, LG has adopted a new group level policy that emphasises the promotion of human dignity for employees and the maximisation of customer satisfaction. Voluntary employee participation in workplace organisational improvements has been identified as a critical success factor. Consequently, the rapid realisation of co-operative labour relations and enlightened ER practices have become recognised as tasks of major significance by member firms and the ER staff of the Group Chairman's Office.

The current situation

To construct an ER system and culture consistent with the Leap 2005 strategy, the following issues were identified as being areas of concern, requiring concerted efforts towards improvement:

1. management characteristics and organisation, including: the delegation of power and authority, communication, training and development, and reward systems;
2. the status of unions, including: support among members, ability of union leaders, and union legitimacy;
3. overall perceptions of ER.

Survey data relating to the above issues were collected from a sample of approximately 11 000 employees of the LG Group in 1993. The firms surveyed were from eight different LG member companies, including six manufacturing firms and two service companies.

CHARACTERISTICS OF MANAGEMENT SYSTEMS
This survey suggested that the principal concern of most LG managers was to avoid wage disputes rather than develop successful and effective systems and methods for encouraging employee participation and/or development.

The dominant management system of the LG Group companies was still based on a hierarchical delegation of power and authority (a direct report culture), with only superficial employee participation in quality control and total productivity management programs. Management was found to be more interested in the short-term use of employees rather than their long-term growth, development and contribution to the company. The management system of the LG Group of firms allows for many cross-functional training programs; however, these programs are not systematically operated, and employee training is still insufficient. Although employee evaluation systems are in place, in most instances compensation (pay) does not reflect evaluation results as it is largely determined by seniority and educational background.

In the area of decision-making, the perceptions of management and labour were very different. The managers who responded to the survey expressed the belief that most employees had sufficient power to do their jobs effectively; however, many employees felt they were given little power or discretion to do their jobs and were merely expected to follow direct orders from their superiors. Many employees also felt that the organisation was so bureaucratic that it was impossible to share information.

Employees and managers also had differing responses in regard to the perceived support and resources given to employee education and training programs. Employees complained that in order to meet their production goals they had to work overtime, leaving no time available to increase their skills through job rotation or skill-training programs.

The survey also found that employee morale was not high, with employees feeling they received no extra benefits by working hard. For example, blue-collar workers said they felt they were discriminated against in promotion. On a scale of 1 to 5, their satisfaction level on promotion opportunities was 2.2, while white-collar workers reported a satisfaction level of 2.7.

The survey also located the following problems:

1. Voluntary participation of employees is difficult in an environment of poor delegation and communication.
2. While the companies surveyed have shown an interest in further developing the skills of their employees to increase productivity, the effort thus far remains insufficient and unsystematic.
3. Current evaluation and reward systems do not motivate employees.

THE STATUS OF UNIONS

According to the results of the survey, the unions at the LG Group face two fundamental problems. First, they lack the solid support of their members. Second, they lack the management and administrative skills necessary for effectively leading their unions.

The main reasons for low employee support for union activity are the frequent power struggles among union leaders and the lack of interest in union activities among younger union members. Even though many union leaders have expressed interest in actively participating in managerial decision-making, they generally do not have an understanding of critical business issues and lack the technical skills necessary to effectively utilise and interpret financial data. At company level, unions clearly recognise and understand the need to raise the level of professionalism in union management and administration, but they have thus far been unable to achieve this objective.

THE PERCEPTION OF EMPLOYMENT RELATIONS

The survey found that, for the most part, union leaders tend to perceive the LG Group and its member companies to be managed in a relatively transparent manner. However, it is also clear that joint efforts between labour and management to improve productivity and quality have been insufficient; more systematic ways for union leaders and members to participate in the management decision-making process need to be provided.

At the workplace level, voluntary participation in quality improvement activities and in work and safety related training programs has been very low, in part because of the ineffectiveness of line management.

During collective bargaining the major issues of concern for employees and the company are wages and fringe benefits. The two key problems generally experienced in the collective bargaining process at the LG Group are that it generally takes too long to reach a final settlement, and additional requests are frequently added to the union's wage and benefit proposal after the final settlement has been reached between the parties.

The plan for improving employment relations at the LG Group

Designing and developing an ER model which could create a competitive advantage for the LG Group companies was the challenge for members of the LG Group management team, particularly the staff from the LG Group Chairman's Office. For example, benchmarking visits were made to General Motors' US Saturn plant which introduced the LG Group to an entirely new concept in terms of creating a system and culture of joint union–management ownership. At Saturn management and workers were integrally involved in the decision-making and implementation processes. LG representatives were highly impressed to find that managers and union representatives worked together, through a process of mutual agreement, when determining and deciding on wage and benefit levels. The ability of Saturn and the United Auto Workers Union to design and successfully implement individual work units, capable of continuously operating on an autonomous or self-directed team basis, also greatly impressed the group.

Similarly Motorola in the US, although a non-union company, also served as an important model for the transformation processes at LG. The group was especially impressed by Motorola's wide variety of employee participation and development programs. These included 'Total Customer Satisfaction Teams' and well designed training programs for blue-collar workers.

Japanese companies were also studied for benchmarking purposes; however, although most of these companies were unionised, the actual unions themselves were weak. In this environment any significant co-operative ER relied primarily on the initiatives and efforts of front-line supervisory leadership.

Despite considerable variation in industries and practices (and the different nomenclature used to describe co-operative and participatory activities), most of the companies benchmarked shared a common core set of values. These values included a strong emphasis on employee and work group autonomy, and on voluntary employee participation in activities to enhance organisational performance. This was seen as the principal foundation and driving force for co-operative relations between labour and management.

The basic concept

As a result of this research and considerable soul searching and planning, the central goal of the LG Group's ER strategy shifted from one of simply trying to maintain a stable and relatively peaceful ER climate (free of disputes and overt conflict) to the far more proactive goal of developing a dynamic atmosphere of 'co-operative labour–management relations'.

The philosophy that has served as the foundation of this significant change is a firm belief that co-operative ER can simultaneously improve company competitiveness and the overall quality of life for employees. This can be achieved by establishing a partnership between management and the union which, by its very nature, facilitates and encourages employees voluntarily to seek opportunities to improve not only their own performance, but also that of the company as a whole. In order to attain maximum competitiveness through co-operation, labour and management must work together as partners in a process of developing a high-performance organisation which: holds individual initiative in high esteem; encourages voluntary participation in organisational problem-solving and improvement activities; and establishes an ER culture of mutual trust by improving negotiation practices and union–management interaction.

In creating co-operative ER, the LG Group seeks to create 'best practice' companies in their respective industries as well as the finest workplaces for employees in terms of providing safe, interesting and exciting jobs. The aim is to create a context in which the philosophy of sharing mutual gains is deeply embedded in company culture and policies.

The plan for transforming labour–management relations at the

Table 11.1 The LG Group's employment relations plan

Period	Pre-1994	1995 to 1997	1998 to 2000
Concept	Hierarchical	Equal	Mutual
Management's perception of labour	Begin to perceive as an asset	Perceived as an asset	Major source of competitiveness
Management's perception of the union and its role	Passive support	Recognition of the union's positive role in the workplace	Partnership
Management's primary concern in dealing with the labour–management relationship	Maintain a stable labour relations climate in order to avoid labour disputes	Build a labour–management relationship founded upon consensus and a spirit of trust and mutual concern	Facilitate voluntary participation of employees and union leaders in management activities
Union characteristics	Weak employee support	Becoming professional	Professional
Primary ER concerns	Basic 'bread and butter' issues	Quality and productivity	Autonomy and participation

LG Group is summarised in Table 11.1. In line with this plan, instituting the reforms necessary for establishing a system of co-operative ER relations began in 1997.

To establish the initial basis and foundation for a co-operative ER culture, a trust-building plan, with a strong emphasis on creating equal relationships among the key stakeholders, was first developed.

The second step in this process was to make co-operative ER the norm rather than the exception at the LG Group, and to also develop a specific plan with steps for action and deadlines for encouraging employees to participate voluntarily.

Once co-operative labour relations in the workplace have been attained, the LG Group can expect to benefit from productivity gains and the increased quality of working life which will be experienced by employees.

The implementation plan

JOB TRAINING

To establish respect for human dignity as the foundation of the LG Group's management philosophy, it was determined that management needed to increase significantly its investment in education and training to enhance the skills, ability and knowledge of its work force. Action plans for accomplishing this objective were as follows:

1. Build educational training centres using skilled lecturers—establish a solid foundation for continuous learning through training and education.
2. Each company to make a concentrated investment in quality education and training by having members of top management participate directly in the development of quality education and training programs and activities—establish the standards and goals for delivering the highest quality to customers.
3. Each LG company to offer a program of education and training which requires only a minimum of standardised training time, combined with customised and individually designed training plans for each employee.
4. The formation of 'Co-operative Labour Relations Education and Training Operations Committees' to help develop management training goals and corresponding educational activities—each company to offer high quality, integrated and complete programs of employee training and development.
5. Each company to design a versatile plan of employee job rotation and skills upgrading through training and education. Such a plan should encourage and enforce a regular program of job rotation among blue-collar workers that introduces different skill levels and standards in co-ordination with individually customised training plans and goals.

Delegation of power

Through effective utilisation of personnel planning skills, workplace redesign and implementation skills, and strengthening workplace leadership through training and education, each company can effectively manage human resources through employee empowerment.

1. Each company should empower each section (the smallest subunit of company organisation) as a unit of management in co-ordination with the simplification of the organisation's seniority structure.
2. The role of managers is to be restructured. The supervisor's role is to be transformed from one of directing to that of coaching and providing professional expertise and guidance to sections and employee teams—significant empowerment of employees.
3. Management should seek to transform the current workplace organisation to a system based on self-directed work teams.

BUILDING FAIR EVALUATION AND REWARDS SYSTEMS
LG companies should identify and eliminate discriminatory and inconsistent ER policies and practices.

1. Management to introduce new personnel plans, with job evaluation based on the principles of skill and ability. This should eliminate the alienation of skilled workers in a system based strictly on seniority and educational background.
2. Enhance and strengthen the system of receiving suggestions, complaints and ideas from clerical workers.
3. Eliminate discrimination based on prejudice, such as job discrimination based on gender.
4. Each company to provide support for each individual's personal goals.
5. Each company to provide competitive welfare and fringe benefits for its employees while maintaining its competitiveness in its respective business field.
6. Company level 'Human Resource Development Committees' should be established and strengthened; the breadth and sophistication of human resource information systems to be expanded.
7. Introduce and successfully implement employee evaluation systems—including customer, subordinate, peer and superior evaluation—which are fair and objective.

SHARING OF INFORMATION

It was decided that the management of the LG Group and company performance should be more open and provide more access to financial performance information and management information systems data. This would encourage employees to become more aware of management policies and give them the capability to contribute and become more involved in management decisions and processes. Specific actions recommended for increasing employee business skills, financial understanding and management capabilities included:

1. *Enhanced Management Information Systems:* Management should increase the opportunity for employees to gain access to information on company performance through the creation of greatly expanded and more participatory internal communication and management information systems.
2. *Shared Ownership of Company Goals and Values:* Management must strengthen and encourage two-way communication between superiors and subordinates, provide greater harmony and communication between departments and other sub-units, activate a wide array of functional collaboration and problem-solving through the creation of joint labour–management task forces, and provide a broader scope of information interchange, such as with the local community and employees' families.

ENHANCING UNION PROFESSIONALISM AND EFFECTIVENESS

Although management at the LG Group had traditionally preferred and actually encouraged a paternalistic relationship with workers and union leaders, it was agreed that a major priority for achieving a higher level of company performance, and also an improved quality of working life for employees, required that managers support union efforts to achieve a greater degree of independence and autonomy while also encouraging the development of an increased level of professionalism on the part of union leaders. Steps recommended for achieving these objectives were as follows:

1. Management is to encourage the union to achieve greater financial independence from the company through increases in union dues and fees, through arbitration and a more open public sharing of union financial information.
2. Union leaders are to be encouraged to strengthen their leadership through leadership education programs and processes.
3. The level of union professionalism is to be raised through training and educational support.
4. Union leaders to be supported in developing standardised labour activities manuals and comprehensive education and training programs.

It was also agreed that the LG Group unions and their leaders would have to take some important steps on their own to increase union credibility, professionalism and the rationalisation of union organisation and administration. Specific actions recommended were as follows:

1. Unions should seek to change the role of union leadership and establish educational programs to teach union leaders how to serve effectively in the role of co-ordinators and advocates to meet employee needs and answer members' questions.
2. Union leaders should develop a stronger consciousness and concern for production performance, product quality and customer service through appropriate quality–education and the formation of a joint 'Labour–Management Quality Planning Committee' and a 'Team Activity Support Committee'. Similarly, a more positive attitude on the part of all union members should be secured through the significant enlargement of channels of direct communications between workers and managers, and through expanded union-sponsored educational programs offered to the general membership.

EMPLOYMENT RELATIONS

In order to achieve a new ER system and culture, a first priority for the LG Group was the facilitation of a significant change in the stereotypical views held by senior management regarding the conduct of ER. A key strategy in this transformation process has been a continuation of the benchmarking LG ER practices and policies against those of the most advanced and progressive companies in the world. The ER managers have also sought to clarify and reaffirm top management's support for, and sincere interest in, creating and continuing to cultivate a co-operative ER culture. They also strengthened the role of leading ER executives and their staff at the firm level, and worked to establish common group-wide standards of fairness in the conduct of management's roles in bargaining and the implementation of ER practices. These include:

1. completing and formalising the channels used in collective bargaining through establishing wage and result level rules for negotiations;
2. creating joint 'Labour–Management Co-operative Committees' for improving production quality and production efficiency;
3. improving the techniques used in collective bargaining, such as encouraging pre-bargaining meetings and problem-solving, and introducing techniques of win/win and mutual gains bargaining;
4. increasing the bargaining authority of ER managers and the top management of individual LG Group companies;
5. publicly supporting a philosophy of ER co-operation and fairness on the part of management and union leaders in the conduct of negotiations and the process of collective bargaining;
6. encouraging managers and union leaders to set the tone for a co-operative ER culture through their daily interaction and work together on labour–management issues and problems;
7. opening up the process of evaluating management strategy to union leaders by inviting them to attend and participate in management strategy meetings;
8. re-establishing the norms and practices of collective bargaining by working together with union leaders in collaboratively setting the basic principles of collective bargaining and the roles of bargaining in the ongoing operations of the firm and individual workplaces;
9. instituting labour–management collaboration meetings for engaging in joint problem-solving and decision-making related to quality, production, wage levels and other ER problems.

LG Electronics: Towards more co-operative labour relations

LG Electronics (LGE), a subsidiary of the LG group, is a model for the creation of co-operative employment relations at LG. While a number of issues remain to be solved, the story of LGE shows the benefits that can accrue from successfully developing a sustainable healthy partnership between management and labour.

LGE is a global manufacturer of electrical and electronic products, with 59 branches, 18 sales subsidiaries and 31 manufacturing subsidiaries spanning 171 countries. LGE operates 26 R&D facilities at home and abroad in TV, audio and video systems, computers, information systems, multimedia products and thin-film-transistor liquid crystal displays. The acquisition of Zenith in 1995 facilitated advances in digital HDTV, video on demand, CD-interactive products and other multimedia applications.

LGE was established in 1958 and by the late 1990s had approximately 33 700 employees. However, the total had fallen to 22 800 by January 2000. Annual sales in 1999 amounted to 10.5 trillion won (approximately US$9.3 billion as at January 2000) and total capital was 632 billion won (approximately US$559 million as at January 2000). The union which represents LGE's non-managerial work force was established in 1963 and by 1997 had 17 000 members, but membership was only 11 200 in early 2000. As well as its main headquarters, the LGE union has eight branches established at workplaces located throughout South Korea.

LG's Second Management Revolution signals a new level of commitment to customer values, high ethical principles and leadership through example. The goal for the individual LG Group companies, including LGE, is to successfully achieve a transformation to a position of worldwide leadership by the year 2005. By this date LGE is committed to achieving sales of US$74 billion and an average rate of profit of 6% by producing top grade products in terms of both quality and quantity. By providing courteous, quick and responsive service, LGE is committed to ensuring complete customer satisfaction with both LGE products and service. LGE promises its workers a communal labour–management relationship on the basis of trust, mutual respect and the realisation of the vision of all employees.

During the late 1980s LGE experienced two big industrial disputes. These disputes constituted the biggest crisis faced by LGE management since the establishment of the company and resulted in Samsung successfully repositioning itself ahead of LGE as the market leader in the field of consumer electronics. These disturbing events resulted in a significant reduction in LGE's market share, the loss of many important customers and a significant deterioration in product quality. Because of these stoppages distrust began to spread among some of LGE's most important customers, who lost confidence in the firm's ability to deliver top quality products on time and in the quantities ordered.

In 1987, the year of the first major strike, all work stopped and the dispute lasted for ten days, at a high cost to LGE. From this point ER was increasingly characterised by conflict. In 1989, a second strike occurred that lasted for 39 days. This cost the company very dearly in terms of lost sales.

In spite of the high economic and social costs that resulted from this period of labour–management strife at LGE, some valuable lessons were learnt by management and the union during this period. The 1989 strike served as a 'wake up call' to both parties, alerting them to the very real need to try and create a new and more co-operative approach to ER. External forces, such as the opening up of the South Korean market to foreign electronics products, also accelerated the desire to change the ER culture at LGE. Management began to realise the importance of ER to company success. Management learnt that ER were a core aspect of company management, and they also realised that ensuring customer satisfaction could only be achieved if employee needs were also satisfied. A fair system of evaluation, rewards and discipline upon which everyone could agree was necessary. It was also necessary to create a climate of mutual understanding and respect between the company and its employees: individual rights and responsibilities needed to be clearly identified and protected and a strong sense of shared duty of care and support had to be encouraged and nurtured. Only in these ways could LG achieve a viable approach to ER.

Management changes and transformation

LGE management came to realise that it was essential to build a foundation of mutual respect and trust between labour and management. Therefore, since 1990, LGE has introduced a series of programs for the purpose of establishing a co-operative ER culture. These programs include efforts to build a climate of mutual trust, ensure continuous improvement in employee wages and welfare, and to construct a safe and pleasant working environment.

Recognising that labour is an important company asset, and not a mere factor of production or production expense, LGE began to change its management practices in order to regain the trust of its employees. Of first importance to LGE was the education of all workers on the importance of co-operative ER. To further emphasise the central importance of labour–management relations, the responsibility for ER was shifted from a staff to a line function and co-ordination was greatly strengthened between ER related departments.

In 1989, through holding a 'Oneness Parade', LGE tried to promote harmony and unity between labour and management. Extensive training on economic realities, the business environment, the desirable attitudes of LG workers, teamwork and South Korean labour law was also provided for union officials and employees. In 1990 teams were created to enhance mutual understanding and openness. Other educational programs included training in problem-solving skills (1991), customer satisfaction (1992) and quality innovation (1993).

Since line managers, rather than staff, were considered to be the key agents of change at LGE, the company endorsed the expansion of the role of line managers to include the resolution of everyday grievances and the maintenance of employee motivation. Moreover, various tools were developed to assist line managers in performing their new role more easily, such as the development of employee performance appraisal forms and an on-the-job training (OJT) guidebook.

LGE also strengthened co-operation between the ER staff at the Chairman's Office and the member companies. The role of the Chairman's Office staff was redesigned so that they could concentrate on formulating short and long-term ER strategies, provide support for collective bargaining at member firms and develop group-wide welfare programs. ER staff at individual workplaces began to focus their efforts on resolving employee grievances, administering Labour Relations Committees at the factory level and collecting employees' opinions. In addition, LGE constructed a more rapid and efficient system of information sharing. This included regular and irregular meetings among staff members and line managers to share information and ideas, and communication vehicles such as the company newsletter, *Labor Relations Bulletin*. This has helped to ensure that major issues are communicated to all employees working at LGE's numerous work sites.

Continuous improvement in wages and employee welfare

LGE has continually monitored wages and employee welfare and has striven to improve the total quality of life for its employees. For example, realising the importance of employee housing needs LGE has, since 1989, provided loans for home purchases at lower than market interest rates. Other efforts have included more travel opportunities for employees, provision of educational fees for children, group life insurance, wedding anniversary gifts and medical insurance. These welfare programs were designed to reflect the varying needs of employees as they progress through different life-cycle stages. Through the years these programs have continued to expand. Thus, LGE recently adopted a flexible working time schedule and a biweekly five-day working system.

Construction of a pleasant and safe working environment

LGE has upgraded its factories and offices to make them safe and more pleasant places in which to work. Nine teams, with the role of educating employees on important safety issues and safety-related programs, have been created. As a result of these efforts, LGE received an award from the national government for its superior workplace safety record. LGE has also made substantial investments in creating environmentally friendly management practices. It has established a committee to deal with environmental issues, and has also made large investments in developing environmentally friendly products and technologies.

Union activities

The 1989 crisis, a period of frequent and large-scale strikes, also caused the LGE union to rethink its relationship with management and the company. The union has recognised the need to develop a 'co-operative relationship' with management. Various efforts made by LGE management have helped change the union's position. The union has voluntarily chosen to participate in a variety of innovations to help raise productivity and enhance product quality. The union has also launched a campaign with the specific purpose of trying to create a new workplace culture. The campaign promotes respect for the company, elimination of inefficiencies, improvement of the company's image, revitalisation of the organisation and active involvement in management innovations. In addition, union leaders have also voluntarily served in the role of sales representatives for LGE. Through engaging in these activities, the union has increasingly evolved in its role as a natural partner of management. In LGE's new vision the role of the union is to become one of a trusting and productive partner working together with management on the tasks of improving company competitiveness and the quality of working life for LGE employees.

The LGE union has also made 'A Resolution for Coexistence and Co-prosperity'. This resolution promotes innovations which increase competitiveness and enhance the quality of life through productive ER with more participation and co-operation. It was established through a bargaining settlement reached in 1993. The main points of this resolution are as follows:

1. In order to achieve the goals of the company and its vision for the future, labour and management must work together voluntarily in a spirit of co-operation.
2. A competitive edge will be developed by creating the best-selling

products through intensive research and development and innovation.

3. The salary and ranking system must be restructured to ensure that employees have a better quality of life and have pride in their role as LG workers.

4. Keeping a healthy labour–management relationship requires that both parties respect each other's rights.

Under the slogan 'The Company which has a union has a greater competitive advantage than the company without', the union at LGE has sought to actively and voluntarily participate in developing management innovations and creating a new ER culture. For example, in putting its new philosophy into practice, the LGE union voluntarily organised a maintenance team that went on a special service tour. Union members have also become actively involved in actually selling the products they produce on the streets of South Korea in an effort to promote the company and increase sales volume. An Innovation Team for improving productivity was created within the union at the Gumi monitor plant, with the specific purpose of increasing productivity by 200%.

Creating a new ER culture

Such efforts from both sides resulted in the joint creation of a 'Charter of Labour Relations', announced in 1995. The Charter includes:

1. a reinforcement of the commitment to build a labour–management partnership and create a new labour–management culture;

2. creation of a flexible and creative organisational culture that provides employees with the finer things in life and a quality working environment in which high potential individuals can become high performance individuals; and

3. a commitment to manage the company with integrity.

LGE's joint declaration of the 'Charter of Labour Relations' of 1995 appears to have been reasonably successful. During the post-1997 financial crisis, management and labour agreed on a wage freeze and drastic cuts in fringe benefits. On the other hand, LGE increased its investment in training and continued to communicate with the union and its members. Further, LG improved product and services quality, partly as a result of the partnership between management and labour; LGE recorded a sales revenue of US$9.3 billion and a net profit of US$177 million in 1999. It is expected that the sales revenue and especially profits will increase in the following years.

LGE has also declared a new corporate vision, 'Digital LG'. The main themes of this vision are:

- digital technology leadership;
- globalisation;
- creating value for people; and
- innovative reorganisation.

The successful implementation of this vision will depend on many factors including the changing nature of ER. For example, after the expected record high profit of 1999, the union may demand a high wage increase during the year 2000 bargaining session. The current government's political, economic, and social reform initiatives will impact on the corporate governance system of *chaebols*. The full implications of the government's initiatives for LGE's employment relations are not yet completely clear.

Conclusions

This chapter has briefly examined ER challenges faced by the LG Group and described the new model of ER that LG has developed to achieve higher productivity and an improved quality of working life. As a successful example of this process, the experiences of LGE were presented. The LG group is trying to restructure its labour–management relationship so every member of the group fully realises that the only way to survive is through management innovation, with labour and management voluntarily and wholeheartedly participating in innovation activities.

The major implications of this case study can be summarised as follows. First, without management innovation, co-operative ER cannot be achieved. For labour–management relations to be a positive-sum game, these innovations should enable the company to achieve superior performance and the capacity to provide employees with better rewards.

Second, much time and effort is required from top management to develop a constructive labour–management culture. The ER department cannot achieve the development of co-operative employment relations by itself. The labour–management relationship should be viewed as a profit-creating relationship, rather than a cost-creating one.

Third, the company should support increased independence and professionalism on the part of the union, and provide education for union leaders. A union that lacks professionalism is unable to get the full support of its members and lacks effective management strategies for administering union business because of a high turn-over of union officials.

Fourth, to be successful all these activities should be conducted consistently and systematically over time. Many companies only seriously consider the labour–management relationship when faced by a critical problem, such as a strike. Such focused attention tends to fade when the strike is settled. The LG Group has chosen a different path and spent a year analysing its ER, the optimal structure for creating a co-operative labour–management model, and a plan and a schedule for the implementation of the model. So far the LG Group has been successful in implementing this process as planned, with the continuous support and attention of top management.

12 Employment relations at a Taiwanese semiconductor firm: TSMC

Meiyu Fang

According to Porter (1998), 'clusters' are striking features of every national and regional state; they are also found in the cities of industrialised nations. Clusters are geographic concentrations of interconnected companies and institutions in a particular industry. Silicon Valley and Hollywood are well known examples of clusters.

In 1970 the government of Taiwan invested massively to develop the Hsin-Chu Science-Based Industrial Park. The Industry Park, located near Taipei, became the centre of the third largest high-tech industry in the world. In the late 1990s it accounted for a third of Taiwan's manufacturing exports and a major share of the world's computer production. Total revenue from the Park comprised 47% of Taiwan's export earnings (*Statistics Quarterly* 1997). Certain industries in the Park have been offered special privileges, including tax reductions; however, due to its success, the Park is rapidly filling. In the late 1990s the Park housed 240 firms generating a combined annual revenue of approximately US$12 billion.

Taiwan's investment in infrastructure and new equipment to increase its chip-making capacity reflects its aim to expand its presence in the semiconductor industry. Taiwan has about a 9% share of the world memory chip market. This appears relatively small compared with South Korea's 40% share. Taiwanese semiconductor firms invested an amount equal to their revenues in 1997, whereas South Korean firms invested less than 40%. In absolute terms, for the first time Taiwan spent more on increasing its semiconductor capacity than South Korea. A reduction in capital spending by South Korean firms—such as Samsung, LG Semicon and Hyundai Electronics—was in part due to the Asian economic crisis. Japanese firms are also spending less and are paying Taiwanese companies to make chips for them on a contract basis. It is predicted that Taiwan's share of the world memory chip market may increase to more than 15% (*The Economist* 1998).

A new development, the 'pure foundry', which focuses on integrated circuit (IC) manufacturing services, has become an industry in its own right. The fabrication process used to be integrated with other steps in the chip-making processes. Then firms began to separate into the different sections of the production process, such as silicon manufacturing, IC packaging, and testing (Wilson 1996). Taiwan's share of the world market for such foundry work is expected to reach 70% (*The Economist* 1998).

Taiwan Semiconductor Manufacturing Company

Taiwan Semiconductor Manufacturing Company (TSMC), located in the Hsin-Chu Science-Based Industrial Park, is a joint venture between the government of Taiwan, Philips Electronics NV of the Netherlands and private investors. Established in 1987, it was the world's first dedicated foundry operator. According to a survey conducted by *Common Wealth Magazine* (1998), TSMC, with revenues of US$1.3 billion, ranked eleventh among the top 1000 manufacturing companies in Taiwan. TSMC currently operates five fabrication factories in the Industrial Park. A new manufacturing centre that will employ an estimated 2000 workers is also planned for Tainan, in southern Taiwan. TSMC has also invested overseas. WaferTech, established in 1996 and located in the US, was a joint venture between TSMC and several long-standing customers. It was operating at full capacity by 1998.

The work force at TSMC grew from approximately 1000 workers in 1987 to almost 6000 in 1999. Because the semiconductor industry usually requires more research and development (R&D) employees than other industries, its work force generally exhibits a higher than average level of education. In TSMC, 40% of the work force have completed high school, 38% have junior college or college degrees and over 20% have Masters or PhD degrees. More than 60% of the work force are less than 30 years old. The average age of the TSMC work force is approximately 33 years.

Virtual foundry

One feature of TSMC is that the firm's charter precludes it from designing or manufacturing its own IC products. According to the Chairman of TSMC, Dr Morris Chang, TSMC's long-term vision is to offer a comprehensive range of services including a 'Virtual Fab' for TSMC's customers around the world. It is generally acknowledged that the capital investment entry level into the semiconductor industry is at least US$1 billion, to which must be added a fixed cost of US$600 million per year for equipment (Wilson 1996). The barriers for entry into this industry are very high. Not only does the technology demand high levels of expertise, but to win business, dedicated foundries must not have an ownership link with any firm that designs or manufactures its own IC products. Bob Tsao, Chairman of United Microelectronics Co., stated, 'It is not easy for a big company to have the expertise of being flexible about customers' needs while maintaining high-quality manufacturing' (Wilson 1996:28).

TSMC turned the above barriers to entry into its own special competitive advantage and developed the concept of the 'Virtual Fab'. Under this arrangement, TSMC acts as the customers' own manufacturing facility. The 'Virtual Fab' is an integrated system whereby TSMC's clients access the technology, information and support they need. Therefore, customers can gain access to a manufacturing operation without the huge investment and maintenance required of an in-house facility. Moreover, customers monitor the manufacturing progress of their IC orders through interconnected and interactive computer systems.

TSMC envisioned the concept of the specialist foundry, creating what has become a multibillion dollar industry. TSMC has committed more than US$14 billion towards capacity expansion and leading edge facilities over the next decade: by the year 2000 it was producing more than two million 8-inch equivalent wafers. From 1992, until the Asian economic crisis hit in 1997, TSMC was booked to capacity. Seventy per cent of TSMC's customers are non-foundry chip companies, so TSMC can break even, irrespective of a given customer's silicon cycle. The annual revenues of TSMC grew dramatically during the 1990s, with sales reaching US$1 billion in 1996.

TSMC workers are encouraged to exhibit pride in their organisation and the culture is energetic and results driven. The Human Resource (HR) Division is guided by the ten business philosophies created by the founder, Morris Chang (see Table 12.1). In many Taiwanese companies the business philosophy is not taken very seriously by the workers; however, in TSMC workers are encouraged to implement these philosophies in their daily operations and policy-making.

Performance management and development

Because of the profits being realised in the semiconductor industry, more semiconductor firms have turned to the foundry business for

Table 12.1 TSMC's ten business philosophies

1. Integrity
We tell the truth. We believe the record of our achievements is the best proof of our merit. Once we make a commitment, we devote ourselves completely to meeting that commitment. We compete with competitors to our fullest within the limits of the law. We also respect the intellectual property rights of others. We maintain an objective, consistent and impartial attitude with vendors.

2. Focusing on the core business: IC foundry
We are a dedicated IC foundry, and do not distract ourselves with other pursuits.

3. Aiming at the world market
Our target is, and has always been, the global market. We recognise that the semiconductor business has no national boundaries, and that to be competitive anywhere we must be competitive around the whole world.

4. Pursuing long-term strategies
We truly believe that a person, or a company, that does not plan carefully for the future will soon face challenges in the present. We believe that if we do a good job of long-term planning and execution we will greatly reduce the need for crisis management.

5. Treating customers as partners
At TSMC, customers come first. Their success is our success, and we value their ability to compete as we value our own.

6. Building quality into all aspects of the business
Every TSMC employee is responsible for providing the highest quality service. Our greatest goal is to achieve and maintain complete customer satisfaction.

7. Constant innovation
Innovation is the wellspring of TSMC's growth. It is vital to all sectors of our business, from strategic planning, to marketing, management, technology, and production.

8. Creating a dynamic and enjoyable working environment
To retain talented people who share our goals and interests, we work hard to foster a dynamic and enjoyable working environment.

9. Keeping communication channels open
TSMC has implemented an open-style management system designed to keep all lines of communication open in the working environment. Everyone welcomes constructive criticism and is willing to seek improvement in his or her working role.

10. Caring for employees and shareholders and being a good corporate citizen
Employees and shareholders are important constituents of our company. Our goal is to provide salary and benefit packages that are above the industry average. We also aim to earn a return on investment above the industry average.

Table 12.2 A benchmark of revenue and operating income in the IC industry

Company	Revenue in US$ billion	Operating income in US$ billion	No. of workers	Revenue per worker (US$'000s)	Operating income per worker (US$'000s)
Intel	25.1	9.89	63 700	394	155
TSMC	1.5	0.54	5 593	276	97
UMC	1.2	0.27	4 252	272	59
TI	9.8	0.62	44 140	221	14

Note: UMC = United Microelectronics; TI = Texas Instrument.
Source: TSMC (1997).

IC manufacturing. Some forecasts predict that by the year 2000 almost 20% of the world's ICs will be produced in foundries. As a pioneer in the semiconductor foundry industry, TSMC believes that foundry manufacturing services will continue to play an increasingly important role in the IC industry.

In spite of optimistic predictions for the future of the foundry business, the economic slump in 1996 saw the price of memory chips fall. Consequently, many memory chip manufacturers began to lose money, while the Asian economic crisis in 1997 made the situation worse. Consequently, the total market value of the semi-conductor industry worldwide decreased by approximately 10% in 1997, but TSMC was still able to record a 14% growth in sales in that year. After it peaked in 1995, some commentators believed that the four-year cycle of the semiconductor industry would come to an end; however, the evidence is mixed. The strategy of TSMC is to keep the organisation lean and flexible so the firm can quickly profit from future upturns in the market.

TSMC often benchmarks its productivity with other leading competitors, such as Intel, Texas Instrument and United Microelec-tronics Co. As shown in Table 12.2, in the late 1990s TSMC's revenue per worker was US$276 000, which was relatively good compared with its competitors. For instance, the total revenue of Texas Instrument was US$9.8 billion, which was more than six times that of TSMC's total revenue of US$1.5 billion; however, the revenue per worker at Texas Instrument was US$55 000 less than at TSMC. Intel's worker productivity was the best among the manufacturers listed in Table 12.2, with Intel being regarded as a role model organisation by TSMC. TSMC often benchmarks its operations with Intel.

TSMC's sales and operating income per worker decreased from its peak in 1996 (see Figure 12.1), while its production of wafers

Figure 12.1 Sales and operating income per worker

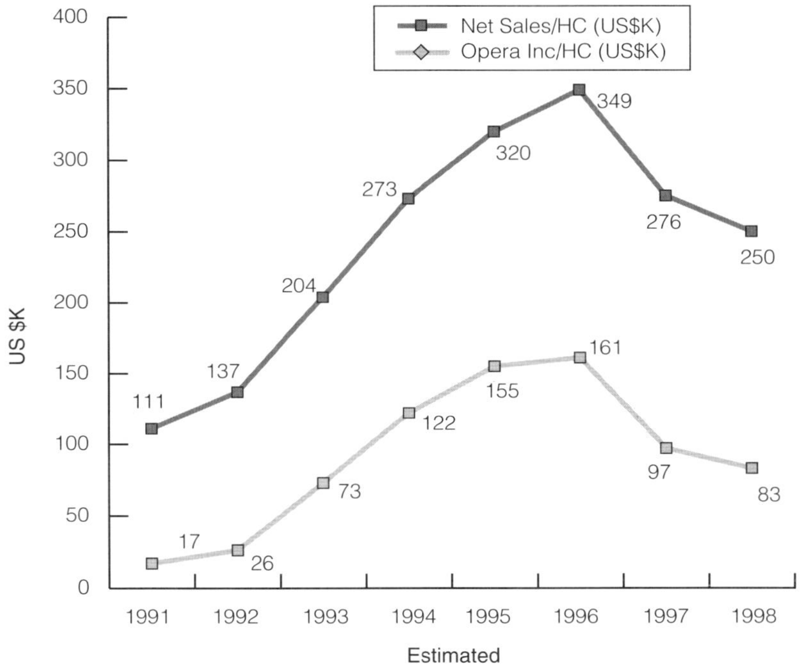

Source: TSMC

per head also went down after 1997 (see Figure 12.2). The slow recovery of the semiconductor industry was partly due to world economic conditions. However, TSMC strove to combat such problems from within and believed that the late 1990s were a good time to examine the competitiveness of the firm, which for much of the 1990s had been busy dealing with its rapid growth. Therefore, the HR division initiated a new program in 1998, entitled 'Performance Management & Development' (PMD), to restructure the performance management process.

The main theme in PMD is multiple-source performance evaluations, with the final evaluation being a combined result from several review processes. In addition to performance management, TSMC believes that employee development is the key activity in PMD because a good development plan can increase workers' competencies, which will contribute to the firm's performance. Mr Wu, Director of the HR Division, believes that the traditional training curriculum, designed and based on a training needs survey, is not

Figure 12.2 Wafer production per worker

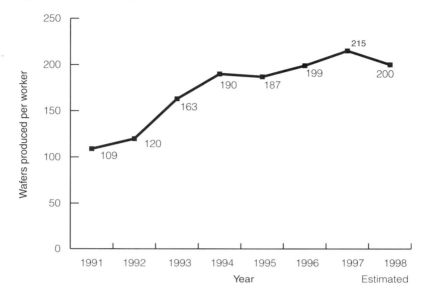

Source: TSMC

as effective as job based training. Instead of asking what the training needs are, the top level supervisor should have a clear mind about the kind of competencies that will contribute to a winning organis-ation. It should be the top level managers' responsibility to communicate the required professional or core competencies to their subordinates. The subordinates then have a few days to think about the goals, before coming back to discuss them with their supervisor. Supervisors should have a good understanding of how their workers operate. In sum, the PMD is a results driven program.

At the first phase, the HR Division was reorganised into two sections: the 'Centre of Excellence' and the 'Site Service'. The 'Centre of Excellence' is responsible for making strategic HR plans and delivering HR expertise. The 'Site Service' is responsible for the delivery of HR functions, such as staffing, compensation and employee relations. The short-term goal of PMD is to enhance current on-line communication within the firm. The long-term goal is to integrate and globalise the HR system.

The five principles of PMD are as follows:

1. people are the most important asset;
2. maximise employee performance and potential;

3. provide a supportive environment to develop employees;
4. align individual goals to team and corporate goals;
5. create a culture of meritocracy and strive for excellence.

Implementation schedule of PMD

The HR Division and all line managers are involved with the implementation of PMD. The HR Division first communicated the concept of PMD to the line managers, and their departments, in face-to-face meetings. Second, the HR Division announced the PMD change processes to all workers. Third, HR staff and line managers began to work together to carry out the necessary education and training programs to implement the program. Fourth, the line managers began to implement the PMD with their subordinates, assisted by the HR Division. Supervisors and subordinates have been engaged in the PMD process through goal setting, development plans, feedback and coaching. Finally, the HR Division collects, consolidates and reviews the results of the PMD process.

There are four types of performance reviews in PMD: periodic, mid-year, cross-team and joint reviews. The periodic and mid-year reviews monitor ongoing performance evaluations and help to create a development plan. The purpose of the ongoing performance reviews is to avoid unexpected results at the end of the year. The mid-year review starts with an interview between the worker and his or her immediate supervisor. The purpose is to review the worker's accomplishments, update goals and identify the support or resources required for the worker to achieve his or her goals. The department head has the responsibility of identifying high and low performers and providing corrective action for the low performers. In the final stage, a cross-review team examines and discusses the decisions made by the mid-year review. Usually, the HR division will participate and facilitate the divisional review meetings.

The objectives of the cross-team reviews are to provide the opportunity to learn across different teams, to set standards of fairness and to develop an 'action plan' for poor performers. The section heads will identify the best and worst performers in lower job grades, while the department heads will identify the best and worst performers in higher job grades. Their decisions with regard to the good and poor performers are then forwarded to the cross-team reviewers. After passing through the cross-team review, the head of the department or the division grants the final endorsement. The cross-team review is conceptually similar to the idea of a 360°

feedback on performance, except that there is no evaluation from the subordinates in PMD.

The last performance review scheme is a joint review that emphasises teamwork and customer orientation. First, the line managers decide who should become members of the joint review team. The most appropriate candidates are usually the workers' supervisors and major customers. The timing for the joint review is in the period from January to February, when new projects are beginning or new goals are being set. Then the joint reviewers observe and coach the workers' performance from March to December. The joint reviewers give performance feedback to the workers at the beginning of the following year.

New evaluation scale for performance

In addition to a clear behavioural definition for each performance level, a forced distribution of the frequency in each level is also necessary for the purpose of distinguishing good and poor performers. Therefore, less than 10% of the whole division get 'outstanding'; 25% to 45% get 'excellent'; 50% to 70% get 'good'; 5% get 'improvement needed'; and 5% get 'unacceptable'. The unacceptable performers will be rotated to a job in which it is hoped they can make progress and are given a period of time to show some improvement in their performance. If no progress has occurred after a certain date, the workers may be asked to leave.

The five levels of performance standards as outlined in the PMD are as follows:

1. *Outstanding:* Workers with this rating usually perform more than their job requirements, can work independently and require little guidance or assistance from others.
2. *Excellent:* Workers sometimes meet or exceed job requirements, but still require some direct supervision or guidance. Generally they can work independently.
3. *Good:* Workers can meet their job requirements, but also require some direct supervision or guidance.
4. *Improvement needed:* Workers cannot consistently meet the job requirements. They might require some improvement of performance. They might require a greater amount of supervision and guidance to produce adequately.
5. *Unacceptable:* Workers with such ratings usually perform below their job requirements. There is a lack of interest in improving performance. This group of workers has difficulty in doing the job as indicated. Unless some improvement within a specified period occurs, it is likely that their jobs would be terminated.

Performance reinforced

TSMC's remuneration (compensation) system includes a fourteen-month annual salary, the quarterly incentive bonus and the yearly profit sharing. None of them directly links with individual performance. In other words, the good performers and poor performers might be rewarded with similar amounts of compensation. The salary level in Taiwan is based on a combination of a worker's education, tenure and/or work experience—profit sharing is linked to the firm's financial performance. Therefore, the difference in pay between good and poor performers should be more significant, as there is little incentive for workers to make greater efforts if compensation packages and/or career advancement opportunities do not recognise individual performance. The next step for the PMD process is to make pay structures better reflect the differences in the efforts that workers put into their jobs. Thus, the differences between key performers and poor performers will become more significant.

PART V

An international institutional perspective

13 The APEC forum: Human resources development and employment relations issues

Nigel Haworth and Stephen Hughes

The Asia Pacific Economic Co-operation (APEC) forum was created in 1989. It comprises twenty-one economies with a combined Gross Domestic Product (GDP) of over US$16 trillion in 1996 and 45% of global trade. APEC's emergence reflects economic and geopolitical developments on the international stage. Asia's phenomenal industrialisation and export success since World War II has been one factor promoting regional linkages. The Cold War created another framework for regional collaboration, paradoxically reinforced by the end of that confrontation. If trade liberalisation and support for the outcome of the Uruguay Round of negotiations on tariff reductions associated with the General Agreement on Tariffs and Trade (GATT) is the fundamental purpose of APEC, a range of associated issues has also arisen. Some of these issues are not controversial—for example, talks on energy, transport and telecommunications policies may be seen as complementary to the trade liberalisation agenda. Similarly, a focus on the environment strikes a universal chord, if with different resonances.

Specific human resources development (HRD) issues fall within this broadly uncontroversial category of APEC concerns, but broader employment relations (ER) including human resources management (HRM) issues are less obviously perceived as legitimate. For economic and political reasons, some ER issues are more problematic and often divisive—for example, migration policies, labour standards, human rights and security issues. APEC traditionally sought to overcome the problems raised in relation to the latter group of issues by attempting to keep its agendas firmly focused on trade liberalisation and its subsequent benefits. In particular, HRD policies promoted within the APEC agenda reflected the belief frequently expressed within APEC circles that HRD issues are central to the maximisation of trade liberalisation's advantages.

Since 1997, however, a combination of factors has led to a

widening of issues addressed in the HRD area. These factors include the emergence of a strong focus in APEC on economic and technical co-operation (the ECOTECH agenda), the impact of the 1997–98 Asian financial crisis, and the desire, particularly on the part of the US government, to extend APEC's activities to include issues such as labour standards.

The context of APEC's development

There are six processes which intersect in the creation and operation of APEC and which directly or indirectly impinge on HRD/HRM issues. These are:

- contemporary internationalisation
- economic crisis and restructuring in the OECD (Organisation for Economic Co-operation and Development) economies
- trade liberalisation and the outcome of the Uruguay Round
- contemporary regional bloc formation
- Asian economic growth and internationalisation
- international neo-regulation

While space constraints do not permit a detailed discussion of this intersection, some introductory points may be usefully made. First, postwar internationalisation has not only resulted in a growing international economic integration on the basis of transnational investment, but also has caused a parallel internationalisation of HRD/HRM issues, policies and practices. The growth of international trade has focused attention on issues such as comparative and competitive advantage, productivity and flexibility which, through their impact on production systems, have contributed to the internationalisation of HRD/HRM issues. The internationalisation of management training has also contributed to this process.

Second, the economic reversals faced in particular by many OECD economies since the 1970s have given rise to a standard set of policy prescriptions for recovery—that is, the model based on deregulation, reduced state intervention and market processes. In the HRD/HRM context, a subset of this standard package has developed, based on deregulated labour markets, flexible labour strategies and reformed bargaining regimes, and parallel reforms in training and education. While there is no automatic translation of these packages from the OECD economies to the broad Asian region, their existence substantially conditions the debate in APEC about HRD/HRM developments, particularly in relation to the interventions by the US, Japan, Canada, Australia and New Zealand. The Asian financial crisis has firmly focused the attention of affected economies' policy-makers on these packages as they search for routes out of the crisis.

Third, trade liberalisation has been promoted as a panacea for contemporary economic ills. Building on the growth of international trade in the post-war period, trade liberalisation meshes completely with the orthodox, 'more market' approach to economic reform, focusing attention on comparative advantage in the international sphere and domestic strategies for international competitiveness. The outcomes of the Uruguay Round have intensified this process, creating a powerful international lobby for trade liberalisation. The search for international competitiveness opens up a range of policy options including 'downward' and 'upward' restructuring, depending on the sector and the economy (Sengenberger 1991). The choice between these broad options has important implications for the mix of national HRD policies put in place and, also, for dominant ER practices.

Fourth, regionalisation of the international economy has advanced. With the emergence of the expanding European Union (EU), ASEAN, NAFTA and, now, APEC (to name only the major economic blocs), regionalised economic strategies have come to be associated to a greater or lesser extent with regionalised social policies. Economic regionalisation brings in its train the possibility of regionalisation of HRD debate and policy formation. In the case of APEC, it is recognised that shared knowledge about HRD issues may improve policy prescriptions and contribute to increased competitiveness. However, also in the case of APEC (and in contrast to the EU), member economies are firmly opposed to the development of complex social policy packages alongside the trade liberalisation focus. In other words, any interest in HRD (and any subsequent impact on ER) is primarily driven by APEC's economic agenda. Nevertheless, the narrow focus of attention in APEC on trade liberalisation is sufficiently wide to include HRD issues as part of an economic and technical co-operation program complementing the liberalisation agenda.

Fifth, a group of East and South-East Asian economies has experienced spectacular economic development and export success since 1960. This success has been based in part on shared policies— for example, a strong export orientation, degrees of state direction of the economy, high savings ratios—and also in part on differing prescriptions—for example, varying levels of dependence on foreign direct investment (FDI), contrasting autonomies of the business sector, differing legitimacies for and styles of labour organisation. HRD policies have been a central theme of this success. The issues confronting these economies included the management of the shift from rural to urban based production, the educational infrastructure required to create the skill base needed for export oriented growth and the servicing technocracy, the provision of appropriate skill mixes as technical parameters shift upwards, policies to deal with age and gender issues, and compensation and social insurance regimes—to name the most obvious. Today, the Asian economies in APEC cover the spectrum between Japan—a mature industrial economy facing HRD problems similar to those in the US and the EU—and Thailand, in the first flushes of industrialisation and coping with the gamut of HRD issues, from urbanisation and labour market formation to advanced technical training.

Of course, the financial instabilities in the Asian region in the late 1990s caused a significant re-evaluation of the 'Asian miracle'. One effect of the crisis was a shift in emphasis within the most affected economies from HRD to short-term measures for dealing with rapidly rising unemployment (Haworth 1998). How this short-term focus ties in with APEC's medium-to-long-term HRD focus is an issue still to be resolved.

Sixth, there is what may be called contemporary neo-regulation, by which is meant the range of international provisions imposing conditions and standards on international economic activities. Primarily at intergovernmental level on the basis of bilateral or multilateral arrangements, but also now as a result of non-governmental organisations' (NGO) arrangements with companies, regulation of, for example, investment, trade, intellectual property, environmental issues, labour standards, human rights related issues and quality regimes is in place or under consideration. Much of this international regulation emerges as a direct consequence of the need to patrol the outcomes of internationalisation and its partial erosion of national sovereignty. Also, it frequently results in significant consequences for HRD regimes, not only in obvious contexts such as labour standards, but also in relation to other, less immediately obvious contexts. For example, the management and production skills appropriate to sound environmental outcomes are often deemed to be different from those currently in place in many APEC economies. As a result, much effort is invested in the consideration of the management of sustainable development in APEC deliberations.

APEC: Organisation and modalities

The intersection of these processes resulted in the formation of APEC in 1989. Four aspects of APEC should be particularly understood in the context of this chapter. These are:

- the inter-governmental relationship
- the debates about membership and purpose
- the trade liberalisation agenda
- the HRD agenda

APEC is an inter-governmental organisation that primarily reflects the positions adopted by the administrations of the member economies. It maintains good relations with associated regional bodies with wider membership—for example, the Pacific Economic Co-operation Council (PECC) and the Pacific Basin Economic Council (PBEC)—but sustains the more rarefied status appropriate to a forum of sovereign states (despite the nomenclature issues surrounding the 'Three Chinas'). The inevitable consequence is that policy issues addressed by APEC are defined by state-level political agenda rather than, directly, by other interest groups. Furthermore, APEC deliberations are conducted primarily by officials charged with the delivery of state government agenda. The effect is to establish debate around government defined orthodoxies—for example, the policy imperatives of export based industrialisation from the ASEAN economies, the defensive postures of the US State Department and the Office of the Trade Representative, and the regional integration and development agenda of the Japanese government.

The membership and purpose of APEC are subject to subtle, nuanced debate. This is particularly evident in the conceptualisation of 'open regionalism'—the analytical basis underpinning the APEC process. Open regionalism responds to economic argument that open, free-trading economies will attain higher levels of welfare than protected economies and that collective efforts—such as APEC—to promote openness will induce transnational welfare maximisation. That said, the politics of APEC membership and purpose belie such a straightforward analysis. The Australian government, which claims to have initiated APEC's formation, began its move into Asia not only for trade purposes but also for wider, strategic reasons (in part as a response to US geopolitical initiatives). Similarly, Japan, which some commentators believe to have been the real force behind APEC's creation, combined wider strategic issues with an economic integration agenda in its pro-APEC stance. Japan's interest in certain key issues—for example, technology, quality, and APEC's Economic and Technical Co-operation agenda—is seen by some to reflect Japan's interest in creating the 'conditions of existence' for greater intra-regional FDI. The ASEAN economies, while sharing strategic and economic integration perspectives, also manifested clear reservations about the extent of APEC—that is, the partners with which they wished to ally. The US was initially lukewarm about membership and it continues to be hard to dispel the view held by many Asians that the US is in APEC primarily to further its own sectional trade policy directions while establishing wider strategic relationships with Asian economies. New Zealand is in APEC because it sees little alternative to a close political and economic relationship with the growing Asian economies.

This underlying ambiguity about the purpose of membership is seen not only in the membership moratorium which is in place (and the extraordinary array of economies which perceive themselves as potential APEC members) but also in the definition of APEC's purpose. The formal vision of APEC defines three purposes:

* trade and investment liberalisation
* trade and investment facilitation
* economic and technical co-operation

The first two purposes are in principle straightforward and reflect the role adopted by APEC as a regional focus for the World Trade Organisation (WTO)/GATT agenda. Through APEC agencies such as the Committee on Trade and Investment, trade liberalisation is assiduously promoted.

The Osaka Action Agenda laid out nine principles designed to achieve 'free and open trade and investment no later than the year 2010 in the case of the industrialised economies and the year 2020 in the case of developing economies'—the 2010/2020 goal. These principles were to be put into effect in a framework built from individual member economy action plans. These action plans were to contain concrete steps for the short to medium-term achievement of liberalisation in defined key areas—tariffs, non-tariff protection, services, telecommunications, transportation, energy, tourism, investment, standards and conformance, customs procedures, intellectual property rights, competition policy, government procurement, deregulation, rules of origin, dispute mediation, mobility of business people, implementation of the Uruguay Round outcomes, and information gathering. These action plans, and their collective counterparts, were discussed at the 1996 Manila APEC meetings. The varying and uniformly conservative content of the individual action plans highlights the difficulties experienced in member economies in moving from the level of platitudes to specific actions.

For our purposes, it is sufficient to note that the trade liberalisation agendas outlined above are indirectly concerned with ER issues. Rather, HRD impacts derive from the implementation of policies which emerge from the liberalisation agenda. In this context, the role of the APEC HRD Working Group (HRDWG) merits consideration.

The APEC HRD Working Group

The HRDWG was established in 1990 and has completed, or is involved in, approximately 80 APEC-wide projects. Its choice of direction is determined by an action program laid out in detail in the 1994 Bogor Declaration, which highlights the centrality of HRD issues in APEC activities. The precepts guiding APEC's HRD work were specified in Beijing in 1995 as follows:

- The development of human resources [contributes] to the attainment of economic growth and development [underscoring] the importance of designing regional approaches to human resources development.
- Sustainable development depends upon the successful implementation of policies that integrate economic, environmental and social objectives. It is important to integrate environmental objectives into education and training programs to enhance environmental management and technical skills.
- The accelerating globalisation of industry creates a prime opportunity to encourage the establishment and growth of domestic industry and to nurture a highly efficient and productive industrial structure . . . policy dialogue on human resource development, information access, technology sharing, the availability of finance and market access should be enhanced.

Three features of these precepts should be highlighted—the idea that a regional HRD strategy might be put in place in the context of globalisation, the integration of HRD issues with environmental and social ones, and the focus on small and medium-sized enterprises (SMEs). The idea of a regional HRD strategy reflects the impact of many of the forces which shaped the emergence of APEC—internationalisation, regional bloc formation, agendas for sustained growth and competitiveness and particular national agenda, as in the case of Japan, for example. Unlike the EU, however, APEC has adopted an informal non-binding organisational structure which depends for its effect on a willingness on the part of member economies to commit to a strategy. While the logic of shared experience of education and training issues may be obvious, and while measures to facilitate mobility of qualifications may be similarly desirable, the creation of a structure able to deliver such benefits effectively is a difficult task.

The link between HRD and environmental issues reflects the broader impact of them on growth strategies, particularly since the recognition accorded in the Uruguay Round to environmental issues. Environmental concerns in management training and decision-making have a strong presence in HRDWG work, often driven by an

Australian focus on this area. At the 1996 APEC Ministerial Meeting on Sustainable Development, held in Manila, three major themes emerged:

- sustainable cities/urban management
- clean technology/clean production
- sustainability of the marine environment

Responding to these concerns, the HRDWG has been involved in activities in relation to project management for sustainable development, the future of industrial technology HRD, and the HRD elements in economic environmental impacts.

The integration of APEC's HRD strategy with its focus on SMEs is a reflection of APEC's stated belief in the significance of SMEs in regional growth. SMEs were placed in the forefront of APEC policy at the 1993 Seattle Leaders' Meeting. Estimates suggest that SMEs constitute approximately 99% of APEC's enterprises, contribute between 30% and 60% of GDP, employ between 40% and 80% of APEC's workforce, are responsible for 70% or more of net employment creation and contribute approximately 35% of direct exports. From an APEC HRD perspective, the key issues affecting SMEs have been identified as gaps in much management training and development. It is argued that more skilled managers in SMEs will be better able to take advantage of the liberalised trading environment. Sharing of information (particularly about 'best practice'), development of training programs specific to SMEs, appropriate technological transfers, reduced compliance costs, strategies to increase SME productivity performance, and better access to capital are the types of initiatives deemed necessary to build on SME strengths. A key initiative in relation to HRD in the SME area is the recommendation from the Third APEC SMEs Ministers' Meeting (Cebu, 1996) to establish an APEC Centre for Technology Exchange and Training for SMEs (ACTETSME).

The HRDWG priority areas

The Beijing statement specified eight priority areas which the HRDWG was to address in its work. These were:

- a quality basic education for all
- regional labour market analysis
- increasing the supply and quality of managers, entrepreneurs and training in the areas central to economic growth
- reducing skill deficiencies and unemployment by designing appropriate training priority areas and outcomes
- improving the quality of curricula, teaching methods and materials

- improving access to skill acquisition in the bloc
- preparing individuals and organisations for rapid economic and technological change
- trade and investment facilitation and liberalisation

To achieve progress in these priority areas, member economies were to engage in policy dialogues within the HRDWG, while developing an exchange of information in key areas and promoting professional HRD practices and standards. The Osaka Action Agenda took these priority areas and attached to each programs designed to produce specific and appropriate outcomes (see Figure 13.1).

Apart from these programs, the HRDWG was also required to respond to a further seven initiatives based on APEC leaders' and ministerial initiatives (for example, the Business Volunteer Programme, ACTETSME and the APEC Education Foundation) and a range of one-off, HRD related activities promoted by other APEC groups (for example, training courses on clean coal technologies, health and quality issues in the fish products sector, HR in the telecommunications sector, and health management and disease control in sustainable shrimp culture). As we shall discuss below, 1997 saw a crucial amendment of the priority areas specified in Beijing.

The HRDWG institutional framework

The institutional framework adopted in the HRDWG to achieve these goals is an important consideration. Until January 2000 the HRDWG oversaw the activities of five subgroups:

- Business Management Network (BMN)
- Industry Technology Network (HURDIT)
- Economic Development Management Network (NEDM)
- Education Forum
- Labour Market Information

The BMN focused primarily on executive education and development and brought together management trainers from public and private sector training establishments and colleges in a wide range of training and education based projects. It was managerialist and technicist in its general thrust. Illustrating this, at the 1995 Beijing meeting, projects accepted by the BMN included an annual get-together of entrepreneurs within the bloc, research into technical management and HRD support in the region, cross-cultural management of trade dispute resolution and the cross-cultural management of collaborative research and development.

HURDIT focused on a range of issues, including technological and professional standards, skills issues, the sharing and transfer of high-technology knowledge and technology management training.

Again, to illustrate its scope, projects accepted at its 1995 Beijing meeting included an exchange of information on competencies for engineering, strategies for HRD and the environment industry technology, and a seminar on industrial technology education. It was also technicist in its approach to issues.

NEDM focused on regional labour market issues as they related to HRD. It had a technical policy orientation and was closely related to the growing activity on labour market information signalled at the 1996 APEC HRD Ministerial Meeting held in Manila. Projects sponsored by NEDM included economic/environment training for policy advisors, linkages between labour markets and education, the internationalisation of SMEs and HRD in the Asia-Pacific region, and public/private sector collaboration in HRD.

The Education Forum focused on education systems and their capacity to respond to changing labour market demands. It looked particularly at performance, quality and mobility matters within education systems. Projects under its auspices included the improvement of understanding of cultures in APEC.

The Labour Market Information group was a forum in which APEC economies could share and exchange information on labour market trends and prospects, policies and programs, analytical techniques and relevant methods. The hope was that such activities would improve the functioning of labour markets within the APEC economies.

Completing the overview of the HRDWG institutional framework, three cross-cutting themes should be noted:

- HRD for SMEs
- HRD for Sustainable Development
- Lifelong Learning

The first two themes have been discussed above. Lifelong learning is an umbrella concept capturing the range of issues raised by the need for the region's workforce to respond to rapid structural and technological change.

Characterising the role of the HRDWG

The purpose of the HRDWG is to provide two types of outputs: practical training and up-skilling materials (particularly for executives and government officials), and materials appropriate to policy-making. The application of both types of output is intended to develop the responsiveness of public and private sector institutions and individuals to the needs of internationalisation and competitiveness. The mode of HRD seen as appropriate for the region was originally unitarist (cf. Fox 1974). The inter-governmental nature of

APEC tended to generate a top-down view of appropriate HRD developments, drawing substantially on economic and managerial orthodoxies for their intellectual underpinnings.

The origin of this view can be explained by the shared perspectives on internationalisation among APEC members. A commitment to international economic integration unites APEC members, notwithstanding the different routes travelled to this perspective. The practical issues addressed by the HRDWG may only be placed in APEC programs on the basis of consensus among the members. This consensus traditionally supported a technicist, developmental approach to HRD issues in the region.

The consensus becomes apparent when we consider issues on which there continues to be no consensus, or on which there is agreement about their inappropriateness for consideration. Such an issue is labour migration, where there is no consensus in APEC HRD discussions. For many member economies, labour migration is a significant issue. Some members are substantial net exporters of labour. Other members are importers of labour to a greater or lesser extent. Many members are in the international labour market in terms of demand for specific skills. In all economies, labour mobility is tied in closely with immigration policy and the question of citizenship. One aspect of mobility has uniform support. The unrestricted movement of business people in the region is agreed to be a worthwhile goal. To this end, all members were asked to make provision for mobility of business people in the individual action plans submitted to the Manila Leaders' Meeting. The unrestricted movement of other types of employees is not treated similarly in APEC's HRD discussions. A commitment to market liberalisation is not extended to the labour market in general and, consequently, labour mobility is not taken up by the HRDWG. On occasions, when the topic has arisen in working group discussions, delegations from member economies opposed to this discussion have made their views known forcefully and have effectively vetoed further discussion.

A similar response to discussion of public sector reform and its management has been observed. While it is not as controversial an issue as labour mobility, some member economies have expressed reservations about the appropriateness of discussion about the public sector in relation to the activities of the HRDWG. Hence, in both these cases, a consensus does not exist and the issues are either marginalised or excluded from the agenda.

There are, however, other issues which by their nature were originally deemed either to be so controversial that they ought not to be raised for fear that they would undermine progress in areas of consensus, or where they were seen to be national concerns not appropriate to regional level discussion. Labour standards illustrate the former, national industrial relations systems the latter. While labour standards have been an issue for many years, they came to the fore once more in the debates around the Uruguay Round. Indeed, the 1994 Marrakech agreement which concluded the Uruguay Round was made possible in part by the last minute compromise on labour standards which saw a joint committee of the International Labour Organisation (ILO) and the to-be-formed World Trade Organisation (WTO) established to consider international labour standards and their linkage to the international trading regime. Since then, the idea that labour standards should be patrolled internationally on the basis of enforcement by trade sanctions has divided the international community. On the one hand, countries such as Norway, France and, particularly, the US, have promoted a body of core labour standards tied into the international trading regime. They have been supported in this by much of the international trade union movement. In opposition has been an alliance of employer organisations, some Third World unions and, most obviously, a range of countries drawn from the developed and developing worlds. Thus, New Zealand, the UK and Australia aligned with, for example, India, Malaysia and Singapore in opposition to the standards–trade linkage. The terrain of the debate is complex, covering a range of moral arguments and much technical economic argument. APEC encompasses the two extremes of the debate, captured in the positions of the US and Malaysia. Such is the intensity of the debate that it was effectively excluded from all APEC debate, except perhaps at the highest level. Since 1997, this exclusion has appeared to be less certain (see below).

Individual country's ER systems are an example of an issue deemed to be national and so not subject to regional debate. Here a clear distinction is made between labour market issues—conceived in technical and developmental terms—and ER issues—understood in terms of the political nature of ER in member economies. This distinction carries greater weight with many Asian economies than it does with Australia, New Zealand, Canada and the US. In the latter economies, ER regimes are 'mature', articulated with the broader political system and, generally, economistic in character. In other words, labour market policies and the ER systems engage within a system of inclusive political regulation.

In many Asian economies, ER are not so ordered. Labour market policies oriented towards increased growth and export performance may clash with the demands for representation, bargaining rights and improvement in well-being. Many APEC economies have felt the pressure of rising expectations during stages of economic development when national planning has deemed such pressure to be unwise or illegitimate. The history of bargaining and union formation in South Korea from the 1960s onwards illustrates this process. Indonesia is facing similar pressures. The People's Republic of China is acutely aware of the challenge emerging around independent labour organisations in the context of demands for political reform. It is the explicit relationship between bargaining systems and their associated organisations and the political process (particularly democratisation) which makes ER issues so difficult for APEC. Hence, it is not surprising that APEC should choose a technicist, developmental labour market approach to HRD and effectively ignore the broader ER issues which inevitably arise. The inter-government nature of APEC ensures that this is the case.

APEC and employment relations issues

This characterisation of APEC permits a brief discussion of APEC and regional ER practices. Two points emerge from this discussion. At a practical level, APEC, through the HRDWG, is engaged in extending across the region a range of shared managerial practices in areas such as cross-cultural management, quality issues, training and education provisions, technology transfer and utilisation. Given the economic importance and size of APEC, the progress of these types of management development takes on particular significance. In this, the role of business people should be recognised, particularly as it emerges through the work of the APEC Business Advisory Council (ABAC), on which sit senior business people from all member economies and which produced for the Manila Leaders' Meeting a 'business agenda' for APEC.

Second, APEC's commitment to trade liberalisation and market openness provides the context for these managerial practices to emerge and defines to a large extent their content. Thus, APEC is in the early stages of developing a regional framework for managerial training and practice which is explicitly predicated on a trade liberalising, neo-classical economic framework. It is interesting to consider what the outcome of this framework might be in terms of ER. One obvious benefit will follow the emphasis placed in the HRDWG and elsewhere on cross-cultural management issues. The extent and quality of the commitment within APEC to this dimension of management is notable and may come to influence a new generation of management education and training within the APEC economies. Given the nature of management education in the past, it is possible that it will be the 'Western' economies that will benefit most from this cross-cultural expertise as they increasingly operate in Asia. One very significant area of cross-cultural management in APEC outputs is the management of culturally diverse or different workforces, a central ER consideration.

Public sector management is another area which may experience change as a result of APEC-derived management development. Shared experience between government officials meeting in the many APEC events is the source of exchange of ideas and practices. The 'management of liberalisation' is an implicit sub-text to all APEC deliberations allowing, incidentally, economies such as New Zealand a voice far more powerful than the size of its economy would suggest because of experience of deregulation and liberalisation. ER strategies for the state sector are an element in these deliberations.

The APEC focus on SMEs is important in ER terms. The SME theme cuts through all APEC agendas and the up-skilling of SME management is a particularly significant emphasis in APEC discussion. SMEs are represented as the flexible heart of export success, job creation and technological innovation. Consequently, they are also characterised in terms of flexible ER practices. It requires little imagination to extend APEC debates on SMEs to conclusions about the need to protect SMEs from compliance costs of many kinds. Such protection becomes a policy touchstone with significant ER consequences. On the positive side, management training appropriate for SMEs may advance and become a valuable resource in the region. On the negative, an over-emphasis on the reduction of compliance costs and on management training may bring adverse consequences for labour in SMEs in terms of bargaining power and representation. As noted above, there is no concomitant APEC agenda for industrial relations or labour standards rounding off the SME strategy.

Technology is another key theme with ER consequences in the APEC agenda. Technology transfer, training in appropriate technologies, quality and technology and the management of technology are variously central in APEC debates. Here again, the tenor of the debate within APEC is managerialist and production oriented. Two key debates are not yet present in APEC analyses of technological issues. The first is the debate about to what ends technology may be put. Little discussion has emerged round the choice between 'upward' and 'downward' restructuring and the consequent implications for technological innovation. This is not surprising in that, first, the implicit assumption is that this is a choice for the manager and, second, across the APEC economies there is little consensus about the need for a focus on 'upward' restructuring. Economies such as New Zealand, seen as advanced in the deregulatory reform process, still display a preference for 'downward' restructuring when faced by adverse international circumstances. Other economies, still taking advantage of relatively cheaper labour costs and placing great emphasis on labour intensive, assembly line production, are similarly in the main committed to 'downward' restructuring approaches. In ER terms, then, the APEC technology agenda promotes quite different outcomes, depending on the strategic direction of the member economies.

APEC's work on education systems merits comment. There is in this dimension of APEC's work a clear commitment to the functional orientation of education systems towards the needs of production. This is seen most clearly in the focus on curriculum development in the sciences and technology and on the interface between business and education promoted in various APEC groups. There is little new in this, in so far as development strategies for industrialising economies have traditionally sought to link education systems to the development needs of the economy. In this sense, APEC is simply reinforcing a process well established since World War II. However, if we consider the power relations between APEC member economies, the potential for the regional direction of education provision to fall under the sway of dominant funding economies must be recognised. Member economies will presumably address this possibility in their consideration of APEC outputs in the field of education.

Labour-related issues

At its January 1997 meeting held in Sydney, the HRDWG was galvanised by strong US pressure to include labour and labour-related issues in the HRDWG process. The pressure arose from the Clinton Administration which has consistently supported a pro-labour standards position in international agencies. It also reflected a transfer in responsibility for the HRDWG in the US to the Department of Labour. In the APEC HRD Ministerial Meeting held later in 1997, the priorities laid down in Beijing were amended to include the following:

> Priority 7—Enhancing the quality, productivity, efficiency and equitable development of the labour forces and work places in member economies

This innocuous wording, by its explicit mention of labour forces, has shifted the ground on which the HRDWG operates. Already, the US and Canadian delegations to the HRDWG include as a matter of course representatives from their countries' central trade union confederations. Other economies, willing or not, are, as a result of

this priority, engaged in dialogue with their central union confederations about the form of labour's participation in the HRDWG.
Simultaneously, the International Confederation of Free Trade
Unions (ICFTU), through various regional bodies (the Asia Pacific
Regional Organisation—APRO and the Asia Pacific Labour Network—APLN), is developing contacts with, and strategies for,
APEC. It remains to be seen what the full impact of this shift will
be, but it is clear that the original unitarism of the HRDWG is now
challenged by an increasingly plural membership.

By 1999, the US pressure for the inclusion of labour standards
in particular, and labour-related issues in general, in trade-related
international fora was even stronger. In July 1999, the US took a
firm line in the third APEC HRD Ministerial Meeting in Washington,
promoting a range of initiatives that appeared to be 'labour-friendly'.
These initiatives reflected a strong commitment by the Clinton
Administration to the active consideration of labour interests in
international trade matters. However, the pressure exerted by the US
in APEC on labour-related issues was much less than its forceful
support for a trade–labour standards link in the December 1999
WTO meeting in Seattle. Reports of that meeting suggest that the
expected problem—agriculture—was at the point of solution, but
the Clinton Administration insistence on a trade–labour standards
link contributed significantly to the collapse of the meeting. In the
light of the Seattle meeting, we can infer that the focus on labour
issues within APEC is part of a much larger US agenda on trade
and labour issues.

Reflecting the outcome of the Washington Ministerial meeting,
but also responding to a wish on the part of some APEC member
economies that the HRDWG become more effective in its activities,
significant changes in the structure of the HRDWG were agreed in
its January 2000 meeting in Sapporo, Japan. The five subgroups
described above were replaced by three new subgroups. The new
Education Network continues the established focus on education
development in the region. The Capacity Building Network (CBN)
combines the erstwhile BMN and HURDIT into one, responsible
for the promotion of human capacity building and the strengthening
of markets in the APEC region by means of, *inter alia*, improved
productive processes, enterprise productivity and adaptability, and
management and skill development. The Labor and Social Protection
Network (LSP) is to foster human capacity building, social integration and strong and flexible labour markets by means of information
exchange, policy development initiatives, a focus on workplace
conditions and practices and on strong social safety nets. This
structure marks a concerted shift towards workplace-based issues, a
recognition of the impacts of the 1997 crisis on the Asian region

(particularly in relation to social and labour market impacts), and an emerging focus (originally defined during the Auckland APEC Leaders' Meeting in 1999) on the need to strengthen markets in the region.

Conclusions

We began by situating APEC in terms of global political and economic shifts since World War II. APEC is seeking to build on many of these processes to take advantage of growth in international trade. The intellectual underpinning of this strategy is an orthodox neo-classical economic model in which trade liberalisation maximises welfare. HRD policies appropriate to this model are concerned with training and educational provision appropriate to flexible labour markets, technological adaptation, high productivity, international competitiveness and SMEs. APEC, particularly through the HRDWG, is promoting such policies in a technicist, managerialist framework. The inter-governmental nature of APEC and the consensus around ER issues between member economies reinforces this outcome. Consequently, related HRM issues—bargaining systems and labour standards, in particular—were initially excluded from APEC's deliberations on two grounds: first, they are national concerns around which no consensus exists; second, they are policy areas which to an extent challenge the prescriptions of the trade liberalisation model and, therefore, would disrupt APEC's deliberations. They also focused attention on tensions around membership of APEC which might undermine the trade liberalisation agenda.

Whether the consensus could be maintained was always an issue. Just as environmental issues had wormed their way into mainstream importance in the WTO and APEC, it was possible that the excluded dimensions of ER—we might characterise them as the 'political' aspects of ER—might also find a way to the table. In a model which stresses internationalisation and integration, the attempt to define arbitrarily some issues as not open to international scrutiny was perhaps always doomed. The opening up to labour representation in the HRDWG and the inclusion of labour related matters in the HRDWG's priorities reveals the difficulty in trying to 'ring-fence' HRD issues. How far this opening will progress will depend on the ability of those supporting labour representation to create a new, broader consensus between APEC members.

Table 13.1 Output from APEC's HRD Working Group

Priority	Examples of outputs
High quality instruction in key subjects	Case studies on teacher induction Case studies on teacher development Case studies on teaching/work environments Approaches to the improvement of science education Approaches to technological innovation in teaching
Analysis of labour market issues	Linkages between labour market and education Role/status of women in social and economic development Capacity building in key basic industries HRD database in conjunction with PECC
Management/strengthening of SMEs	Symposia on HRD and marketing for SMEs Training to improve productivity in SMEs Promotion/conduct of on-the-job training programs for SMEs
Management and promotion of sustainable development	Human resources for sustainable development (audits, case studies, human resources capacity plan) Sustainable development courses for higher education Certification programs for environment managers
Executive education and development	Cross-cultural technology transfer issues Training courses for Economic Development Zone managers Annual get-together of entrepreneurs University–industry co-operation Technology management and HRD support
Cross-cultural management	Cross-cultural management curriculum and country profiles Cross-cultural issues in international joint ventures Organisational strategy and HRD in the cross-cultural context Cross-cultural management of collaborative research and development
Industrial technology education	HRD outlook and strategies in industrial technology Research and networking in the food sectors Best practice information technology education Technology management program for SMEs

Priority	Examples of outputs
Lifelong learning	Database on lifelong learning activities Conference on lifelong learning approaches and initiatives
Monitoring performance of education systems	Expansion and improvement of education statistics Information sharing on performance indicators Creation of a performance measurement framework
Mobility of persons and information exchange for HRD and economic growth	Best practice/training in accreditation, curriculum development and certification Exchanges in higher education Networking for education and HR policy-makers Creation of the APEC Study Centres Continuing development of University Mobility in the Asia Pacific (UMAP) Exchanges of education officials Accreditation, curriculum development and certification of professions
Management for organisational change	Managing corporate change in APEC economies Public sector reform and the management of change
Liberalisation/facilitation of trade in services	Materials on appropriate trade dispute mediation
Standards and conformance	Promotion of quality assurance systems
Intellectual property rights	Training needs in IPR

Source: The authors.

Notes

Chapter 1 Industrialisation, democratisation and employment relations in the Asia-Pacific

1. The authors acknowledge that earlier versions of this chapter were presented at conferences jointly with Chris J. Leggett, to whom we are most grateful; he played a very significant role in developing the ideas in it.
2. For a diverse selection of introductions to the field, albeit from the perspective of English-speaking industrialised market economies (IMEs), see from the US: Katz & Kochan (1992); Dunlop (1993); from Australia: Gardner & Palmer (1997); Deery et al. (1997); Keenoy & Kelly (1998); from Canada: Chaykowski & Verma (1992); and from Britain: Gospel & Palmer (1993); Blyton & Turnbull (1998).
3. This notion is of course controversial and subject to a range of criticisms; nevertheless, such a hypothesis can provide a useful way of helping to organise a discussion of comparative ER. See Kerr, et al. (1973); Kerr (1983); Poole (1986) and Bamber & Lansbury (1998).
4. A term used by Morgan Stanley's China economist Andy Xie when discussing 'the status quo of entrenched relationship economies'. The term implies that while many hitherto successful Asian economies were pro-business, they were not always pro-market. Instead, many Asian firms gained a competitive advantage over rivals because of privileged access to bank loans and monopoly licences (Sender 1998).
5. See Dabscheck (1995:100–104). In contrast with earlier British traditions of voluntary collective bargaining, Australian employment relationships have long been regulated by legally binding arbitrated industrial awards. An award is a legally enforceable determination of employment terms and conditions in a firm or industry, which has been arbitrated or certified by an IR commission or similar, either at a national or state level. An award may apply at either a national, state, industry, enterprise, workplace and/or occupational level.

226

Chapter 2   Changing approaches to employment relations in Australia

1. The authors acknowledge that this chapter draws on Davis, E. & Lansbury, R. 1998, 'Employment relations in Australia', in Bamber & Lansbury (1998). The present chapter focuses on the Australian *federal* jurisdiction. Deery et al. (1997) probably is the most established textbook, while Moorehead et al. (1997) provides the most comprehensive set of data on Australian industrial relations. Textbooks that have a slightly more practical orientation include Fox et al. (1995) and Sappey & Winter (1992). The federal Department of Employment Workplace Relations and Small Business publishes leaflets on various aspects of the federal jurisdiction and also provides information on its web page (http://www.dwrsb.gov.au/). It has offices in the capital city of each Australian state (phone 1800 068 690). Most of the state equivalents also publish leaflets. Bamber & Lansbury (1998) includes chapters on ER in Australia, Britain, the US, Canada, France, Italy, Germany, Sweden, Japan and Korea. It also includes international and comparative data on these countries, including various labour market and more general statistics. Although it refers primarily to Britain, Hyman (1989) is a useful analysis of industrial conflict. For an analysis of the differing labour laws in the US, New Zealand and each Australian state, see Nolan (1998).

Chapter 3   Changing approaches to employment relations in New Zealand

1. A nation-wide survey conducted for the Industrial Relations Service of the Department of Labour had many more employees on CECs— around 50% of all employees (Industrial Relations Service 1997). Likewise, a 1998 employee survey found that 44% of employees were covered by CECs (Rasmussen, McLaughlin & Boxall 1999).
2. Other estimates, developed by Vic Hall, Victoria University of Wellington, relate productivity growth to the business cycle. These productivity estimates are higher but still not above 2% annual growth (see Kerr 1996 & 1997). A comprehensive, but rather controversial, analysis of productivity growth by Lawrence and Diewart (1999) found that another measure of productivity—multifactor productivity (output divided by labour and capital input)—showed a 1.7% average growth rate between 1993–1998 (the full report can be found on the website of the New Zealand Treasury).

Chapter 4   Changing approaches to employment relations in Japan

1. The Weimar democracy era of German history began after the end of World War I and ended with the rise of Hitler and National Socialism.

2. *Zaibatsu* refers to the financial combines that existed up to the beginning of the post-World War II Occupation of Japan, when they were made illegal. *Keiretsu* refers to the post-World War II enterprises linkages that replaced *Zaibatsu*. These linkages among firms in Japan often include reciprocal stock holdings, exclusive or nearly exclusive parts supplier roles between large and small firms, the exchange of proprietary and technical information, and the transfer of personnel.

3. The 'New Deal' was the slogan of the F.D. Roosevelt U.S. presidency. The only four-term president of the United States, FDR served from the onset of the Great Depression through World War II, dying in office. New Deal labor legislation legalised labor unions, but 'at will' employment and an absence of employment participation mechanisms were reinforced.

4. Most of these cases occurred after the oil shock of the 1970s.

5. The following is a 1979 definition of this practice from a labour law dictionary.

> It is the custom by which one is employed in the same enterprise from post-graduation hiring until retirement. In Japan lifetime employment developed implicitly. Wages, age, and years of work are the basis for the seniority-based wage system. The retirement payment system is based upon the number of years of work. Furthermore, health and welfare facilities within the enterprise brought about a system that increased worker stability. In Europe and in the United States it is normal to freely move to another establishment depending on the labour conditions found. In Japan, which has adopted the lifetime employment system, a change in workplace is a distinctly negative factor for the worker. Accordingly, even with dissatisfaction about low wages and other working conditions, it is not possible to easily switch jobs. However, since 1955, due to the technology revolution, skilled workers have become less needed. Because of this and other factors, management has begun to re-examine the lifetime employment system (Matsuoka 1979:120).

6. A chart of the table data is given on page 166 of the text. Note that the table on page 85 (reference materials section) of the Labour White Paper incorrectly switches data for male and female; this can only be a misprint. I have corrected this error in the table provided in this chapter. The data correctly correspond to the chart found in the text.

7. Listed under Japanese references: Asahi, Jiyu, & Shueisha (1999). The Jiyu annual is oldest: 1999 is the 51st year of publication. Asahi is in its 10th year. The Shueisha volume does not list years of publication.

8. See any of the three information annuals for a Japanese summary of this revision. See Yamakawa (1998) for a good English summary.

9. For an explanation of the origins of provisional dispositions, see Kettler & Tackney (1997).

10. See the web page: http://www.ml.com/woml/press_release/19980418–1.htm

11. Japan maintains among the lowest pay differentials between executives and other employees in the industrialised world.

Chapter 5 Changing approaches to employment relations in South Korea

1. See Appendix 5.1 for the detailed contents of the labour law revision.
2. See Appendix 5.2 for the detailed contents of the agreement.

Chapter 9 Challenges facing unions in South Korea

1. However, a decentralised union movement should not be regarded as the end for the union movement. Historically, new union movements have been formed by overcoming the previous fragmentation (Hyman 1992).
2. For example, as the financial market has been opened to foreign capital in recent years, employment adjustment and downsizing have been an immediate concern for major financial institutions in Korea.
3. Seniority-based promotion and the collective reward system which operated in South Korean companies has in many cases been replaced by the merit-based or individual reward system.
4. Among the agreed issues, the biggest exchange between labour and the government was the acceptance of measures for enhancing labour market flexibility in return for participating in general social reform including corporate restructuring and reform of the taxation system (for details see Korea International Labor Foundation 1998).
5. The role of social corporatism in implementing structural adjustment seems to be limited to the cases of Hungary and Australia in recent years (Hethy 1995; Hampson 1997). However, there was also a 'Dutch miracle' which has been maintained by the combination of neo-classical structural reform and social corporatism (Visser & Henerijck 1997).

Chapter 10 Challenges facing unions in Australia

1. It is gratefully acknowledged that this chapter was edited by Mindy Thorpe.

Chapter 13 The APEC forum

1. A wide range of HRDWG unpublished internal documents were consulted in the preparation of this chapter. This chapter was produced on the basis of work carried out for the University of Auckland project on New Zealand

and APEC, funded by the Foundation for Research, Science and Technology (the most significant New Zealand government research funding agency). For further analysis of the changing consensus within the HRD Working Group see N. Haworth 'APEC HRD and the Social Dimension' APEC Study Centre Consortium Conference *Towards APEC's Second Decade: Challenges, Opportunities and Priorities*, Auckland, May 1999 (see www.auckland.ac.nz/apec/papers/Haworth.html).

References

Chapter 1 Industrialisation, democratisation and employment relations in the Asia-Pacific

Anderson, G. (1991) 'The Employment Contracts Act 1991: An employers' charter?' *New Zealand Journal of Industrial Relations* 16, pp. 127–42

ALU (Asian Labour Update) (1991) *Hong Kong* Asia Monitor Research Centre, June

Bamber, G.J. & Lansbury, R.D. (1998) 'An introduction to international and comparative employment relations' in G.J. Bamber & R.D. Lansbury eds *International and Comparative Employment Relations: A Study of Industrialised Market Economies* Sydney: Allen & Unwin

Bamber, G.J. & Sappey, R.B. (1996) 'Industrial relations reform and organisational change: Towards strategic human resource management in Australia?' in B. Towers ed. *The Handbook of Human Resources Management* rev. edn, Oxford: Blackwell

Benson, J. (1996) 'Management strategy and labour flexibility in Japanese manufacturing enterprises' *Human Resource Management Journal* 6, 2, pp. 42–55

BOK (Bank of Korea) (1990) *Economic Indicators* Seoul: Bank of Korea

Blyton, P. & Turnbull, P. (1998) *The Dynamics of Employee Relations* 2nd edn London: Macmillan

Borthwick, M. (1992) *Pacific Century: The Emergence of Modern Pacific Asia* Boulder Colorado: Westview Press

Boxall, P. (1995) 'Building the theory of comparative HRM' *Human Resource Management Journal* 5, 5, pp. 5–17

Chaykowski, R.P. & Verma, A. (1992) *Industrial Relations in Canadian Industry* Toronto: Dryden

Clegg, H.A. (1960) *A New Approach to Industrial Democracy* Oxford: Blackwell

Dabscheck, B. (1995) *The Struggle for Australian Industrial Relations* Melbourne: Oxford University Press

Deeks, J., Parker, J. & Ryan, R. (1994) *Labour and Employment Relations in New Zealand* Auckland: Longman Paul

Deery, S.J., Plowman, D. & Walsh, J. (1997) *Industrial Relations: A Contemporary Analysis* Sydney: McGraw Hill

Deyo, F.C. (1989) *Beneath the Miracle: Labor Subordination in the New Asian Industrialism* Berkeley: University of California Press

——(1995) 'Human resource strategies and industrial restructuring in Thailand' in S. Frenkel & J. Harrod eds *Industrialization and Labor Relations: Contemporary Research in Seven Countries* Ithaca: ILR Press

Dore, R. (1973) *British Factory, Japanese Factory: The Origins of National Diversity in Industrial Relations* London: Allen & Unwin

——(1979) 'Industrial relations in Japan and elsewhere' in A.M. Craig ed. *Japan: A Comparative View* Princeton: Princeton University Press

Dunlop, J. (1993) *Industrial Relations Systems* rev. edn, Boston: Harvard Business School Press

Elgar, T. & Smith, C. (1994) *Global Japanization* London: Routledge

Elliott, F. (1969) *A Dictionary of Politics* London: Penguin

Farh, J.L. (1995) 'Human resource management in Taiwan, the Republic of China' in L.F. Moore & P. Devereaux Jennings eds *Human Resource Management on the Pacific Rim: Institutions, Practices and Attitudes* Berlin: Walter de Gruyter

Fox, A. (1974) *Beyond Contract: Work, Power and Trust Relations* London: Faber

Frenkel, S. (1993) 'Australian trade unionism and the new social structure of accumulation' in S. Frenkel ed. *Organized Labor in the Asia-Pacific Region: A Comparative Study of Trade Unionism in Nine Countries* New York: ILR Press

Fruin, M. (1992) *The Japanese Enterprise System* New York: Oxford University Press

Gall, G. (1998) 'Independent unionism in Indonesia' *International Journal of Employment Studies* 6, 1, pp. 83–102

Gardner, M. & Palmer, G. (1997) *Employment Relations* 2nd edn, Melbourne: Macmillan

Gilley, B. (1998) 'Buying binge' *Far Eastern Economic Review* (weekly) 20 August 1998, vol. 161, no. 34, pp. 42–4

Goodall, K. & Warner, M. (1997) 'Human resources in sino-foreign joint ventures: Selected case-studies in Shanghai, compared with Beijing' *International Journal of Human Resource Management*, 8, 5, pp. 569–94

Gospel, H.F. & Palmer, G. (1993) *British Industrial Relations* 2nd edn, London: Routledge

Harbridge, R. & Honeybone, A. (1995) 'Trade unions under the Employment Contracts Act: Will the slimming be fatal?' in P. Boxall ed. *The Challenge of Human Resource Management* Auckland: Longman Paul

Harbridge, R. & Moulder, J. (1993) 'Collective bargaining and New Zealand's Employment Contracts Act: One year on' *Journal of Industrial Relations* 35, 1, pp. 62–83

Hsing, You-tien (1998) *Making Capitalism in China: The Taiwanese Connection* New York: Oxford University Press

Hutchings, K. (1996) 'Workplace practices of Japanese and Australian multinational corporations operating in Singapore, Malaysia and Indonesia' *Human Resource Management Journal* 6, 2, pp. 56–69

Jackson, S. (1994) 'Labour issues in China' in S. Jackson ed. *Contemporary Developments in Asian Industrial Relations* Sydney: Industrial Relations Research Centre, University of New South Wales

Katz, H.C. & Kochan, T.A. (1992) *An Introduction to Collective Bargaining and Industrial Relations* McGraw-Hill: New York

Keenoy, T. & Kelly, D. (1998) *The Employment Relationship in Australia* 2nd edn, Sydney; Harcourt Brace

Kerr, C. (1973) *Industrialism and Industrial Man: The Problems of Labor and Management in Economic Growth* rev. edn, London: Penguin

——(1983) *The Future of Industrial Societies: Convergence or Continuing Diversity?* Cambridge: Harvard University Press

Kerr, C., Dunlop, J.T., Harbison, F. & Myers, C.A. (1975) *Industrialism and Industrial Man* London: Penguin

Kim, T. (1995) 'Human resource management for production workers in large Korean manufacturing enterprises' in S. Frenkel & J. Harrod eds *Industrialization and Labor Relations: Contemporary Research in Seven Countries* Ithaca: ILR Press

Knowles, K. (1993) 'A new era of workers' rights' *Southland Magazine* 3, pp. 14–15

Kuruvilla, S. & Arudsothy, P. (1995) 'Economic development strategy, government labor policy and firm-level industrial relations practices in Malaysia' in A. Verma, T.A. Kochan & R.D. Lansbury eds *Employment Relations in the Growing Asian Economies: A Summary*, London: Routledge

Kuwahara, Y. (1998) 'Employment relations in Japan' in G.J. Bamber & R.D Lansbury eds *International and Comparative Employment Relations: A Study of Industrialised Market Economies* Sydney: Allen & Unwin

Kwon, S.H. & Leggett, C. (1994) 'Industrial relations and South Korean chaebol' in R. Callus & M. Schumacher eds *Current Research In Industrial Relations: Proceedings of the 8th AIRAANZ Conference* February 1993, Sydney, pp. 804–34

Lambert, R. (1994) 'Authoritarian state unionism in new order Indonesia' in R. Callus & M. Schumacher eds *Current Research In Industrial Relations: Proceedings of the 8th AIRAANZ Conference* February 1993, Sydney, pp. 86–138

Lee, J.S. & Park, Y.B. (1995) 'Employment, labor standards and economic development in Taiwan and Korea' *Labor, Special Issue Tenth IIRA World Congress* May 31–June 4, pp. 223–42

Liew, L. (1998) 'A political economy analysis of the Asian financial crisis' *Journal of Asian Political Economy* 3, 3, pp. 301–30

Mathews, J. (1994) *Catching the Wave: Workplace Reform in Australia* Sydney: Allen & Unwin

Moore, L.F. & Devereaux Jennings, P. eds (1995) *Human Resource Management on the Pacific Rim: Institutions, Practices, and Attitudes* Berlin: Walter de Gruyter

Nitta, M. (1998) 'Employment relations after the collapse of bubble economy' in J. Banno ed. *The Political Economy of Japanese Society Vol. 2* Oxford: Oxford University Press

OED (*The Shorter Oxford English Dictionary on Historical Principles*) (1973) Oxford: Clarendon Press

O'Leary, G. (1994) 'The contemporary role of Chinese trade unions' in S. Jackson ed. *Contemporary Developments in Asian Industrial Relations* Sydney: Industrial Relations Research Centre, University of New South Wales

Oliver N. & Wilkinson B. (1992) *The Japanisation of British Industry* Oxford: Blackwell

Paik, Y., Vance, C. & Stage, D. (1996) 'The extent of divergence in human resource practice across three Chinese national cultures: Hong Kong, Taiwan and Singapore' *Human Resource Management Journal* vol. 6, no. 2, pp.18– 29

Park, Y. & Leggett, C. (1998) 'Employment relations in Korea' in G.J. Bamber & R.D. Lansbury eds *International and Comparative Employment Relations: A Study of Industrialised Market Economies* Sydney: Allen & Unwin

Poole, M. (1986) *Industrial Relations: Origins and Patterns of National Diversity* London: Routledge

Poon, T. (1996) 'Dependent development: The subcontracting network in Hong Kong and Taiwan compared' *Human Resource Management Journal* vol. 6, no. 2, pp. 38–49

Roberts, H.S. (1986) *Roberts' Dictionary of Industrial Relations* 3rd edn (prepared by Industrial Relations Centre, University of Hawaii at Manoa), Washington, DC: The Bureau of National Affairs

Schak, D.C. (1997) 'Taiwanese labour management in China' *Employee Relations: The International Journal* vol. 19, nos 4 & 5, pp. 365–73

Sender, H. (1998) 'Asian indigestion' *Far Eastern Economic Review* (weekly) 1 October 1998, pp. 10–15

Suzuki, S. (1995) 'Tradition and modernity in Japanese management: On industrialization and the groupism management in Japan' in A. Hing, P. Wong, & G. Schmidt eds *Cross Cultural Perspectives of Automation* Berlin: Sigma

Ungar, J. & Chan, A. (1995) 'China, corporatism and the East Asian model' *Australian Journal of Chinese Affairs* vol. 33 (January), pp. 29–53

Verma, A., Kochan, T.A. & Lansbury, R.D. eds (1995) 'Lessons from the Asian experience' *Employment Relations in the Growing Asian Economies: A Summary* London: Routledge

Verma, A. & Yan, Z. (1995) 'The changing face of human resource management in China: opportunities, problems and strategies' in A. Verma, T.A. Kochan & R.D. Lansbury *Employment Relations in the Growing Asian Economies, A Summary* London: Routledge

Vogel, E.F. (1980) *Japan as No. 1: Lessons for America* Tokyo: Charles E. Tuttle

Wager, T. & Gilson, C. (1996) 'Workforce reduction in Australia and New Zealand' *Human Resource Management Journal* vol. 6, no. 2, pp. 86–96

Walsh, P. & Ryan, R. (1993) 'The making of the Employment Contracts Act' in R. Harbridge ed *Employment Contracts: New Zealand Experiences* Wellington: Victoria University Press

Warner, M. (1996) 'Human resources in the People's Republic of China' *Human Resource Management Journal* vol. 6, no. 2, pp. 30–41

Wilkinson, B. (1994) *Labour and Industry in the Asia-Pacific: Lessons from the Newly-Industrialised Countries* Berlin: Walter de Gruyter

Wright, C. (1995) *The Management of Labour: A History of Australian Employers* Melbourne: Oxford University Press

Chapter 2   Changing approaches to employment relations in Australia

ABS (Australian Bureau of Statistics) (1984) *Trade Union Statistics, Australia, December 1983* Cat. no. 6323.0, Canberra: ABS

——(1997a) *Trade Union Members, Australia, August 1996* Cat. no. 6325.0, Canberra: ABS

——(1997b) *Labour Statistics, Australia, 1997* Cat. no. 6101.0, Canberra: ABS

——(1997c) *Industrial Disputes, Australia* Cat no. 6321.0, Canberra: ABS

——(1998) *Employee Earnings, Benefits, and Trade Union Membership Australia* Cat no. 6310.0, Canberra: ABS

——(1999) *Labour Force Australia* Cat. no. 6203.0, Canberra: ABS

AIRC (Australian Industrial Relations Commission) (1991a) *National Wage Case,* April, Print J7400, Melbourne: AIRC

——(1991b) *National Wage Case* October, Print K0300, Melbourne: AIRC

——(1993) *National Wage Case* October, Print K9700, Melbourne: AIRC

ALP–ACTU (Australian Labor Party–Australian Council of Trade Unions) (1983) 'Statement of accord by ALP and ACTU regarding economic policy', Melbourne: ALP–ACTU

Bamber, G.J. & Lansbury, R.D. eds (1998) *International and Comparative Employment Relations* 3rd edn, Sydney: Allen & Unwin

BCA (Business Council of Australia) (1989) *Enterprise-based Bargaining Units: A Better Way of Working* Melbourne: BCA

——(1991) *Avoiding Industrial Action* Melbourne: BCA

Beggs, J.J. & Chapman, B.J. (1987) 'Australian strike activity in an international context: 1964–1985' *Journal of Industrial Relations* 29, 2, pp. 137–49

Bennett, L. (1994) *Making Labour Law in Australia: Industrial Relations, Politics and Law* Sydney: The Law Book Company

Callus, R., Morehead, A., Cully, M. & Buchanan, J. (1991) *Industrial Relations at Work: The Australian Workplace Industrial Relations Survey* Canberra: AGPS

Chapman, B.J. & Gruen, F.H. (1990) 'An analysis of the Australian consensual incomes policy: the prices and incomes accord' in *Paper* Canberra: Australian National University Centre for Economic Policy Research, p. 221

Coelli, M., Fahrer, J. & Lindsay, H. (1994) 'Wage dispersion and labour market institutions: A cross country study' *Reserve Bank Economic Research Discussion Paper* No. 9404, Sydney: Reserve Bank

Cook, P. (1991) 'Address at the launch of *Industrial Relations at Work*', Workplace Australia conference, Canberra: Department of Industrial Relations

Dabscheck, B. (1989) *Australian Industrial Relations in the 1980s* Melbourne: Oxford University Press

——(1995) *The Struggle for Australian Industrial Relations* Melbourne: Oxford University Press

Davis, E.M. (1992) 'The 1991 ACTU congress: Together for tomorrow' *Journal of Industrial Relations* 34, 1, pp. 87–101

——(1996) 'The 1995 ACTU Congress' *Economics and Labour Relations Review* 7, 1, pp. 165–81

Davis, E.M. &. and Harris, C. (eds) (1996) *Making the Link: Affirmative Action and Industrial Relations* vol. 7, Canberra: AGPS, pp. 61–3

Davis, E.M. & Lansbury, R.D. (1988) 'Consultative councils in Qantas and Telecom' *Journal of Industrial Relations* 30, 4, pp. 546–65

Davis, E.M. & Pratt, V. eds (1990) *Making the Link: Affirmative Action and Industrial Relations*, Canberra: AGPS

Deery, S.J., Plowman, D.H. & Walsh, J.T. (1997) *Industrial Relations: A Contemporary Analysis*, 4th edn, Sydney: McGraw-Hill

Dufty, N.F. & Fells, R.E. (1989) *Dynamics of Industrial Relations in Australia* Sydney: Prentice-Hall

Fox, C., Howard, W.A. & Pittard, M.J. (1995) *Industrial Relations in Australia: Development, Law and Operation* Melbourne: Longman Australia

Frenkel, S. (1990) 'Australian trade unionism and the new social structure of accummulation', Paper presented to the Asian Regional Congress, International Industrial Relations Research Association, Manila

Hagan, J. (1981) *The History of the ACTU*, Melbourne: Longman Cheshire

Hyman, R. (1989) *Strikes* 4th edn, London: Macmillan

Jost, J. (1994) 'Time for unions to pay their dues' *Australian Business Monthly* March, pp. 24–8

Karpin, D. (1995) *Enterprising Nation: Report of the Industry Task Force on Leadership and Management Skills* Canberra: AGPS

Kelty, W. (1991) *Together for Tomorrow* Melbourne: ACTU

Lansbury, R.D. & Davis, E.M. (1992) 'Employee participation: Some Australian cases' *International Labour Review,* 131, 2, pp. 231–48

Lever-Tracy, C. & Quinlan, M. (1988) *A Divided Working Class: Ethnic Segmentation and Industrial Conflict in Australia* London: Routledge & Kegan Paul

Moorehead, A., Steel, M., Alexander, M., Stephen, K. & Duffin, L. (1997) *Changes at Work: The 1995 Australian Workplace Industrial Relations Survey* Melbourne: Longman

Nolan, D.R. ed. (1998) *The Australasian Labour Law Reforms: Australia and New Zealand at the End of the Twentieth Century* Sydney: Federation Press

OECD (Organisation for Economic Cooperation and Development) (1997) *Historical Statistics* Paris: OECD

Plowman, D. (1989) *Holding the Line: Compulsory Arbitration and National Employer Coordination in Australia* Melbourne: Cambridge University Press

Quinlan, M. (1996) 'The reform of Australian industrial relations: Contemporary trends and issues' *Asian Pacific Journal of Human Resources* 34, 2, pp. 3–27

Quinlan, M. & Bohle, R. (1991) *Managing Occupational Health and Safety in Australia: A Multidisciplinary Approach* Melbourne: Macmillan

Ross, P. K. & Bamber, G.J. (1998) 'Changing employment relations in former public monopolies: Comparisons, contrasts and strategic choices at New Zealand Telecom and Telstra' in R. Harbridge, C. Gadd & A. Crawford (eds) *Current Research in Industrial Relations: Proceedings of the Twelfth AIRAANZ Conference,* Association of Industrial Relations Academics of Australia and New Zealand (AIRAANZ), Wellington, New Zealand, February, pp. 309-317

Sappey, R.B. & Winter, M. (1992) *Australian Industrial Relations Practice* Melbourne: Longman Cheshire

Sutcliffe, P. & Callus, R. (1994) *Glossary of Australian Industrial Relations Terms* Sydney: Australian Centre for Industrial Relations (ACIR), University of Sydney; Brisbane: Australian Centre in Strategic Management, Queensland University of Technology

Women's Bureau (1993) *Women and Work* Canberra: Department of Employment, Education and Training

Chapter 3   Changing approaches to employment relations in New Zealand

Anderson, G. (1996) 'Introduction' *New Zealand Journal of Industrial Relations* 21, 1, pp 1–5

Armitage, C. & Dunbar, R. (1993) 'Labour market adjustment under the Employment Contracts Act' *New Zealand Journal of Industrial Relations* 18, 1, pp. 94–112

Boston, J. (1984) *Incomes Policy in New Zealand: 1968–1984* Wellington: Victoria University Press

Boxall, P. (1990) 'Towards the Wagner framework: Change in New Zealand industrial relations' *Journal of Industrial Relations* 32, 4, pp. 523–43

——(1993) 'Management strategy and the Employment Contracts Act 1991' *Employment Contracts: New Zealand Experiences* R. Harbridge ed. Wellington: Victoria University Press

Boxall, P. & Haynes, P. (1992) 'Unions and non-union bargaining agents under the Employment Contracts Act 1991: An assessment after 12 months' *New Zealand Journal of Industrial Relations* 17, 2, pp. 223–32

——(1997) 'Strategy and trade union effectiveness in a neo-liberal environment' *British Journal of Industrial Relations* 35, 4, pp. 567–91   .

Bradford, M. (1997) 'Curb judicial activism to make the ECA work as parliament intended' *The Independent* 14 March, pp. 8–9

Brook, P. (1990) *Freedom at Work: The Case for Reforming Labour Law in New Zealand* Auckland: Oxford University Press

——(1991) 'New Zealand's Employment Contracts Act: An incomplete revolution' *Policy* 7, pp. 12–14

Campbell, G. (1997) 'The Max factor' *The Listener* 3 May, pp. 24–6

——(1998) 'For richer or poorer' *The Listener* 8 August, pp. 18–21

Carroll, P. & Tremewan, P. (1993) 'Organising employers: The effects of the Act on the Auckland Employers Association' in R. Harbridge ed. *Employment Contracts: New Zealand Experiences*, Wellington: Victoria University Press

Clark, H. (1993) 'Employment Relations—The New Direction under Labour' *New Zealand Journal of Industrial Relations* 18, 2, pp. 153–62

Crawford, A., Harbridge, R., & Walsh, P. (1999) 'Unions and Union Membership in New Zealand: Annual review for 1998' *New Zealand Journal of Industrial Relations*, 24, 3, pp. 383–95

Deeks, J., Parker, J. & Ryan, R. (1994) *Labour and Employment Relations in New Zealand* Auckland: Longman Paul

Dumbleton, A. (1996) 'The Employment Tribunal–Four years on' *New Zealand Journal of Industrial Relations* 21, 1, pp. 21–33

Easton, B. (1996) 'Productivity puzzle' *The Listener*, 27 July, p. 51

——(1997) 'The economic impact of the Employment Contracts Act' Paper presented to 1997 IRR Industrial Relations Conference, Auckland

Farlow, D. (1989) 'Occupational safety and health: The employers perspective' *New Zealand Journal of Industrial Relations* 14, 2, pp. 189–94

Grills, W. (1994) 'The impact of the Employment Contracts Act on labour law: Implications for unions' *New Zealand Journal of Industrial Relations* 19, 1, pp. 85–101

Harbridge, R. (1993) 'Bargaining and the Employment Contracts Act: An overview' in R. Harbridge ed. *Employment Contracts: New Zealand Experiences*, Wellington: Victoria University Press

——(1997) 'Recent industrial disputes and the impact on future industrial relations management' Paper presented to 1997 IRR Industrial Relations Conference, Auckland

Harbridge, R. & Crawford, A. (1996) 'The Employment Contracts Act and collective bargaining patterns: A review of the 1995/96 year' in R. Harbridge, A. Crawford & P. Kiely eds *Employment Contracts: Bargaining Trends & Employment Law Update 1995/96* Report, Industrial Relations Centre, Victoria University of Wellington, pp. 5–52

——(1997) 'The Employment Contracts Act and collective bargaining patterns: A review of the 1996/97 year.' in R. Harbridge, A. Crawford & P. Kiely eds *Employment Contracts: Bargaining Trends & Employment Law Update 1996/97* Report, Industrial Relations Centre, Victoria University of Wellington

Harbridge, R. & Honeybone, A. (1995) 'Trade unions under the Employment Contracts Act: Will the slimming be fatal?' in P. Boxall ed. *The Challenge of Human Resource Management* Auckland: Longman Paul

Hodgson, P. (1999) 'Labour's Labour Relations' *New Zealand Journal of Industrial Relations* 24, 2, pp. 173–80

Holt, J. (1986) *Compulsory Arbitration in New Zealand—The First Forty Years* Auckland: Auckland University Press

Howard, C. (1995) *The Interpretation of the Employment Contracts Act* Wellington: New Zealand Business Roundtable

Hunt, G. (1996) 'Employment Court judges need to fall into line with free market' *National Business Review*, 17 May, pp. 13

Industrial Relations Service (1996) *Contract* 18

——(1997) *Contract. Special Edition* November

James, C. (1986) *The Quiet Revolution* Wellington: Allen & Unwin

Janes, N. & Rasmussen, E. (1998) 'The road to international competitiveness? The current state of industry training in New Zealand' Paper presented at the 12th AIRAANZ Conference, Wellington

Kelsey, J. (1997) *The New Zealand Experiment* Auckland: Auckland University Press

Kerr, R. (1996) 'Employment, productivity and growth all blossom under the Employment Contracts Act' *NZ Herald* 5 October, p. A17

——(1997) 'NZ must wise up to employment growth obstacles' *The Independent* 7 March, pp. 8–9, 42

Kiely, P. (1996) 'Employment law update' in R. Harbridge, A. Crawford & P. Kiely eds *Employment Contracts: Bargaining Trends & Employment Law Update 1995/96* Report, Industrial Relations Centre, Victoria University of Wellington, pp. 53–77

Lamm, F. (1994) 'Chronicle' *New Zealand Journal of Industrial Relations* 19, 3, pp. 331–45

Lawrence, D. & Diewart, E. (1999) 'We're not doing that badly' *NZ Herald* 11 August 1999, pp. A15

McLaughlin, C. & Rasmussen, E. (1998) 'Freedom of choice and flexibility in the retail sector?' *International Journal of Manpower* 19, 4, pp. 281–95

Mealings, A. (1998) *New Zealand and Norway: A Comparative Analysis of Workplace Reform Practices* masters thesis, Department of Management & Employment Relations, University of Auckland

Meyers, B. (1996) 'Industry training in New Zealand in the 1990s' Research essay, Department of Management & Employment Relations, University of Auckland

National Party (1990) *Election Manifesto* Wellington: National Party

NZCTU (New Zealand Council of Trade Unions) (1996) 'Election backgrounder nos. 1–12' *Papers* Wellington

OECD (1993) *OECD Economic Surveys: New Zealand 1993* Paris: Organisation for Economic Cooperation and Development

Philpott, B. (1996) 'A note on recent trends in labour productivity growth' Paper, Victoria University of Wellington, October

Rasmussen, E. (1995) 'Chronicle' *New Zealand Journal of Industrial Relations* 20, 2, pp. 227–36

——(1997) 'Workplace reform and employee participation in New Zealand' in R. Markey & J. Monat eds *Innovation and Employee Participation through Works Councils*, Aldershot: Avebury

Rasmussen, E. & Boxall, P. (1995) 'Workforce governance' in P. Boxall ed. *The Challenge of Human Resource Management* Auckland: Longman Paul

Rasmussen, E. & Deeks, J. (1997) 'Contested outcomes: Assessing the impacts of the Employment Contracts Act' *California Western International Law Journal* 28, 1, pp. 283–304

Rasmussen, E. & Jackson, A. (1996) 'Employment relations in the New Zealand banking industry' Paper presented to the OECD-MIT research network on banking, Auckland, May

Rasmussen, E. & Lamm, F. (1999) *An Introduction to Employment Relations in New Zealand* Auckland: Longman Paul

Rasmussen. E. & McIntosh, I. (1998) 'Chronicle' *New Zealand Journal of Industrial Relations* 23, 2, pp. 119–31

Rasmussen, E., McLaughlin, C. & Boxall, P. (1999) 'A survey of employee experiences and attitudes in the New Zealand workplace' *New Zealand Journal of Industrial Relations* (forthcoming)

Rasmussen. E. & Schwarz, G. (1995) 'Chronicle' *New Zealand Journal of Industrial Relations* 20, 3, pp. 336–47

——(1996) 'Chronicle' *New Zealand Journal of Industrial Relations* 21, 2, pp. 201–10

Rasmussen, E., Wailes, N. & Haworth, N. (1996a) 'Where are we and how did we get here? Skills, skills shortages and industry training in New Zealand' in R. Fells & T. Todd eds *Current Research in Industrial Relations: Proceedings of the AIRAANZ Conference* Perth, Australia, pp. 473–84

——(1996b) 'Industrial relations and labour market reforms in New Zealand' *Human Resources Development Outlook 1995–1996* Melbourne: Monash University

Robertson, B. (1996a) 'The arguments for a specialist employment court in New Zealand' *New Zealand Journal of Industrial Relations* 21, 1, pp. 34–48

——(1996b) 'Judges should stick to their legal knitting' *National Business Review* 21 June, p. 16

Roth, B. (1978) 'The historical framework' in J. Deeks et al. eds *Industrial Relations in New Zealand* Wellington: Methuen

Ryan, R. (1995) 'Workplace reform in New Zealand—The state of play' Report, Wellington: Workplace New Zealand

Savage, J. (1996) 'What do we know about the economic impact of the Employment Contracts Act?' *NZEIR Working Paper 96/97* Wellington: NZ Institute of Economic Research

Savage, J. & Cooling, D. (1996) 'A preliminary report on the results of a survey on the Employment Contracts Act' *NZIER Working Paper 96/7* Wellington: NZ Institute of Economic Research

Skiffington, L. (1996) 'The role of specialist legal institutions in bargaining under the Employment Contracts Act 1991: Saboteurs or saviours?' *New Zealand Journal of Industrial Relations* 21, 1, pp. 49–66

Statistics New Zealand (1995) *Labour Market 1994* Wellington: Statistics New Zealand

——(1996) *Labour Market 1995* Wellington: Statistics New Zealand

——(1997) *Labour Market 1996* Wellington: Statistics New Zealand

——(1998) *Key Statistics. July 1998* Wellington: Statistics New Zealand

——(1999a) *Labour Market 1999* Wellington: Statistics New Zealand

——(1999b) *New Zealand Now: Incomes* Wellington: Statistics New Zealand

——(1999c) *Key Statistics, November 1999* Wellington: Statistics New Zealand

Visser, J. (1991) 'Trends in union membership' *OECD Employment Outlook* Paris: OECD, pp. 97–134

Wailes, N. (1994) 'The case against specialist jurisdiction for labour law: The philosophical assumptions of a common law for labour relations' *New Zealand Journal of Industrial Relations* 19, 1, pp. 1–15

Walsh, P. (1993) 'The state and industrial relations in New Zealand' in B. Roper & C. Rudd eds *State & Economy* Auckland: Oxford University Press

——(1994) 'An "unholy alliance": The 1968 nil wage order' *New Zealand Journal of History* 28, 2, pp. 178–93

Walsh, P. & Fougere, G. (1987) 'The unintended outcomes of the arbitration system' *New Zealand Journal of Industrial Relations* 12, 3, pp. 187–98

Walsh, P. & Ryan, R. (1993) 'The making of the Employment Contracts Act' in R. Harbridge ed. *Employment Contracts: New Zealand Experiences* Wellington: Victoria University Press

Wevers, F. (1995) 'Managerial perception of the quality of human resource management practice in New Zealand' Report, Auckland: NZ Institute of Management

Wevers International Ltd/Centre for Corporate Strategy (1996) 'The New Zealand Index of Human Resource Management and Organisational Effectiveness' Report, Auckland: NZ Institute of Management

Whatman, R., Armitage, C. & Dunbar, R. (1994) 'Labour market adjustment under the Employment Contracts Act' *New Zealand Journal of Industrial Relations* 19, 1, pp. 53–73

Chapter 4   Changing approaches to employment relations in Japan

Abegglen, J.C. (1958) *The Japanese Factory: Aspects of Its Social Organization* Glencoe: Free Press

——(1958b) *Nihon no Keiei (Management in Japan)* Tokyo: Diamond

Abraham, K.G. & Houseman, S.N. (1989) 'Job security and work force adjustment: How different are U.S. and Japanese practices?' *Journal of the Japanese and International Economies* 3

Aoki, M. (1986) 'Horizontal vs. vertical information structure of the firm' *The American Economic Review* 76 (December)

——(1987) 'The Japanese firm in transition' in K. Yamamura & Y. Yasuba eds *The Political Economy of Japan Vol. 1: The Domestic Transformation*, Stanford: Stanford University Press

——(1988) *Information, Incentives and Bargaining in the Japanese Economy* Cambridge: Cambridge University Press

Araki, T. (1994) 'Flexibility in Japanese employment relations and the role of the judiciary' in H. Oda ed. *Japanese Commercial Law in an Era of Internationalization*, London: Graham & Trotman

Asahi (1999) *Chiezo (The Asahi Encyclopedia of Current Terms)* Tokyo: Asahi Shinbun Press

Chuma, H. (1999) *Rodo keizai (Labour economics)*, Imidas, Tokyo: Shueisha, pp. 139–48

Cole, R.E. (1971a) *Japanese Blue Collar* New Haven: Yale University Press

——(1971b) 'Labour in Japan' in B.M. Richardson & T. Ueda eds in *Business and Society in Japan* Praeger: New York

——(1971c) 'The theory of institutionalization: Permanent employment and tradition in Japan' *Economic Development and Cultural Change* 20

——(1972) 'Permanent employment in Japan: Facts and fantasies' *Industrial and Labour Relations Review*

——(1973) *British Factory-Japanese Factory: The Origins of National Diversity in Industrial Relations* London: Allen & Unwin

——(1979) *Work, Mobility, and Participation,* Berkeley: University of California Press

——(1986) *Flexible Rigidities: Industrial Policy and Structural Adjustment in the Japanese Economy 1970–1980* Stanford: Stanford University Press

Dore, R., Bounine-Cabal, J. & Tapiola, K. (1989) *Japan at Work: Markets, Management and Flexibility* Paris: Organization for Economic Co-operation and Development (OECD)

Economic Planning Agency (1994) *Economic Survey of Japan: 1993–1994 (English translation 1995)* Tokyo: Printing Bureau, Ministry of Finance

Gordon, A. (1985) *The Evolution of Labour Relations in Japan: Heavy Industry, 1853–1955* Cambridge: Harvard University

Gould, W.B. (1984) *Japan's Reshaping of American Labour Law* Cambridge: MIT Press

Hanami, T.A. (1985) *Labour Law and Industrial Relations in Japan* Antwerp: Kluwer Law and Taxation Publishers

Hanrei jijo (Legal precedent times) (1961) 270: 11–26

Jiyu Kokumin Sha (1999) *Gendai Yogo no Kiso Chishiki (Fundamental knowledge of Current Terms)* Tokyo: Jiyu Kokumin Sha

Kettler, D. & Tackney, C. (1997) 'Light from a dead sun: The Japanese lifetime employment system and Weimar labour Law' *Comparative Labour Law and Policy Journal* 19, pp. 101–41

Koike, K. (1983) 'Internal labour markets: Workers in large firms' in Taishiro Shirai ed. *Contemporary Industrial Relations in Japan* Madison: University of Wisconsin Press

——(1987) 'Human resource development' in K. Yamamura & Y. Yasuba eds *The Political Economy of Japan, Vol. 1: The Domestic Transformation* Stanford: Stanford University Press

——(1988) *Understanding Industrial Relations in Modern Japan* London: Macmillan

——(1991) *Shigoto no keizaigaku (The economics of work)* Tokyo: Toyo Keizai

——(1995) *The Economics of Work in Japan* Tokyo: LTCB International Library Foundation, English translation of Koike (1991)

Koike, K. & Inoki, T. (1991) *Skill Formation in Japan and Southeast Asia* Tokyo: University of Tokyo Press

Koshiro, K. (1994) 'The link between labour—management relations and job security: Employment fluctuations under the "lifetime employment system"' Paper prepared for the Japan/U.S. Human Resource Network Conference, (New York)

Labour Affairs Office Tokyo, Metropolitan Shinagawa Ward (Tokyo To Shinagawa Rosei Jimusho) (1998) Last year's deepening employment conditions and transitions in the metropolitan Tokyo labour administration over the 50 postwar years (Kinnen no shinkokka suru koyo josei to sengo 50 sunen no torosei gyosei no suii) Tokyo: Shinagawa Ward Metropolitan Tokyo Labour Affairs Office

Lex/DB case (1997) 28021615 (proprietary data base listing)

Levine, S.B. (1958) *Industrial Relations in Postwar Japan* Urbana: University of Illinois Press

——(1965) 'Labour markets and collective bargaining in Japan' in W.L. Lockwood ed. *The State and Economic Enterprise in Japan* Princeton: Princeton University Press

——(1983) 'Careers and mobility in Japan's labour markets' in D. W. Plath ed. *Work and Lifecourse in Japan* Albany: State University of New York Press

Levine, S.B. & Kawada Hisashi eds (1980) *Human Resources in Japanese Industrial Development*, Princeton: Princeton University Press

Lockwood W. ed. (1965) *The State and Economic Enterprise in Japan* Princeton: Princeton University Press

Markey, R. & Monat, J. (1997) *Innovation and Employee Participation through Works Councils: International Case Studies* Sydney: Avebury

Matsuoka, S. (1979) *Rodoho kojiten (A Small Dictionary of Labour Law)* Tokyo: Chuo Keizaisha

MOL (Ministry of Labor) (1995) *Japan's Current Labour—Management Communications (Nihon no roshi komunikeshion no genjo)* Ministry of Labor Policy Secretariat Survey Section, Tokyo: Ministry of Finance

Nihon Rodo Kenkyu Kiko (1998) *Rodo Hakusho* Tokyo: Nihon Rodo Kenkyu Kiko

Nitta, M. (1997) 'Employment relations after the collapse of the bubble economy' in Banno Junji ed. *The Political Economy of Japanese Society, Vol: 2, Internationalization and Domestic Issues* Oxford: Oxford University Press

Rodo Hanrei (Labour law precedent) (1987) *Ikegai Iron Works Case (Ikegai tekko jiken)* October 15

Sano, Y. (1995) *Human Resource Management in Japan* Tokyo: Keio University Press

Shimada, H. (1983a) 'Employment effects of incremental employment subsidies' *Highlights in Japanese Industrial Relations: A Selection of Articles from the Japan Labour Bulletin* Tokyo: Japan Institute of Labour (first published February 1981 in *Bulletin* 20 p. 2)

——(1983b) 'Japanese industrial relations—A new general model? A survey of English-language literature' in T. Shirai ed. *Contemporary Industrial Relations in Japan* Madison: University of Wisconsin Press

——(1989) 'Japan's industrial culture and labour—management relations' *Searching for a New System in Industrial Relations*, Proceedings of the 30th Anniversary International Symposium Tokyo: Japan Institute of Labour

——(1992a) 'Japan's industrial culture and labour—management relations' in S. Kumon & H. Rosovsky eds *The Political Economy of Japan, Vol. 3: Cultural and Social Dynamics* Stanford: Stanford University Press

——(1992b) 'Structural change and industrial relations: Japan' in A. Gladstone, H. Wheeler, J. Rojot, F. Eyraud & R. Ben-Israel eds *Labour Relations in a Changing Environment* Berlin: Walter de Gruyter

Shimada, H., Seiki, A., Furugoro, T., Sakai, Y. & Hosokawa, T. (1983) 'The Japanese labour market: a survey' *Japanese Economic Studies,* 11 (Winter), p. 2

Shitara, K. (1998) *Kaisha to no tatakaikata oshiemasu (I'll Teach You 'How to Fight' Your Company)* Tokyo: Gendai Shorin

Shueisha (1999) *Imidas (Innovative Multi-Information Dictionary, Annual Series)* Tokyo: Shuei Sha

Sugeno, K. (1992) *Japanese Labour Law* Tokyo: University of Tokyo Press

——(1993) 'Japan: the state's guiding role in economic development' *Comparative Labor Law Journal* pp. 302–20

Tackney, C.T. (forthcoming) ' "Managing" Japanese management: A study of the 1988 Labour Union Coup at Okuma Corporation, a machine tools manufacturer', Proceedings of the August 1998 North America Case Research Association Conference, University of New Hampshire, Durham, New Hampshire

——(1995) 'Institutionalization of the lifetime employment system' PhD dissertation, Industrial Relations Research Institute, University of Wisconsin, Madison, Ann Arbor: UMI. 9608158

——(1998) 'The legal ecology of "Japanese management" and its transnational diffusion' in *Globalisation and regionalism: employment relations issues in the Asia Pacific*, Proceedings of the International Employment Relations Association 6th Annual Conference, 15–17 July 1998 held at the University of Wollongong NSW Australia. pp. 335–41

Taira, K. (1970) *Economic Development and the Labour Market in Japan* New York: Columbia University Press

Taira, K. & Levine, S.B. (1985) 'Japan's industrial relations: A social compact emerges' in H. Juris et al. eds *Industrial Relations in a Decade of Economic Change* Madison: Industrial Relations Research Association

Takahashi, Y. (1997) 'The labour market and lifetime employment in Japan' *Economic and Industrial Democracy*, 18

Yamakawa, R. (1998) 'Special topic: Overhaul after 50 years: the Amendment of the Labour Standards Law' *Japan Labour Bulletin* 37, 11, 1 November

Yanagawa, M., Furuyama, H., Ogata, S., Takashima, R. & Saito, H. (1950) *Hanrei rodo ho no kenkyu (Research in Labour Law Legal Precedent)* Tokyo: Romu Gyosei Kenkyujo

Chapter 5   Changing approaches to employment relations in South Korea

The Bank of Korea (various issues) *Balance of Payments*

The Bank of Korea (various issues) *National Incomes*

Choi, J.J. (1989) *Labour and the Authoritarian State: Labour Unions in South Korean Manufacturing Industries* Seoul: Korea University Press

Choi, K.-S. & Jung, J. (1997) 'Women's interrupted labour market experience: Problems and policy suggestions' *Korean Journal of Industrial Relations* vol. 7

Fields, G. (1992) 'Changing labour market conditions and economic development in Hong Kong, Korea, Singapore and Taiwan' (mimeo)

Korea Labour Institute (various issues) *Quarterly Labour Review*

Lindauer, D. (1991) et al. *Korea: The Strains of Economic Growth* Cambridge, MA: Harvard Institute for International Development

Mazumdar, D. (1990) 'Korea's labour markets under structural adjustment' World Bank Working Paper No. 554

Office of Statistics, Korea (various issues) *Monthly Statistics of Korea*

Park, D.J. (1992) 'Industrial relations in Korea' *The International Journal of Human Resource Management* 3, 1 May, pp. 105–23

Park, Young-bum (1994) 'State regulation, the labour market and economic development: South Korea' in Gerry Rodgers ed. *Workers, Institutions and Economic Growth in Asia* Geneva: International Institute for Labour Studies

——(1995) 'Economic developmental globalization, and practices in industrial relations and human resource management in Korea' in A. Verma, T.A. Kochan & R.D. Lansbury eds *Employment Relations in the Growing Asian Economies* London: Routledge

——(1998) 'The Financial Crisis in Korea: Industrial Relations Connection', *Perspectives on Work* vol. 2, 2, pp. 37–41

Park, Young-bum and Leggett, C.J. (1998) 'Employment relations in the Republic of Korea' in G. Bamber & R. Lansbury eds *International and Comparative Employment Relations* 3rd edn, Sydney: Allen and Unwin

Park, Young Chul (1998) 'Financial crisis and macroeconomic adjustments in Korea', 1997–98 (mimeo)

Topel, R. & Kim, D. (1992) 'Labour markets and economic growth; lessons from Korea's industrialization: 1970–90' Paper presented at the Universities Research Conference: *The Labour Market in International Perspective*, National Bureau of Economic Research

Vogel, E.F. (1991) *The Four Little Dragons: The Spread of Industrialization in East Asia*, London: Harvard University Press

Woo, S.H. (1996) 'Approaching the 21st century: Perspectives on Korean industrial relations' Proceedings of the International Industrial Relations Association 3rd Asian Regional Congress September 30–October 4, 1996, Taipei, vol. 4, pp. 155–76

World Bank (1997) *The East Asian Miracle*, World Bank: Washington DC: World Bank

Yoo, I. (1994) 'Labour institutions and economic development in South Korea' in Gerry Rodgers ed. *Workers, Institutions and Economic Growth in Asia* Geneva: International Institute for Labour Studies

Chapter 6   Changing approaches to employment relations in Taiwan

CEPD (1999) *Statistical Data Book* Republic of China: Council for Economic Planning and Development

Chung C. (1998) *The Internationalisation of Small and Medium Businesses in Taiwan* Taipei: Chung Hua Institution for Economic Research

COL (Council of Labour Affairs) (1997) *A Survey of Workers' Attitudes on Labour Management Relations in Taiwan* Republic of China: Council of Labour Affairs

——(1998a) *A Survey of Industrial Unions In Taiwan 1997* Republic of China: Council of Labour Affairs

——(1998b) *A Survey of Year End Bonus in Private Enterprises* Republic of China: Council of Labour Affairs

——(1999) *Yearbook of Labour Administration 1998* Republic of China: Council of Labour Affairs

DGBAS (1998) *Report on the Work Experiences in Taiwan 1997* Republic of China: Directorate-General of Budget, Accounting and Statistics

——(1999) *Yearbook of Manpower Survey Statistics of Taiwan Area 1998* Republic of China: Directorate-General of Budget, Accounting and Statistics

DLA (1996) *Survey of Workers' Attitudes on Work and Employment Relations in Taiwan Province* Department of Labour Affairs, Taiwan Provincial Government

Huang, Hui Ling (1996) 'The formation and development of trade unions outside of the legal system' *Labor–Management Relations* 15, 1, pp. 19–30

Labor (1998) 95, April

Lee, Joseph S. (1980) 'An empirical study of the functioning of the labor market in Taiwan' *Academia Economic Papers* 8, 1, March, pp. 171–244

——(1988) 'Stages of economic development and labor relations: The case of the Republic of China' *Proceedings on Conference on Labor and Economic Development* Taiwan: Chung-Hua Institution for Economic Research

——(1995) 'Economic development and the evolution of industrial relations in Taiwan: 1950–1993' in A. Verma, T. Kochan & R. Lansbury eds, *Employment Relations in the Growing Asian Economies* London: Routledge

Lee, Joseph S., Huang, T.C. & Cheng, C.C. (1998) *The Path to Skill Acquisition For Workers in High-Tech Industry in Taiwan:* Institute of Human Resource Management, National Central University Taiwan

Ministry of Economic Affairs (1998) *Monthly Bulletin for Industry* Republic of China: Ministry of Economic Affairs

Chapter 7   Changing approaches to employment relations in the People's Republic of China

Bell, M., Khor, H. & Kochhar, K. (1993) *China at the Threshold of a Market Economy* Occasional Paper No. 107 Washington: International Monetary Fund

Benson, J. & Zhu, Y. (1999) 'Markets, firms and workers: the transformation of human resource management in Chinese State Owned Enterprises', *Human Resource Management Journal*, 9, 4, pp. 58–74

Chan, A. (1993) 'Revolution or corporatism? Workers and trade unions in post-Mao China' *The Australian Journal of Chinese Affairs* 29, 1, January, pp. 31–61

——(1995) 'Chinese enterprise reforms: convergence with the Japanese model?' *Industrial and Corporate Change* 4, 4, pp. 449–70

Chen, Y. (1997) *Xiang Shehui Zhuyi Shichang Jingji Zhuanbian Shiqi De Gonghui Lilun Gangyao Yu Pingshu (The Outline and Analysis of Trade Union Theory in the Transition Period Toward Socialist Market Economy)* Beijing: People's Press

Child, J. (1994) *Management in China During the Age of Reform* Cambridge: Cambridge University Press

Dong, K.Y. (1996) *Labour Market Policy in China* Beijing: China People's University

Feng, L.R. (1982) *Laodong Baochou Yu Laodong Jioye (Labour Reward and Employment)* Beijing: China Prospect Press

Geng, L. (1992) 'Jiji Tuijing Shehuai Baozhang Zhidu Gaige' (Promoting the reform of the social security system) in China Enterprises Management and Training Centre ed. *Qiye Zhuanhuan Jingying Jizhi: Lilun Yu Shijian (Changing the Function of Enterprise Management: Theory and Practice)* Beijing: China People's University Press

Goodall, K. & Warner, M. (1997) 'Human resources in Sino-foreign joint ventures selected case-studies in Shanghai, compared with Beijing' *International Journal of Human Resource Management* 8, 5, pp. 569–94

Granick, D. (1990) *Chinese State Enterprises: A Regional Property Rights Analysis* Chicago: University of Chicago Press

Han, J. & Morishima, M. (1992) 'Labour system reform in China and its unexpected consequences' *Economic and Industrial Democracy* 13, 2, pp. 233–61

Hu, T.W. & Li, E. (1993) 'The labour market' in W. Galenson ed. *China's Economic Reform*, San Francisco: 1990 Institute, pp. 147–76

Huang, S.J. (1996) *Guoyou Qiye Chanquan Zhidu Biange (The Reform of State-Owned Enterprises' Ownership and Managment System)* Beijing: Economic Management Press

ILO (1996) *China: Employment and Training Policies for Transition to a Market Economy* Geneva: International Labour Office

Kaple, D. (1994) *Dream of a Red Factory: The Legacy of High Stalinism in China* Oxford: Oxford University Press

Korzec, M. (1992) *Labour and the Failure of Reform in China*, London: Macmillan

Lee, L.T. (1986) *Trade Unions in China*, Singapore: Singapore University Press

Leung, W.Y. (1988) *Smashing the Iron Rice Pot: Workers and Unions in China's Market Socialism* Hong Kong: Asia Monitor Resource Centre

Li, J. (1998) 'Diversified forms for materializing public ownership' *Beijing Review*, January 5–11, 1998, pp. 13–16

Li, T.C. (1992) 'Zhuanhuan qiye jingying jizhi de xuanze (The choice for changing enterprise management systems)' in China Enterprises Management & Training Centre ed. *Qiye Zhuanhuan Jingying Jizhi: Lilun Yu Shijian (Changing Enterprise Management Systems: Theory and Practice)* Beijing: China People's University Press

Lim, L.L., Sziraczki, G. & Zhang, X.J. (1996) *Economic Performance, Labour Surplus and Enterprise Responses: Results from the China Enterprise Survey* Geneva: International Labour Office, Labour Market Papers 13

Lu, X.B. & Perry, E.J. (1997) *Danwei: The Changing Chinese Workplace in Historical and Comparative Perspective* New York: M.E. Sharpe

Ng, S.H. & Warner, M. (1998) *China's Trade Unions and Management* London: Macmillan

Poole, M. (1997) ' Industrial and labour relations' in M. Warner ed. *IEBM Concise Encyclopedia of Business and Management* London: International Thomson Business Press, pp. 264–82

Sziraczki, G. & Twigger, A. (1995) *Employment Policies for Transition to a Market Economy in China* Geneva: International Labour Office, Labour Market Papers 2

Unger, J. & Chan, A. (1995) 'China, corporatism, and the East Asian model' *The Australian Journal of Chinese Affairs* 33, January, pp. 29–53

Walder, A. (1996) *China's Transitional Economy* Oxford: Oxford University Press

Warner, M. (1986) 'Managing human resources in China' *Organization Studies* 7, 4, pp. 353–66

——(1992) *How Chinese Managers Learn* London: Macmillan

——(1995) *The Management of Human Resources in Chinese Industry* London: Macmillan

——(1997a) 'Management–labour relations in the new Chinese economy' *Human Resource Management Journal* 37, 4, pp. 30–43

——(1997b) 'Culture, organisation and work in China: The societal effect' Working paper, Judge Institute of Management Studies, The University of Cambridge

——ed. (1999) *China's Managerial Revolution* London: Frank Cass

——ed. (2000) *Changing Workplace Relations in the Chinese Economy* London: Macmillan

White, G. (1987) 'The politics of economic reform in Chinese industry: The introduction of the labour contract system' *The China Quarterly* 111 pp. 365–89

Yamashita, M. (1989) *Gendai Kigyo No Romu Kanri (Modern Enterprise Labour Management)* Tokyo: White Peach Press

Yuan, L.Q. (1990) *Zhongguo Laodong Jingji Shi (The History of Chinese Labour Economy)* Beijing: Beijing Economic Institute Press

Zhu, Y. (1992) 'The Role of Export Processing Zones in East Asian Development: South Korea, Taiwan, China and Thailand' Ph. D. thesis, Melbourne: University of Melbourne

——(1995) 'Major changes under way in China's industrial relations' *International Labour Review* 124, pp. 36–49

Zhu, Y. & Campbell, I. (1996) 'Economic reform and the challenge of transforming labour regulation in China' *Labour and Industry* 7, pp. 29–49

Chapter 8   Changing approaches to employment relations in Indonesia

Bhoka, W. (1995) 'Peningkatan UMR 1995 belum sebanding dengan inflasi (The increment of 1995 minimum wages isn't a balance to inflation)' *Media Indonesia* (daily newspaper), 23 April

Deyo, F.C. (1989) *Beneath the Miracle: Labor Subordination in the New Asian Industrialism*, Berkeley: University of California Press

Etty, T. (1990) 'Trade union rights in Indonesia: Problems, concerns and challenges for (inter)national labor', International Department, the Netherlands Trade Union Confederation (F.N.V.), Paper presented to the SPSI/ICFTU-APRO Seminar on International Labour Standards, Jakarta

——(1997) Interview with Tom Etty during the ILC 1997, Geneva

Ford, M. (forthcoming) 'Continuity and change in Indonesian labour relations in the Habibe Interregnum' *The Southeast Asian Journal of Social Science*, September 2000

Hadiz, V.R. (1997a) 'Labor policy may be defective' *The Jakarta Post* (daily newspaper), 7 May

——(1997b) *Workers and the State in New Order Indonesia* London/New York: Routledge

Ingleson, J. (1986) *In Search of Justice: Workers and Unions in Colonial Java 1908–1926* Asian Studies Association of Australia, Singapore: Oxford University Press

ILO (International Labour Organisation) (1997) *Report of the Committee of Experts on the Application of Convention and Recommendations* Report III (Part 1A), Geneva: International Labour Office

Kompas (daily newspaper) (1997a) 'RUU naker seharusnya atur tindak pidana korporasi (Manpower Bill should provide sanctions for corporations)', 22 August

——(1997): 'DPR Menyetujui RUUK menjadi Undang-Undang (Parliament agrees to enact Manpower Bill to become Manpower Law)', 12 September

Manning, C. (1993) 'Structural change and industrial relations during the Soeharto period: An approaching crisis?' *Bulletin of Indonesian Economic Studies*, vol. 29, No. 2, August pp. 59–95

——(1996) 'Labor standards and economic development: the Indonesian case' in J.S. Lee ed. *Labor Standards and Economic Development* Taipei: Chung-Hua Institution for Economic Research

Mantra Magazine (1995) 'Interview with Muchtar Pakpahan', Jakarta, April

Media Indonesia (1997) 'RUU ketenagakerjaan kebiri hak pekerja (Manpower Bill ignores workers' rights)', 1 March

Ministry of Manpower (1985) *Manual on the Implementation of Pancasila Industrial Relations* Jakarta: Ministry of Manpower

——(1997a) *The Right to Organise in Indonesia* Jakarta: Ministry of Manpower

———(1997b) *The Right to Organise in Indonesia: An Amendment* Jakarta: Ministry of Manpower

Prawironoto S. (1974) 'Hubungan perburuhan pancasila sebagai wahana menuju ketenagakerjaan kerja dan stabilitas sosial ekonomi untuk pembangunan nasional (Pancasila industrial relations: Towards maintaining industrial harmony and socio-economic development)', Paper presented at the National Seminar on Industrial Relations) Jakarta: Ministry of Manpower

Republika (daily newspaper) (1997) 'Pernyataan 11 LSM: RUU ketenagakerjaan agar dibatalkan (Statement by 11 NGOs: Draft on labor regulations has to be postponed)', 25 February, p. 7

Richardson, J.H. (1958) 'Indonesian labor relations in their political setting' *Industrial and Labor Relations Review* XII, p. 1

Schwarz, A. (1997) 'Indonesia after Soeharto' in *Foreign Affairs*, July/August 76, p. 4

Shamad, Y. (1995) *Hubungan industrial di Indonesia* (Industrial relations in Indonesia) Jakarta: Bina Sumberdaya Manusia

Sijabat, R.M. (1995) 'Rapid economic growth passes workers by' *The Jakarta Post,* 26 December p. 5

Silaban, R. (1997) Interview during the ILC 1997, Geneva

Simanungkalit, P. (1997) Interview during the ILC 1997, Geneva

Soepomo, I. (1974) 'Hubungan perburuhan pancasila sebagai wahana menuju ke ketenangan kerja dan stabilitas sosial ekonomi untuk pembangunan nasional (Pancasila industrial relations: Towards maintaining industrial harmony and socio-economic development)', Paper presented at the National Seminar on Pancasila Industrial Relations, Jakarta: Depnakertranskop

Sudarwo, I. (1995) 'Interview with Iman Sudarwo, Former General Chairman of SPSI' *Media Indonesia*, 25 December p. 9

Sudono, A. (1974) 'Hubungan perburuhan pancasila sebagai wahana menuju ketenagakerjaan kerja dan stabilitas sosial ekonomi untuk pembangunan nasional (Pancasila industrial relations: Towards maintaining industrial harmony and socio-economic development)', Paper presented at the National Seminar on Industrial Relations, Jakarta: Ministry of Manpower

Thamrin, J. (1995) 'Development policy' in D.R. Harris ed. *Prisoners of Progress: A Review of the Current Indonesian Labor Situation* Leiden: Indonesian Documentation and Information Centre (INDOC)

Tjandraningsih, I. (1995) 'Between factory and home: Problems of women workers' in D.R. Harris ed. *Prisoners of Progress: A Review of the Current Indonesian Labor Situation* Leiden: Indonesian Documentation and Information Centre (INDOC)

Chapter 9 Challenges facing unions in South Korea

Amsden, A. (1989) *Asia's Next Giant* Oxford: Oxford University Press

Appelbaum, E. & Batt, R. (1994) *The New American Workplace* Ithaca: Cornell University Press

Barner, R. (1994) 'The new career strategist' *The Futurist* Sept-Oct, vol. 28, Iss. 5, pp. 8–14

Bridges, W. (1994) *Job Shift: How to Prosper in a Workplace Without Jobs* Reading: Addison-Wesley

Choi, J.J. (1988) *Trade Union Movement and the State (in Korean) Seoul*: Yulum Press

Craver, C.B. (1993) *Can Unions Survive?* New York: New York University Press

Deyo, F. ed. (1989) *Beneath the Miracle: Labor Subordination in the New Asian Industrialism* Berkeley: University of California Press

Frank, R. & Cook, P. (1995) *The Winner-Take-All Society* New York: Free Press

Hampson, I. (1997) 'The end of the experiment: Corporatism collapses in Australia' *Economic and Industrial Democracy* vol. 18, Iss. 4, pp. 539–66

Heckscher, C. (1995) *White-Collar Blues: Management Loyalties in an Age of Corporate Restructuring* New York: Basic Books

Hethy, L. (1995) 'Anatomy of a tripartite experiment: Attempted social and economic agreement in Hungary' *International Labour Review* vol. 134, Iss. 3, pp. 361–76

Hyman, R. (1992) 'Trade unions and the disaggregation of the working class' in M. Regini ed. *The Future of Labour Movements* London: Sage

ILO (1996) *World Employment 1996/97* Geneva: International Labour Organisation

Johnson, C. (1987) 'Political institutions and economic performance: A comparative analysis of the government-business relationship in Japan, South Korea, and Taiwan' in F. Deyo ed. *The Political Economy of the New Asian Industrialism* Ithaca: Cornell University Press

Kang, S.H. (1996) 'The labour movement in Korea after 1987' Unpublished manuscript, Korea Labour Institute

Kim, H.J. (1994) *Industrial Relations in Korea* (in Korean) Seoul: Korea Labour Institute

Kim, K.S. (1995) *The Current Characteristics of Korean Labour Movement and Its Problems* (in Korean) Seoul: Duksan Research Institute

——(1996) The *Industry Union System in Korea: Its Past, Present, and Future* (in Korean) Seoul: Korea Institute of Labour and Society

KLIa (Korea Labour Institute) *Quarterly Labour Review* Seoul: KLI (quarterly)

——b (Korea Labour Institute) *KLI Labour Statistics* Seoul: KLI (annually)

Kochan, T. & Osterman, P. (1994) *The Mutual Gains Enterprise* Boston: Harvard Business School Press

Korea International Labor Foundation (1998) *Handbook of the Social Agreement and New Labor Laws of Korea* Seoul: KILAF

Korea MOLa (Ministry of Labour) *Report on Monthly Labour Survey*, Seoul: MOL (various issues)

——b (Ministry of Labour) *Report on the Labour Demand Survey*, Seoul: MOL (various issues)

Korea NSO (National Statistical Office) (1996) *Annual Report on the Economically Active Population Survey*, Seoul: NSO

——(1999) *Home Page*, Korea NSO Internet page at http://ww.nso.go.kr/eindex.html (as at 14.9.99)

Lee, J.Y. (1995) *Trade Unions in the 1990s in Korea* (in Korean) Seoul: Federation of Korean Trade Unions

Locke, R., Kochan, T. & Piore, M. eds (1995) *Employment Relations in a Changing World Economy* Cambridge: MIT Press

OECD (1994) OECD *Economic Surveys Korea* Paris: OECD

Park. D. & Park, K. (1989) *Trade Unions in Korea Vol. 1* (in Korean) Seoul: Korea Labour Institute

Park. J.S. (1996) *Politics of Production and Workplace Democracy* (in Korean) Seoul: Hanwool Press

Park, Y.B. (1996) *Labour Trends in the 1990s in Korea* Seoul: Korea Labor Institute

Pontusson, J. (1992) 'Introduction: organizational and political—Economic perspectives on union politics' in M. Golden & J. Pontussion eds *Bargaining for Change* Ithaca: Cornell University Press

Tomasko, R. (1990) *Downsizing: Reshaping the Corporation for the Future* New York: American Management Association

Visser, J. & Hemerijck, A. (1997) *A Dutch Miracle: Job Growth, Welfare Reform and Corporatism in the Netherlands* Amsterdam: Amsterdam University Press

UNDP (United Nations Development Programme) (1998) 'Responding to the economic crisis in the Republic of Korea', Working paper prepared for the UNDP by Pak Po-Hi (President, INI SIRCH), May 1998, Seoul: UNDP

Chapter 10   Challenges facing unions in Australia

ACTU Living Wage (1999) *ACTU Written Submission to 1999 Living Wage Hearings*, D.1/1999, ACTU: Melbourne

Bamber G.J. & Lansbury, R.D. (1998) *International and Comparative Employment Relations: A Study of Industrialised Market Economies* Sydney: Allen & Unwin

Horne, D. (1964) *The Lucky Country* Victoria: Penguin

Peetz, D. (1998) *Unions in a Contrary World: The Future of the Australian Trade Union Movement* Melbourne: Cambridge University Press

UK Low Pay Commission (1998) 'Report of the UK Low Pay Commission' HMSO

Chapter 11   Employment relations at a large South Korean firm: the LG Group

LG Group (1994) *LG Labour–Management Relations Long-term Model Report*

LG Electronics (1996) *Labour–Management Strategies for the Second Innovation*

Chapter 12   Employment relations at a Taiwanese semiconductor firm: TSMC

Common Wealth Magazine (1998) 'Top 1000 manufacturing companies in Taiwan', June

Porter, Michael E. (1998) 'Clusters and the new economics of competition' *Harvard Business Review*, November–December

Science Park Administration (1997) *Statistics Quarterly,* September

The Economist (1998) 'Taiwan semiconductors: Nice market, we'll take it', July

Wilson, D. (1996) 'Pure foundry, pure profit' *Electronic Business Today* February

Chapter 13   The APEC forum: Human resources development and employment relations issues

APEC (1995a) *The Osaka Action Agenda* Osaka: Asia-Pacific Economic Co-operation

——(1995b) *Mid to Long Term Action Program for APEC Human Resources Development* Beijing: APEC

——(1996) *Joint Ministerial Statement: Call for Action on Human Resource Development* Manila: APEC

Fox, A. (1974) *Beyond Contract: Work, Power and Trust Relations* London: Faber

Haworth N. (1998) *The HRD Dimension of the Asian Financial Crisis: Towards the Definition of an APEC Response* Paper to the APEC HRD Task Force on the Human Resource and Social Impacts of the Financial and Economic Crisis Symposium, Taipei: June

PECC (1996) *Human Resource Development Outlook* Melbourne: Pacific Economic Co-operation Council

Sengenberger W. (1991) 'The role of labour market regulation in industrial restructuring' in G. Standing and V. Tokman eds *Towards Social Adjustment: Labour Market Issues in Structural Adjustment* Geneva: ILO

Index

253